Suffering and martyrdom in the New Testament

SUFFERING AND MARTYRDOM IN THE NEW TESTAMENT

Studies presented to G. M. Styler by the
Cambridge New Testament Seminar

EDITED BY

WILLIAM HORBURY

Fellow and Dean of Chapel, Corpus Christi College, Cambridge

AND

BRIAN McNEIL

*Wissenschaftlicher Assistent, Katholisch-theologische Fakultät,
University of Vienna*

CAMBRIDGE UNIVERSITY PRESS

CAMBRIDGE

LONDON   NEW YORK   NEW ROCHELLE

MELBOURNE   SYDNEY

Published by the Press Syndicate of the University of Cambridge
The Pitt Building, Trumpington Street, Cambridge CB2 1RP
32 East 57th Street, New York, NY 10022, USA
296 Beaconsfield Parade, Middle Park, Melbourne 3206, Australia

First published 1981

Printed in Great Britain at the
University Press, Cambridge

British Library Cataloguing in Publication Data
Suffering and martyrdom in the New Testament.
1. Suffering – Biblical teaching
2. Bible. New Testament – Criticism,
interpretation, etc.
3. Martyrdom – Biblical teaching
I. Styler, G. M. II. Horbury, William
III. McNeil, Brian IV. Cambridge New
Testament Seminar
231'.8   BS2545.S9   80 40706
ISBN 0 521 23482 4

G.M.S.

SCRIBAE CALLIDO SAPIENTI IVCVNDO

AMICO AMICI

D.D.D.

CONTENTS

Abbreviations   page *ix*

G. M. Styler and the Cambridge New Testament Seminar   *xi*
C. F. D. MOULE

Introduction   I
C. F. D. MOULE

Did Jesus teach that his death would be vicarious as well as typical?   9
J. C. O'NEILL

Imitatio Christi and the Lucan Passion narrative   28
BRIAN E. BECK

The persecution of Christians in John 15: 18 – 16: 4*a*   48
BARNABAS LINDARS SSF

Interchange and suffering   70
MORNA D. HOOKER

On the interpretation of Colossians 1: 24   84
W. F. FLEMINGTON

Preparation for the perils of the last days: 1 Thessalonians 3: 3   91
E. BAMMEL

Maintaining the testimony of Jesus: the suffering of Christians in
the Revelation of John   101
J. P. M. SWEET

Martyrdom and inspiration   118
†G. W. H. LAMPE

Suffering and martyrdom in the Odes of Solomon   136
BRIAN McNEIL

Suffering and messianism in Yose ben Yose   143
WILLIAM HORBURY

What might martyrdom mean?   183
NICHOLAS LASH

Index of authors   199

Index of references   202

Index of subjects   217

ABBREVIATIONS

AGJU	Arbeiten zur Geschichte des antiken Judentums und des Urchristentums
AV	Authorised Version
BDF	F. Blass, ed. A. Debrunner (trans. R. W. Funk), *A Greek Grammar of the New Testament and other Early Christian Literature* (Cambridge University Press, 1961)
BJRL	*Bulletin of the John Rylands University Library*
CBQ	*Catholic Bible Quarterly*
ExpT	*The Expository Times*
GCS	die griechischen christlichen Schriftsteller
HR	*History of Religions*
HUCA	*Hebrew Union College Annual*
JAAR	*Journal of the American Academy of Religion*
JB	The Jerusalem Bible
JBL	*Journal of Biblical Literature*
JJS	*Journal of Jewish Studies*
JQR	*Jewish Quarterly Review*
JTS	*Journal of Theological Studies*
MGWJ	*Monatsschrift für die Geschichte und Wissenschaft des Judentums*
MT	Massoretic Text
NEB	The New English Bible
NovT	*Novum Testamentum*
NTS	*New Testament Studies*
PG	*Patrologiae cursus completus, series graeca*, ed. J. P. Migne
PL	*Patrologiae cursus completus, series latina*, ed. J. P. Migne
RevBibl	*Revue Biblique*
RSR	*Recherches de science religieuse*
RSV	Revised Standard Version

TDNT	*Theological Dictionary of the New Testament*, ed. G. Kittel and G. Friedrich; trans. G. W. Bromiley (Grand Rapids, 1964-)
TEV	Today's English Version
ThS	*Theological Studies*
TLZ	*Theologische Literaturzeitung*
TU	Texte und Untersuchungen
ZTK	*Zeitschrift für Theologie und Kirche*

G. M. Styler and the Cambridge
New Testament Seminar

C. F. D. MOULE

Although it is particularly in connection with the Seminar and by its members that Geoffrey Styler is celebrated in this book, there is a great deal more to him than that. The elegance, skill, wit and devotion exhibited by him in his long service to the Seminar will receive mention directly. But outside and far beyond it, despite his excessively retiring modesty, his qualities are admired by those who have known him in many other roles. At Oxford he had a dazzling record as a 'triple First', a Craven Scholar, and a Liddon Student, and went on, with a Commonwealth Fellowship, to an STM at Union Theological Seminary, New York, *magna cum laude.* After training for Orders at Cuddesdon and going to a Curacy at Heckmondwike, of which he often speaks, he began his Cambridge career as Vice-Principal of Westcott House. There followed the Fellowship at Corpus Christi College, with an involvement in College and University life that has steadily increased. With a flair for administrative detail – in the William Temple tradition, he is a master of Bradshaw's Railway Guide and its successors – Geoffrey, more than any one other person, may claim to have been the architect of the reformed Theological Tripos, having put in days and months of concentrated toil in meeting its demands. If the result was the most complicated set of regulations in the whole of *Ordinances* – clerks in the Old Schools have been known to throw up their hands in despair – that is evidence of the subtlety of the problems solved, not of muddled thinking. Nobody has been quicker than Geoffrey to see when Occam's razor might be applied.

Possessed not only of an acute head for administration but of a fastidious scholarship, Geoffrey has been too much of a perfectionist to rush into print; but the quality of his few publications is high – βαιὰ μέν, ἀλλὰ ῥόδα. His piece on the Synoptic Problem will be noted when we come to the Seminar. In addition, he has one or two papers of a penetrating simplicity in learned journals (e.g. 'Stages in Christology in the Synoptic Gospels', *NTS* 10 (1963–4), 398ff, cited in Mr Flemington's contribution in this volume); and his reluctance to publish was over-come once more by his characteristic generosity in contributing an original essay to the Festschrift that my friends were kind enough to make for me ('The Basis of Obligation in Paul's Christology and Ethics', in B. Lindars and S. S. Smalley (eds.), *Christ and Spirit in the New Testament* (Cambridge University Press, 1973), pp. 175ff). His articles are all constructive, and a devout faith is clearly visible through work that is austerely factual. This is true of a recent paper that he was so good as to show me, as yet unpublished, on christological evidence and its interpretation. In the scholar's account there stands to his credit also, albeit anonymously, the considerable service rendered in the making and revising of the New English Bible.

Another side to his abilities is his musical talent. As Precentor of his College he has presided over the Chapel music with sensitivty and distinction for many years. Generations of Corpus undergraduates have been encouraged to share in making music with Geoffrey and his wife Audrey, and other fortunate friends have been delighted with duets for the piano and violin played by husband and wife with both refinement and verve. In another mode he has been a valued player in the cricket team fielded by the Fellows of his College. Indeed, socially, and especi-ally as President of Corpus, he has shown himself the perfect 'College man' – a graceful host, a master of ceremonial, and a hilariously witty raconteur. (The only complaint of his University lectures that one hears is that they are so full of anecdotes that they tend to be discursive.)

But above all loyalty is the word that comes to mind. Geoffrey's undeviating devotion to his duties as a priest and pastor, his saintly and uncomplaining patience, his self-effacing kindness, and his meticulous efficiency in Theological College, College, and University duties – these have all sprung from the loyalty of Christian discipleship that is at the heart of the man. No wonder he evokes an affection of which he is too modest and retiring to welcome the expression. For once, then, he must allow us to dedicate this little tribute to him.

And what of the Seminar? So far as my investigations take me, the Cambridge New Testament Seminar begins with F. C. Burkitt. I seem to recall the late Dr A. C. Bouquet's saying that V. H. Stanton preceded Burkitt as its President; but I can find no written evidence to this effect; and some remarks by F. J. Foakes Jackson suggest that it was under Burkitt's leadership that it first came into being. In the preface to vol. v of *The Beginnings of Christianity* (London, 1933), Foakes Jackson, des-cribing the early stages of the undertaking that led to the compiling of that massive commentary on the Acts, wrote (p. vii):

'I was fortunate enough to obtain the co-operation of Professor Burkitt, who consented to preside at a Seminar, which was largely attended by scholars of the most varied interests in the University, not only theological, but historical, classical, mathematical, and Oriental. Visitors were often present from Oxford, London, and different parts of England; and as the minutes kept by me as Secretary of the Seminar show, the United States and Canada were not unrepresented. Lake paid frequent visits from Leiden, where he has a professorial chair, to watch the progress of the deliberations'.

I have not been able to pin down the exact date of this Seminar's inception; but in that same preface to vol. v of *The Beginnings*, Foakes Jackson says that preparatory work for the commentary (in which he presumably includes the work of the Seminar) went on for only 'a year or more' before the First World War began. If the Seminar referred to by Foakes Jackson is continuous with Burkitt's Seminar to which, in its latter days, I myself belonged (and this is endorsed by Dr Flew's remarks, shortly to be quoted), then it must have stretched from about 1912 to 1935, when Burkitt died.

In J. F. Bethune-Baker's obituary of Burkitt in the *Proceedings of the British Academy* 22 (1936), 3ff, there is a lively account of the Seminar contributed by R. Newton Flew, which is too good not to quote in full (by kind permission of the British Academy):

'There was nothing in the world quite like "Burkitt's Seminar" for those of us who went regularly and lovingly to it. This was because there was nobody else like the Chairman. There were many learned men around that table in the Library of the Divinity School. But this was Burkitt's Seminar. It was constituted (as many people think that the Church is constituted) from above downwards, through its episcopos or Chairman with all authority and membership cohering in a single visible head. But his papacy was gentle and undisputed. He it was who invited new members with little notes written in his own exquisite handwriting. The impress of his mind was upon every meeting. Indeed without him we dared not and would not meet. Your membership began in awe and was consummated in affection. After all it was terrifying, if you were unlearned and a newcomer, to take your place at that table, or to sit on a chair at the other end of the room and gaze on the learned from afar. But after a time your awe dissolved. Everything was so natural, so easy; perhaps a continental theologian might call it sometimes desultory. These scholars, not unlike ordinary folk, loved to wander sometimes. They followed their

Chairman who could on occasion be charmingly irrelevant. Somebody has dared to say that one of the fruits of the Spirit, which is not found in our text of Galatians, is relevance. The question was one óf the few which was never discussed at the Seminar. On the whole we should have dismissed the suggestion unhesitatingly. We had learnt that the license to be irrelevant was divine. Anyhow, your awe went as you saw the Seminar faring down some inviting alley, and you were emboldened to contribute to the conversion your own mite, perhaps even your jest.

Of course we did solid and concentrated work. We did not forget that the first task of all New Testament study is the discovery of the true text. Few problems of interpretation were left unhandled. The minuteness and thoroughness characteristic of Cambridge scholarship were in evidence at every meeting. From 1924 to 1934 only two books were studied, with the exception of a few months in 1929 spent on the *Testaments of the Twelve Patriarchs*. Five years were given to the Fourth Gospel, and five years to the Acts. Many of the notes garnered and the papers read would have enriched any published commentary, but our Chairman was firm in his stipulation that the Seminar did not meet with a view to the publication of results. It is true that in the pre-war period the Seminar had prepared the way for that great enterprise, *The Beginnings of Christianity*, as Dr Foakes Jackson has explained (vol. v, pp. vii, viii). But in these latter days the Seminar, in Burkitt's intention, was a centre and a meeting place for senior University people, including many incumbents from the town and villages, who wanted to study early Christianity. Among our members in the later years were the Professors of Hebrew and Chinese, two eminent Rabbinic Scholars, a specialist in Coptic, and another in Arabic, some classical scholars, several ex-missionaries, as well as teachers of Biblical, historical, and systematic theology. The Chairman delighted to elicit from the ex-missionaries any analogies or illustrations which might light up the problem before us. The discussions were never better than in the last year. Younger graduates had been drawn in; we seemed to have taken a fresh lease of life. The subject was *Early Jewish Christianity*, and had been carefully planned. Some texts were studied, the sources were sifted, many papers were read. The general conclusion which was gradually being reached would have run counter to certain theories current on the continent, wherein the ghost of the Tübingen hypothesis still stalks abroad.

We had our own ritual. In form we were businesslike. There was a Secretary, a Minute Book and Notes. The meetings were opened by reading the Minutes of the last meeting, wherein the names of the members present were recorded in due academic order, save that (as gallantry demanded) the names of ladies were read immediately after that of the Chairman. After the Minutes came the Notes, recording any fresh theories or conclusions, or any valuable information imparted at the previous meeting which was not readily accessible in published work. Next we proceeded to read the Text on which we were engaged, some one member being deputed to translate from the Greek. Discussion would follow after a paragraph had been translated. A paper might be read. Soon after three o'clock the custodian of the Divinity School would appear. This appearance was an unfailing symbol in the ritual; it meant: "How many will stay for tea?" The Chairman said: "Tea?" Hands were lifted up and counted. Back we went to our text or our discussion till tea came in at four p.m. bringing a certain relaxation. Usually we pursued our appointed topic, but in a freer and more human mood. Perhaps some one would introduce a subject of scholarly concern, not visibly related to our appointed task. No question of theological learning was alien to our Chairman. Memory brings back various inquiries on which one or another of us sought for light. Was there anything in the widespread popular misconception that the ten coins in the parable of Luke xv were part of a woman's headdress? Was there any evidence in the Fathers to prove that Christians were opposed to wife-beating, as Jews undoubtedly were? Once our Chairman suddenly said: "As next Sunday is the second in Advent, may I put in a plea for the omission of a comma?" We sat up, expectant. "I believe that Cranmer wrote: 'Grant that we may in such wise *hear them read*, mark, learn, and inwardly digest them....'." He developed his argument that sixteenth-century congregations could not be expected to read and produced his parallel from the Preface to the Book of Common Prayer. If we were not all convinced, we were all enthralled. It was just like him.

On the very day before he was stricken down, he led his Seminar; he was himself, gay, fresh, adventurous, learned, with that unique and indefinable distinction that was ever his. Who could picture the restless, vivid, darting of that mind down some unexpected avenue, the swift following of the fugitive gleam that might mean light on an old problem, the versatile and pungent wit that adorned the vast learning? These characteristics we knew and admired. But what we hardly realized till our master was taken from us was the atmosphere of affection which had flowed around that Seminar table. The centre and the source of it all was Burkitt himself. The very supposition of the

quenching of such a life by death made death itself seem unreal. One
of our Rabbinic scholars gathered a flower from the Talmud to lay on
Burkitt's grave. "Scholars" said R. Hiyya b. Ashi in the name of Rab,
"know no rest, either in this world or in the world to come; as it is
said 'they go from strength to strength till they appear before God in
time'." And our Rabbinist added his own comment:

> Earth's dreams proved true, earth's phantoms laid,
>   Earth's labours done,
> To visions new, to words unsaid,
>   Now call them on.'

Mr R. S. Cripps, an Anglican clergyman and a Hebrew scholar, the
author of a highly regarded commentary on Amos, was Secretary of the
Seminar for some years, and he passed on his notes to me when, many
years later, he vacated the living of Burwell, which he had held in succession to that of Horningsey. From these it appears that in 1921-2 the
Apocalypse was studied, in 1922-3, the Odes of Solomon, and in 1924
the Hermetica. As far as I recollect, I became a member at the very end,
when, for 1934-5, a typed programme was issued for that study of Early
Jewish Christianity to which Dr Flew alluded. Cripps' notes confirm in
some detail what is hinted at in Dr Flew's reminiscences – that in those
days it was still possible for a body of distinguished scholars to enjoy
exploring together the sort of basic questions that go into the making of
a commentary. Such studies were not so far advanced or so elaborate as
they are today, and speculations and original proposals could be made
without first searching thousands of pages of specialist papers to see
what had already been done. Simply translating and explaining the text
occupied a large proportion of the time. Newton Flew says that publication was not an object; but it was under the stimulus of the Seminar
that the philosopher J. W. Oman, then Principal of Westminster College, was led to the writing of a highly original commentary on the
Apocalypse (*Book of Revelation* (Cambridge University Press, 1923)).
In the preface (p. vii) he wrote: 'A fitting dedication would be, "to the
onlie begetter of the insuing book, Prof. Burkitt's Seminar".'

'My presence at its deliberations on "Revelation" [he continues] was
not due to any particular interest in the subject, but to a vague idea
that, to think about religion, without knowing a little about its documents, is not much more use than to be a pundit on its documents,
without doing a little thinking about religion. In the alembic of its
learning, especially the Semitic erudition of the President, Dr

Abrahams, Dr Stanley Cook and Canon Lukyn Williams, any ideas I had were evaporated, and only mere negations seemed to be left. The book could not be explained as composed of various documents; no known Jewish apocalyptic writing sheds much light on it; no method of interpretation – historical, allegorical, mythological, astrological – gives it any connected or reasonable meaning. This did not increase my interest in the book, but it stirred my antagonism to being baffled by a problem: so, having some leisure in a Christmas Vacation, I set myself to a serious reading of the original.'

Certainly there were giants round that table, even if some of them chose to do exploits in realms with which they were not familiar; and one of the great features of the Seminar, as both Foakes Jackson and Newton Flew observe, was the wide range of specialist learning represented: Stanley Cook, Israel Abrahams, J. O. F. Murray, J. W. Oman, Mrs Adam, Francis Cornford, A. Lukyn Williams, John How, J. M. Creed, A. Nairne, J. W. Hunkin, F. S. Marsh, Herbert Loewe, A. C. Moule (eventually Professor of Chinese) – one could extend the list still further of those who, at one time or another, had been members. But there was also a pleasant ingredient of interested amateurs – country clergy, a returned missionary, and so forth, some of whom I recall from the subsequent days of C. H. Dodd. Such was the cheerful Mr J. J. Butler, formerly in China, but then a Vicar near Colchester, an ardent member of the Bezan Club, always ready to champion a Western reading, and the owner, I think, of the hand-printing press from which several résumés of Dodd's Seminar's work issued.

When C. H. Dodd came to the Norris–Hulse Chair in 1935 (the Norrisian Chair was merged with the Hulsean at the end of Burkitt's tenure), he succeeded to the leadership of the Seminar. The first meeting under his presidency was on 21 October 1936, and he continued to lead it, right through the War and until after his retirement from the Chair, though there was a gap between 14 May 1941 and 3 February 1943, owing to Dodd's attack of tuberculosis. For a very different reason, there was one other small gap. There is a note to 25 April 1945 that 'the meeting arranged for May 9th was cancelled because of the national holiday on the occasion of the German capitulation'. It was shortly after that historic intermission that Geoffrey Styler became Secretary, on 23 May 1945. His predecessors had included A. E. Goodman, Henry Chadwick, and A. G. Widdess. F. W. Dillistone's *C. H. Dodd: Interpreter of the New Testament* (London, 1977) contains a section on the Seminar, based on the reminiscences of some of the members. Those of W. D. Davies (pp. 151f) show, as I myself can testify, that the pleasantly informal, unconstrained, free-ranging inquiry that had characterised Burkitt's Seminar was well maintained. Dodd was a chairman with decided views of his own, but tolerant and hospitable to the views of others. At a meeting on 16 November 1938, a communication purporting to be from Luke the Evangelist was produced, defending the plausibility of the Lucan story of the penitent woman. Since it also defended a reading in codex Bezae, one suspects that this pseudonymous fragment's author was not far off. At another meeting, as W. F. Flemington recalls, Wilfred Knox read a paper criticising the theory, espoused by R. H. Lightfoot, that Mark's Gospel was meant to end at 16: 8.

> 'At the end of the paper [I quote Flemington] Dodd's immediate comment was, "Well, I think that puts paid to Lightfoot." During the discussion that followed, several members urged Knox to publish the paper – what about sending it to the *J.T.S.*? Swiftly came Dodd's comment, "Oh no, that would never do! It would be seething the kid in its mother's milk." (R.H.L. was at that time one of the editors of the *J.T.S.*) So Knox sent it to A. D. Nock in America and it came out in the *Harvard Theological Review* (Vol. xxxv pp. 13ff).'

At these sessions it was always possible (and, again, Mr Flemington's memory confirms this) to get up and rove round the room in order to pull out and consult a Wettstein (a copy of which was presented by A. C. Moule on 28 October 1936) or a reference book, the meeting-place in the Divinity School being then still used as the Senior Library and lined – as, alas, it no longer is – with splendid books. The rabbinic mantle of Israel Abrahams had fallen upon Herbert Loewe, who continued a member of the Seminar until his lamented death, recorded in the minutes of 23 October 1940. By that time, David Daube was well established as a representative of rabbinic studies, both in Herbert Loewe's own rabbinic study-group[1] and in Dodd's Seminar, where he often contributed brilliant notes or papers, delivered with verve and vigour. Once again, publication was not the object; but material from these papers found its way into Daube's *The New Testament and Rabbinic Judaism* (University of London, 1956); and W. L. Knox's two volumes on *The Sources of the Synoptic Gospels* (Cambridge University Press, 1953, 1957), skilfully edited with devoted care after Knox's death by Henry Chadwick, were generated within the Seminar, which listened to him again and again reading studies in this area in his bubbling, rapid,

[1] See R. Loewe in *JJS* 25 1 (1974), 137.

rather inaudible manner. They are dedicated to Professor Dodd and the members of his Seminar. A great deal of Dodd's tenure was devoted to the study of Synoptic sources; and from time to time he would himself gather up the findings in a lucid survey.

On Dodd's cession of the chairmanship, Professor Michael Ramsey (later to become Archbishop of Canterbury) took up the lead, with the proposal that the Seminar should study certain great New Testament words such as faith, hope and charity. It was a promising project, but his chairmanship was fairly brief, and the meetings lapsed when he was called to be Bishop of Durham. It was only after careful deliberation with colleagues and after making certain that no one else was going to do so that I ventured to re-convene the Seminar – not because I felt adequately qualified to lead it, but in order that so fine an institution should not be allowed to disappear. Mr Styler, who had already been Secretary for nearly 8 years, generously consented to continue. Neither of us, I suspect, imagined then that he would stick by the Seminar for 23 more years, and for 381 meetings during my tenure: and this, in addition to a whole year's seminars when Professor Lampe kindly presided during my absence on sabbatical leave; and that he would continue this invaluable ministry on into Professor Morna Hooker's presidency. The Seminar owes him an incalculable debt for faithful regularity, except on the rare occasions when illness or extreme pressure of business compelled him to call upon a deputy. But it is far more than mere regularity. What has made his contribution distinctive has been a concentrated accuracy of reporting combined with an editorial gift that usually made a speaker far clearer than he had seemed at the time (even to himself, let alone to others) and irradiated what were often pedestrian proceedings with pleasant sallies of wit that playfully punctured the turgid or the pompous, though never maliciously or unacceptably.

At the first meeting of my Seminar, on Wednesday, 21 January 1953, I alluded to the untimely death of that promising scholar Richard Heard. (Dodd's Seminar had lost young Alasdair Charles Macpherson as a war casualty.) Those present, besides Mr Styler and myself, were: Professor John Knox of Union Theological Seminary, New York, then on study leave in Cambridge, Doctors J. Y. Campbell, R. H. Strachan, P. Katz (or Walters), P. R. Ackroyd, and J. A. T. Robinson, and Messrs H. Chadwick, M. F. Wiles, C. A. Pierce, E. Randall, N. Birdsall, A. Winter, H. Bird, H. W. Montefiore, A. S. Cripps, and W. F. Flemington. The order is mainly random – perhaps, that of the signatures on the sheet passed round; but I am credibly informed that Geoffrey's classical ear told him that rhythmically 'Mr Flemington and the Secretary' made a good *clausula* and he liked to adhere to it. The Seminar began with some examination of Dom (later Bishop) B. C. Butler's book on the priority of Matthew, and Mr Styler read a paper that was the parent of the notable excursus subsequently printed in my *The Birth of the New Testament*, 1st ed. (London, 1962), an excursus that has come to be acknowledged all over the world as a masterly presentation of the case for Marcan priority. Generously, Geoffrey Styler has devoted much time to a complete revision and rewriting of this study for a new edition of my book.

About half-way through my period, the long tradition of meeting on Wednesdays was discontinued, and Tuesday became Seminar day, to save the Seminar from losing the much-valued presence of Professor G. W. H. Lampe, who then had to attend meetings of the General Board of the University on Wednesdays. The last meeting of my Seminar was, accordingly, on a Tuesday – 18 May 1976. At this session, the Secretary gave a review of the main areas of study covered in the period. They included Mark, parables, criteria in research, liturgical background, Johannine sources, 2 Peter and Jude, the Johannine Epistles, Revelation 1–3, the Pastoral Epistles, Matthew, the Fourth Gospel and Jewish worship, eschatology, miracles, the Epistle to the Hebrews, the Synoptic Problem, christology, the death of Christ, the Church (with special attention to σῶμα, ναός, and Israel), the Holy Spirit and Christ in the early Church, parables (again), and the atonement (again). Perhaps such a mixture only proved a too dilettante method (or lack of method); but it brought back memories of many interesting discussions. It has to be admitted with regret that, during my tenure, the range of expertise within the membership of the Seminar was sadly reduced. Long before the end, it was no longer possible to boast that nearly all the main theological disciplines were represented – not to mention extra-theological disciplines. Also, the proportion of junior members, mostly research students, was greatly increased. Though it may have been mainly my fault that a larger number of senior members was not held, it may have been also due in part to the sad but inevitable increase in specialisation. On the other hand, at least patristics, philosophy, Old Testament studies, and rabbinics are still ably represented, as this volume testifies. Moreover, while Foakes Jackson thought it noteworthy that Burkitt's seminar was visited by British scholars outside Cambridge and even by travellers from Canada and the United States, by my time world-wide exchange and travel had become so easy that a large number of the best known New Testament scholars from the Continent and America read papers at the Seminar. The list does not include Rudolf Bultmann, though he had spoken in Cambridge not many years before; but (not including some who attended the Seminar while they were research students and have subsequently come to hold academic positions abroad), I have noted the following (the list is not exhaustive): John Knox, W. C. van Unnik, Montgomery J. Shroyer, O. Cullman, Christine Mohrmann, H. J. Cadbury, Ragnar Bring, C. C. Richardson, J. Jeremias, Gustav Stählin, F. C. Grant, K. H. Rengstorf, E. Schweizer, P. Nepper-Christensen, C. W. F. Smith, Marcel Simon, W. G. Kümmel, R. W. Farmer, B. Reicke, R. W. Funk, R. Longenecker, Günther Bornkamm, H. K. McArthur, Étienne Trocmé, Jürgen Moltmann, E. E. Ellis, R. H. Fuller, Wayne Rollins, F. W. Beare, A. S. van de Woude, Moody Smith, Roy Harrisville, John Reumann, R. W. Lyon, E. F. Osborn, G. Snyder, Joseph Fitzmyer, E. Lohse, M. Hengel, and Godfrey Ashby. One published volume arose directly from the Seminar – *Miracles: Cambridge Studies in their Philosophy and History* (London, 1965), suitably dedicated to the members and most especially to Geoffrey Styler. Other books, such as Barnabas Lindars' *New Testament Apologetic* (London, 1961), owed something of their impetus to the Seminar, and a considerable number of essays and papers in books or learned journals had their first reading there, notably that excursus by Geoffrey Styler on the priority of Mark.

It is a source of lively satisfaction to me to see the chairmanship pass to my esteemed successor in the Lady Margaret's Chair, Professor Morna Hooker (Mrs Stacey), and to continue to listen to Mr Styler's terse, precise, witty summaries of the proceedings. In days when too much time is spent in the desert of utilitarian committee work, it is a priceless boon that one long-established oasis is still preserved (others, happily, have sprung up in other theological disciplines), where scholars and students may refresh themselves by tasting waters, whether or not they turn out to be medicinal. A tribute, incidentally, is owed to all past Secretaries and to the 'stand-ins' who have done faithful service on the occasions when Geoffrey Styler was forced to be absent. But nobody has contributed more than Geoffrey himself to the life and liveliness of this agreeable institution during his thirty-five years as Secretary, and we rejoice to insist – say what he will – on honouring his modest and retiring genius. When this book is presented, we must see to it that, for once, someone else writes up the proceedings, lest he should disparage his share in them.

Introduction

C. F. D. MOULE

Any and every 'browser' who picks up this book in a shop will find himself painfully involved in its subject, even if he totally repudiates the way in which it is handled in theology or in Christian devotion: inevitably – for suffering in some measure is the lot of us all, and innocent suffering is witnessed daily on television screens, while suffering bravely accepted because of one's convictions is never far from our consciousness. The question is what to do with suffering, and how to meet it.

Each of the contributors to this book studies some aspect of this theme, in the New Testament or in related literature. Added together, the essays present us with a spectrum that, within its chosen limits, is illuminating. How did Christians of the New Testament period interpret the sufferings of Jesus? How did they see the relation of their own sufferings to his? How much light is thrown on their own struggles and on their reflections on them by the way they present their story? How far does early Jewish and Christian literature subsequent to the New Testament period differ from or agree with New Testament thought? Finally, and urgently, by what processes may a modern reader interpret the mind of antiquity and come to grips with it in his own day?

Dr O'Neill holds that to interpret the death of Jesus as making its impact by no more than example (an 'exemplarist' theory of atonement) is alien to Jesus' own thinking. Jesus saw his death, he believes, as not merely exemplary but expiatory and vicarious – a service rendered to others that they could not do for themselves. But Dr O'Neill also believes that, in this, Jesus associated with himself his inner circle of followers. It was to them, and not to hearers in general, that the challenge to share the Cross was addressed; and the original form of the saying '*The* son of man came...to give his life a ransom for many' was, he believes: '*A* son of man came...to give his life as an act of cleansing for the benefit of many.' Although the sacrifice of Christ is unique and indispensable, the chosen few who have offered their lives with their Lord in this way do render a service to others in showing them how to receive the gift and in stimulating them to receive it.

Whether or not one follows Dr O'Neill in his view of the original form of that saying, the involvement of the believer with the sufferings of Christ sounds a very clear note in Paul's letters; and Professor Hooker, pursuing a theme on which she has already written elsewhere (see p. 70, n. 2), urges the importance of recognising that the suffering of Christ is not vicarious in the sense of exempting the Christian. Christ's death is indeed once for all; but its implementation is a continuing process. Professor Hooker believes that commentators are mistaken when, in Colossians 1:24, they insist that Paul's 'filling up what is lacking in the afflictions of Christ' is to be put in a quite different category from the suffering of Christ himself. It was precisely failure to accept involvement in Christ's suffering for which Paul reproved some of the Christians at Corinth.

Mr Flemington, though probably agreeing with Professor Hooker in her main contention, offers an interpretation of that particular passage, Colossians 1:24, which, if anything, increases the difference between the sufferings of Christ and the sufferings of the Christian. Paul is filling up what is lacking not in the Church's afflictions collectively, still less in Christ's own suffering, but in what he himself must undergo for Christ's sake: the lack that has yet to be supplied is in the appropriation of Christ's afflictions for himself personally and in his own life. Interestingly, Mr Flemington points out that, in the original version of Charles Wesley's famous hymn, 'O thou who camest from above', the last line read

<blockquote>And make my sacrifice complete.</blockquote>

It was altered, probably by John Wesley, to

<blockquote>And make the sacrifice complete.</blockquote>

Another difficult Pauline text on suffering is examined by Dr Bammel. Returning to an Epistle on which he has written before (p. 98, n. 51), he seeks the precise reference of the Apostle's exhortation 'under all these hardships, not to be shaken' (1 Thessalonians 3:3, NEB). Can the verb σαίνεσθαι, by no means abundantly attested in this sense, be illuminated from Jewish apocalyptic and mysticism? Dr Bammel argues a fascinating case for its signifying the physical tremor felt by the mystic in his visions and by all humanity when the Last Things come to pass. The passage is a warning against this reaction to the imminent end. Its prohibition of premature ecstasy, a reminder of how closely the primitive Church's views of suffering may be associated with apocalyptic Judaism, ties in with the epistle's ethical approach to eschatology, which Dr Bammel describes as typical of Christianity.

St Luke, it is often claimed, gets as near as any New Testament writer to presenting the death of Jesus as simply a martyrdom – as a noble example of suffering bravely borne in God's name – and not explicitly as anything more. Mr Beck, minutely examining Luke's Passion narrative, finds the alleged parallels with martyrologies in the main less than convincing. But, with scrupulous honesty, he acknowledges a possible martyrological note at two points. First, the disciples sleep in the garden because of λύπη, usually rendered 'grief'. But in this context 'grief' scarcely makes sense. It would be more natural to interpret it as 'pain', thus indicating that the disciples had shared in Christ's 'wrestling' (ἀγωνία); in which case, the actual reference to his 'wrestling' – a martyr-theme – in Luke 22: 44, though textually uncertain, is given plausibility. Secondly, the Lucan form of the centurion's confession, 'This man was righteous', is presented in Luke as something by which the centurion 'glorified' God – a term that, in this context, seems to indicate a Christian confession. Is not the centurion, then, acknowledging Jesus as 'the righteous sufferer' – a martyrological trait? Thus, there is at least something, though less than is sometimes alleged, in the view that Luke is presenting Christ as the arch-martyr.

It is well known that the early Christians, in their own sufferings for their allegiance to the faith, did not always, if ever, fully attain the noble ideal of the Sermon on the Mount, which bade them love their enemies. Sometimes, alas, they fell sadly far short. Professor Barnabas Lindars traces, in John 15: 18 – 16: 4, a stage of redaction at which Church and Synagogue are in bitter conflict; while 1 John, he thinks, represents a later stage when the separation between the two is complete, and the Fourth Gospel's christological test has become stereotyped and internalised. It is an instance of how subsequent conflict may leave its mark on the interpretation of Jesus.

Mr Sweet, on the other hand, presents an interpretation of the Revelation that may show another kind of Christian reaction to conflict. What is the interrelation of victory and sacrifice in this writing? Mr Sweet has devoted many years' attention to this question and has written strikingly on it in his commentary on the *Revelation* (London, 1979). He holds that the Apocalypse sees the effectiveness of the Christian Gospel as lying essentially in the maintaining by Christians of the testimony given by Jesus: *their* testimony, if you like, to *his* testimony – to Jesus' witness to

3

reality. Now, is such witness redemptive or only vindicative? In spite of the impression given by a superficial reading of the Apocalypse – that vindication, not to say vindictiveness, is the uppermost theme – he argues that the apparently vindictive passages and the statements about the impenitence of the opponents of Christ express only that destruction that falsehood brings upon itself. By the Christian witness conversion and healing are brought. For, paradoxically, the nations that are said to be exterminated, eventually bring their tribute into the heavenly city; and whereas the apocalyptist *hears* of the conquering *lion*, what he *sees* turns out to be the sacrificial *lamb*; while the blood that is shed turns out to be not that of the opponents, but Christ's blood and (derivatively) that of the martyrs. So the victory is 'Christian' rather than 'Maccabaean' after all. The final victory of truth over illusion is grounded in sacrifice.

Professor Lampe, traversing a wide field from the Maccabees to patristic literature, discusses the understanding of the witness borne by martyrs as the work of the Spirit of God, and thus as essentially due to the prophetic gift of inspiration. He is able to show how closely martyrdom is associated with prophecy in Hebrew–Jewish sources, and equally how often Christian sources see the witness of one who confesses Christ in the face of opposition as dependent on the advocacy of the Spirit, while, conversely, they see apostasy as demon-inspired sin against the Spirit. This observation enables him to throw fresh light on several much-debated passages in the New Testament and in patristic writers. It helps to unravel the knotty tangle into which the various Zechariahs are brought in the traditions. It yields useful criteria for deciding what is meant by Timothy's witness, and by Christ's, with which it is compared (1 Timothy 6: 12ff); and by the much discussed Revelations 19: 10: is this the witness originally borne by Jesus (subjective genitive), or the witness borne by others to him (objective genitive)? Professor Lampe, following several converging clues, comes down in favour of the latter, against Mr Sweet's conclusion (p. 104). This essay, as well as offering a fascinating commentary on several *cruces* in Jewish and Christian martyrology, throws a two-span bridge across from the Old Testament and Judaism to the New Testament and from the New Testament to post-biblical Christian thought. For instance, Professor Lampe observes that both Maccabaean and early patristic views see in martyrdom an internal triumph, within the martyr's heart, of what is noble over what is base – a kind of 'anthropology' of martyrdom, as he calls it. And this, in its turn, ties in with the late Jewish interpretation in Yose ben Yose of miracle as, in a sense, man's work, pointed out by Dr Horbury (p. 155). On the other hand, there are contrasts between Christianity and Judaism: one interesting conclusion arising from this study is that Jewish witness is seen predominantly as defensive, while Christian interpreters often find a redemptive element in the action. This (perhaps one may be allowed to observe) is in keeping with a doctrine of the death of Christ that is more than simply exemplary.

Out beyond the New Testament, again, Dr McNeil examines the theme of suffering and martyrdom in the Judaeo–Christian hymns called the *Odes of Solomon*. Here, too, the way of the Cross is the only way of victory, first for Christ and then for his followers. The serenity and confidence of the *Odes* are anything but cheaply bought. Moreover, the theme, by being associated with that of baptism, is given a more than individual dimension and is related to the whole body of Christ.

Dr Horbury, in a highly original study of a little-known Jewish poet, traces the connection between suffering and messianic hope. Yose ben Yose, a writer of perhaps the fifth century, in the Amoraic period, mourns the communal sufferings of servitude and the loss of the Temple-service. For consolation, he looks to the end of the servitude as deduced from the Danielic scheme of the four kingdoms, and to the bridal imagery of the Song of Songs. He views suffering as punitive, probative and meritorious, without drawing clear or consistent lines between these. In any case, he is not producing homilies addressed *to* the Synagogue: rather, he is voicing, in song, *from* the Synagogue, its confessions, its aspirations, and its hopes of redemption. Thus, martyrdom, and the Synagogue's suffering generally, are seen as punishment for the nation's sin; yet, they are also meritorious, and they win release. A particularly interesting aspect of these hymns for the New Testament student, as Dr O'Neill's discussion of the subject shows (pp. 13–15), is their treatment of the binding of Isaac. The willing obedience of Abraham and Isaac counts as the priestly offering of a victim who freely gives himself. Thus, sacrifice and atonement lie close to each other, as in much Christian thinking. Yet, there is no suffering for the Messiah, and Yose's emphatic theocentrism is perhaps in conscious reaction against Christian interpretations of the suffering of Christ. Yose and the New Testament writers both draw on the Old Testament use of bridal imagery to describe redemption; but, even though Yose boldly projects human feelings on to the divine Bridegroom – who is God himself, rather than the Messiah – the Christian writers distinctively emphasise the sufferings of the Bridegroom – for they envisage him, by contrast, as the crucified Christ. The fact that Yose, in the rabbinic period, so strongly takes up the themes of suffering, sin, sacrifice and redemption, which are prominent in the New Testament, is significant, Dr Horbury believes, for assessment of the development of Judaism during and after New Testament times.

But what is one to make of all this? Professor Lash asks penetrating and disturbing questions about New Testament interpretation. It is a fatal over-simplification, he says, to imagine that the New Testament scholar tells us what the text *meant*, leaving it to others to say what it *means* – as though he were the first runner in a relay-race and only had to hand the original meaning, like a baton, to the systematic theologian who will carry it on. In reality, 'What did it mean?' is itself a complex question. Does it ask 'What did it mean to the author?' or 'to the hearers?' And, anyway, how can one begin to answer such a question without some inkling of its importance to the perennial human predicament, and so to the present? At every stage, even the most basic, interpretation rather than report is inevitable. It is not a relay-race moving in one direction, not a matter of successive stages. Rather, it is a dialogue, a case of mutual interdependence, a moving back and forth. Furthermore, it is no good to confine oneself to the detection of meanings. One cannot evade the question of truth: 'Was Jesus – were the New Testament writers – right?' It is not modesty but evasion of duty to dodge the question of ultimate authority. Some metaphors applied to exegesis are simply inadequate. Goods imported from abroad for consumption at home, or, conversely, tourists travelling to foreign parts – these will not do. One needs to find something more dynamic. Mr Flemington (p. 90) is justified in citing Maximilian Kolbe's voluntary death for the sake of another as a real interpretation of Pauline theology. God's act is not an act of explanation but of transformation. In the last analysis, all interpretation must be interpretative *practice*. It is the *performance* of a symphony that is its only adequate interpretation.

Reflection on these essays presents the reader once again with the enigma of undeserved suffering. An atheist, assuming a random universe, avoids this particular problem, though (many would agree) at too high a price. But from a theist's standpoint, can any sense be made of it at all? Probably not, on the level of rational argument. But some consolation and much strength may be found, and clearly have been found again and again, in the conviction that somehow suffering (however outrageous and inexplicable) can be turned to good account. Somehow it need not be wholly useless, pointless, destructive, or negative. If it is accepted – not supinely but positively and affirmatively – good seems to spring from it, both for the sufferer and for others: 'semen est sanguis Christianorum'. The Acts of the Alexandrine pagan martyrs lack the depth of religious martyr-stories: they are chiefly protest. But at the very least, a life laid down in defiance of tyranny is a blow struck for freedom. And on a deeper and more mysterious level many religious thinkers have seen something reparative and salvific in a death that bears positive witness to faith in an ultimate good. In some sense, the martyr achieves a benefit for others, over and above the gift of his courageous example.

Moreover, in some measure it must be the power of God in him – so a religious observer would say – that enables him to endure. This leads on to christology. Why is it that there is a strong stream in the Christian tradition that, when it comes to interpreting the death of Jesus, refuses to stop even at the martyr's achievement? Not content to describe Jesus as rendering the service of a martyr, it affirms, in his case, something more and different. If Luke comes as near as any New Testament writer to presenting the death of Christ as a martyrdom, yet even Luke's story is still recognisably different. The New Testament writers see Jesus as offering himself 'for' or 'on behalf of' others in some special, some absolute, sense. In some relative sense, no doubt, God is in and with all who valiantly suffer for the truth, and, for that matter, in all those who are simply overtaken by cruelty, without courage or martyr-heroics. But in the case of Jesus it is more than simply that God is in and with him. Because of what, on other grounds, Christians believe Jesus to be, he is in an absolute degree God's own suffering; God's decisive and ultimate giving of his very self in love for the world, and therefore God's transforming, creative power.

A Christian estimate of Christ seems to involve the recognition of this distinctive and decisive character in his death. However true it is that God always has been, and always will be, with and in all his servants in their sufferings, yet it appears that at a particular time in the history of planet Earth there comes a person who is totally loyal to the will of God and who fully and undeviatingly accepts the consequences, and who thus crowns and completes the work of reconciliation achieved throughout time and space by the energy of God's creative love. All martyrs receive and transmit this reparative energy of God's forgiveness; but Christ, as no one else, is one with God in creating it: in him are effected its initiation, its toilsome application, and its consummation.

Does this distinctive understanding of Christ and of his work match the tenor of these essays? Would Professor Lash recognise it as a justifiable conclusion from responsible dialogue with the normative documents? Is it this that Dr O'Neill believes Jesus' actual words to have implied? Is it this that makes baptised membership in the body of

Christ of special import? Is it this that distinguishes a fully and distinctively Christian interpretation of suffering from Yose ben Yose's? Is it this by which we have to judge the marks of controversy between Church and Synagogue or Church and State? Is it this that makes commentators chary of interpreting Colossians 1 : 24 as though Paul's sufferings were in themselves redemptive? And is this so integral a part of the texture of Christian faith and devotion that the expositor cannot discount it, even when he tries to ask himself the purely historical question what an evangelist or the writer of an epistle originally meant? Perhaps not all the essayists would wish to answer 'Yes.' But the questions are worth asking.

If the answer is 'Yes', however, it is still impossible, if one is doing justice to the earliest and most authentic evidence of Christian understanding, to isolate Jesus' life and death and resurrection from the rest of mankind, as though his achievement were vicarious in an exclusive sense. Rather, there is an interchange and interlocking that unites all sufferers with Christ, not exempting them but taking them triumphantly through their sufferings – associating, not equating, their effect with that of his work. No courageous witness to truth, whether within or outside a consciously espoused Christian faith, can be far from the Cross of Christ. Yet, neither could it exist – so Christians will affirm – but for a God whose forgiving love is Christ.

Did Jesus teach that his death would be vicarious as well as typical?

J. C. O'NEILL

Christians and many non-Christians agree that Jesus' death was a model of self-sacrificing love. They hold that his words, his life, and his death formed a seamless robe: he taught love; he acted out love; and he died displaying love. The non-Christians who hold this view of Jesus do not see any reason to become Christians, for they reject the notion that Jesus' death was a sacrifice made on their behalf. Self-sacrifice, yes; but sacrifice, no.

What is particularly interesting is that many Christians, too, wish to eliminate the idea that Jesus' death was a sacrifice for others. I well remember the long and sensitive discussions that went on in Professor Moule's Seminar in 1968–9 and again in 1974–5 about just this point. Geoffrey Styler defended the retention of the term 'sacrifice' by patiently insisting that the idea of sacrifice was the only term that applied directly to the work of Christ (for all the other terms applied to mankind's situation before and after the work of redemption); while Professor Moule, equally patient, argued that sacrificial language should be left behind.

To leave sacrificial language behind is not necessarily to endorse a merely exemplarist interpretation of the death of Christ. Some other way may well be found for emphasising the centrality of Christ's work than saying that he offered his life in sacrifice to the Father. Jesus' death can be held up as an archetype of what happens when perfect love meets evil, and believers can be invited to leave self behind and to adopt this archetypal love. Or, from a slightly different point of view, Jesus' death may be seen as the perfect example of God's reconciling and healing power, and believers may be invited to become incorporated into the new humanity Jesus represents.

Yet, however important the role of Christ in the various systems proposed for interpreting the Gospels without using the language of sacrifice, all these systems agree that the idea that the Son offered himself to the Father must be avoided.

9

I suppose that Christians who avoid sacrificial language want to avoid saying that the Father needed the Son's sacrifice before he was willing or able to forgive sinners. That, however, is not the only interpretation of Christ's death as a sacrifice. The Father may have needed no more than true repentance and sincere worship, but the nation that already knew all that (through Moses and the prophets) may yet themselves have needed something more before they would return and be reconciled; in that sense, the Son's death may have been necessary, and necessary precisely as a sacrifice.

The language of sacrifice may not immediately appeal to us, but it does not entail the view that the Father needed the Son's death before he could forgive.

My task in this paper is not to explore any further the possible views that might be taken of the death of Christ, whether sacrificial or non-sacrificial, but rather to ask, What did Jesus himself intend by willing to die?

The crucial issue is, How was his death 'for others'? Granted he loved others and invited them to join him in some way, did he also mean to do for them something they could not do for themselves? If he meant his life to be a sacrifice to the Father, he must have meant others to benefit from *not* doing what he had to do; at the heart of sacrificial worship is the fact that the worshippers give a costly sacrifice that is yet far less costly than themselves. Did Jesus think that his death was a sacrifice for others in this sense? If we find that he did, we may even be able to go further and explore in what way he thought his death was a sacrifice for others, and to ask whether or not he saw himself as an innocent victim who willingly accepted the punishment for sin that others deserved. But the crucial question remains, Did Jesus die sacrificing himself to the Father for the sins of the world? Did Jesus think that his death would do for mankind what no one else could do?

It is, of course, difficult to discover the intentions of anyone else at all, but, strangely enough, it may be easier for a figure in history like Jesus than for someone nearer in time but less significant. I would even dare to say that Jesus' intentions in going up to Jerusalem to die can be worked out quite simply by listing all the possible explanations, and by eliminating all but the one that fits the broadly agreed facts about his life and about current Jewish expectations. On that test, he is unlikely to have gone to Jerusalem to die except to offer his life to the Father in sacrifice.[1] Nevertheless, that approach cannot by itself sustain the full

---

[1] See C. F. D. Moule, *The Origin of Christology* (Cambridge University Press, 1977), pp. 109f for a report of a lecture in which I tried this approach, with Professor Moule's own reply.

weight of proof. Unless Jesus' own words betrayed the same intention, we could not be content with a case based only on the more general probabilities. If his words betrayed no sense that he saw his death as vicarious, we should be on very shaky ground indeed if we affirmed that his death was in fact vicarious or piacular.

I began to write this paper assuming that of course Jesus intended his death to be a universal model or example, and I thought my task was simply to show that he also meant his death to be a sacrifice for others; but, the more I examined the Gospels, the more clearly I saw that my assumption was wrong, or at least misleadingly inaccurate. Once we examine exactly how Jesus intended his death as a *model*, we recover compelling evidence that he must have meant his death to be a sacrifice.

The discovery I made was that there is very little evidence that Jesus saw his death as the model of self-sacrificing love that all his followers should copy. The sayings that appear to support the idea that his death was intended as the type of the Christian life teach rather, on closer examination, that his death was meant to be expiatory.

The plan I shall follow is this. I shall first examine all the sayings in which Jesus speaks of others' taking up the Cross, and I shall try to show that these sayings were restricted in application to a limited number of followers and were not meant for all. Then I shall examine the sayings about service, including the much-disputed ransom saying in Matthew 20: 28 and Mark 10: 45, and try to show that they apply only to Jesus and his limited circle, and that they imply vicarious service for others.

I shall try to prove that although Jesus did see his own death as exemplary, it was only an example for a limited number of those who believed in him; and that his own death and the death of those followers who were ready to be martyred he saw as vicarious for Israel and the Gentiles.

First, then, I shall discuss the two sayings about taking up a cross, and a third saying that is not normally associated with these two but that I shall argue belongs also with the Cross sayings.

The Cross sayings are, first, 'And whoever does not take his cross and follow after me is not worthy of me' (Matthew 10: 38, for which Luke has: 'Whoever does not carry his own cross and come after me cannot be my disciple', 14: 27); and, secondly, 'If anyone wants to come after me let him deny himself and bear his cross and follow me' (Matthew 16: 24, for which Mark has: 'If anyone wants to follow me, let him deny himself and bear his cross and follow me', 8: 34, and Luke in the Codex Vaticanus: 'If anyone wants to come after me, let him deny himself and carry his cross every day and follow me', 9: 23).

The difficulty is this. The Cross sayings seem to imply that everyone would know what was meant by taking up one's own cross and following some leader who was also carrying his cross, and could apply that language to himself. Such language, however, seems to imply that 'taking up the cross' was either a Jewish or Gentile catch-phrase for self-denial. If there were no such catch-phrase current, which Jesus could use and his disciples understand, and there does not seem to be, then the proverbial-type language must imply that Jesus himself had already been crucified; in other words, the Cross sayings were made up by the early Church and put on to Jesus' lips. If Jesus did say such a thing, he could only have been referring specifically to the typical punishment meted out by Romans and Roman client-kings, but then he would be inciting his followers to join him in a deliberate plot to incite Roman execution, and that does not fit in with the generally pacific tenor of Jesus' teaching.

We are in a dilemma. If the sayings have a religious meaning, they are inauthentic. If the sayings have a straightforward political meaning, they are untypical, and consequently also unlikely to be authentic.

However, when we look closely at the details of the sayings, they do not really fit either the religious interpretation or the political interpretation that I have just suggested. The political interpretation will not do, because the sayings place all the emphasis on the willing acceptance of the burden and the willing following of Jesus. If Jesus meant his followers to court Roman execution he would have had to specify the steps to be taken that would lead to condemnation; once condemned, Roman criminals had no choice about whether they would carry their crosses or not, and no choice about where they were to go. It was possible to choose to follow a leader to court, but not possible to choose to take the cross and follow a leader to the place of execution.

But the religious interpretation is also unlikely. The Cross language is 'applied' to Christians in the early Church, but always with reference to the actual crucifixion of Jesus (Romans 6: 2–14; 1 Corinthians 2: 2; Galatians 6: 14; Philippians 3: 10; Colossians 2: 12–15; 3: 3; 2 Timothy 2: 11 etc.). The Cross sayings, however, concentrate all attention on the taking, bearing and following, and the disciples are asked to take their own crosses, not Jesus'. Furthermore, there is something ridiculous in the image of all Christians carrying crosses after Jesus, a ridiculousness we do not normally see because we spiritualise the language and covertly change the picture so that there is only one cross in view, the Cross of Jesus.

The very details of the sayings compel us to look for another interpretation. This interpretation will have to match two features of the sayings, their emphasis on the voluntary taking and bearing of the Cross to follow Jesus voluntarily; and their emphasis on the taking and the bearing and the following rather than on the actual crucifixion.

Arnold Meyer at the end of the nineteenth century drew attention to the evidence that yields an interpretation that fits these two features. He cited rabbinic evidence by which the verse in Genesis 22: 6, which says, 'And Abraham took the wood of the burnt offering and laid it upon Isaac his son', was interpreted, 'as he who carries his cross on his shoulders' and, in another place, 'He was like him who goes to be consumed with his wood on his shoulders' (Gen. R. 56.3 (35*c*); Pesikta Rabbati 31.2 (143*b*); Tanhuma Wa'era 46, ed. S. Buber (Wilna, 1885), vol. II, p. 114).[2]

Philip R. Davies and B. D. Chilton have argued that Isaac was regarded simply as an *exemplary* martyr in Jewish sources roughly contemporary with the New Testament. The Jewish teaching that the offering of Isaac was an expiatory and redemptive act for all Israel was not earlier than the second century A.D., and arose in response to an Isaac–Jesus typology and to the Christian doctrine of the atonement.[3]

They do not deny, however, that 4 Maccabees contains references to expiatory martyrdom. The question then will be, Are the references to Isaac merely exemplary, or does the context show that Isaac's offering of himself is more than a good example of readiness to accept martyrdom?

All but one of the references to Isaac in 4 Maccabees occur in the long account of the martyrdom of the seven brothers and their mother (chapters 8–18; the only other reference to Isaac is in 7.14). Of course Isaac's willing acceptance of death is held up as an example (13.12), but this is only the first of many references to Isaac. The mother of the seven sons in encouraging them to die is compared to Abraham (15.28); she called on her sons to offer themselves 'in sacrifice' like Isaac (16.19f); she is extolled as one whose child-bearing was from the son of Abraham (17.6); and she reminded her sons that their father when he was alive used to teach them of Isaac who was 'offered as a burnt-offering' (18.11).

We notice two things. Isaac's self-offering is not only an example, but also a sacrifice and a burnt-offering; and Isaac's offering is a recurrent

---

[2] Arnold Meyer, *Jesu Muttersprache* (Freiburg i. B. and Leipzig, 1896), p. 78; H. L. Strack and P. Billerbeck, *Kommentar zum Neuen Testament aus Talmud und Midrasch*, vol. I (Munich, 1922), p. 587; A. Schlatter, *Der Evangelist Matthäus* (Stuttgart, 1929), pp. 35of; R. Bultmann, *Die Geschichte der synoptischen Tradition*, 2nd ed. (Göttingen, 1931), pp. 173f; English translation by John Marsh, 2nd ed. (Oxford, 1968) pp. 16of. See Tertullian, *Adv. Marc.* III. 18.2; *Adv. Iud.* 10.6.

[3] See Davies and Chilton, 'The Aqedah: A Revised Tradition History', *CBQ* 40 (1978), 514–46; Davies, 'Passover and the Dating of the Aqedah', *JJS* 30 (1979), 59–67.

theme throughout the passage. Granted these two points, it is hard to agree with Dr Davies and Dr Chilton that the seven brothers follow Isaac only in following his example and not in intending to achieve what Isaac intended. It is said that the offering of the seven brothers and their mother was to purify their country, to be a ransom for their nation's sins, to be blood shed as propitiation, and to lead to the deliverance of Israel by God (17.22; cf. 18.3–5). If the seven brothers and their mother acted with the example of Isaac's sacrifice before their eyes, surely it is natural to assume that what they are said to have achieved by sacrifice is the same as what Isaac was assumed to have achieved by sacrifice. The references to Isaac in a passage about expiatory deaths are not incidental or casual; the whole passage is saturated with the image of Isaac's sacrifice.

The argument that the later rabbis only adopted the idea that Isaac was a sacrificial offering because the Christians had already made Isaac a sacrificial offering prefiguring Jesus is hard to sustain.[4] Dr Davies and Dr Chilton would have to meet two objections. First, they would have to explain why the Jewish thinkers who, on their hypothesis, were trying to neutralise Christian apologetics, introduced the idea that Isaac in taking the wood on his shoulders took on his *cross*. Why did they make the parallel as specific as this, when there was no need to refer to crucifixion at all in their counter-propaganda? Secondly, Dr Davies and Dr Chilton would have to explain why the Christian thinkers who, on their hypothesis, were creating a doctrine of the propitiatory suffering of Isaac as a type of the propitiatory suffering of Christ, attached this notion to someone in the Old Testament who did not in fact die. The lamb caught in the thicket would have been more obvious. It is only likely that they would compare Christ to Isaac if actual martyrs, who also offered their lives as propitiatory sacrifices, had already been compared to Isaac in pre-Christian Judaism. And for that, as I have already argued, there is good evidence.

If Jesus was referring to the sacrifice of Isaac, all the details in the sayings fall into place. Later Jewish exegesis of the sacrifice of Isaac (exemplified in the early synagogal poetry quoted below) strikingly emphasised Isaac's willing acceptance of his sacrifice.[5] The story of

---

[4] The early Christian references are to be found in Barnabas 7.3; Melito of Sardis, *On the Pascha* 59; 69; fragments 9–12; 15.21; Irenaeus, *Adv. Haer.* IV.5.4 (ed. W. W. Harvey (Cambridge University Press, 1857), II, 157); Tertullian, *Adv. Marc.* III.18.2; *Adv. Jud.* 10.6.

[5] See below, pp. 169–71, and G. Vermes, 'Redemption and Genesis xxii – The Binding of Isaac and the Sacrifice of Jesus' in *Scripture and Tradition in Judaism: Haggadic Studies* (Leiden, 1961), pp. 193–227.

Abraham and Isaac further perfectly matches an emphasis on taking the wood and journeying, without there necessarily being a death at the end: Isaac did not have to suffer, although he was fully ready to do so.

There is one further point that helps confirm this interpretation. Matthew 10: 38 says that he who takes his cross and follows Jesus is 'worthy' of him. This is no vague sentiment, but has particular application to those who are ready to accept martyrdom: the last of the seven brothers put to torture and death at the command of Antiochus Epiphanes was exhorted by his mother to be 'worthy' of his brothers, and the martyrs in Revelation are said to be 'worthy' (2 Maccabees 7: 29; Revelation 3: 4; 16: 6; cf. Wisdom 3: 5).

The term 'the cross' is quite appropriate to the story of Isaac. The wooden cross could easily have been spoken of as the wood of sacrifice before the time of Jesus, because already Jews had been crucified for their faith, and the ambiguity of 'wood' and 'tree' had already been used to connect the tree in the garden of Eden with the staff upon which the brazen serpent had been lifted up in the wilderness.[6] The martyrs' deaths before the time of Jesus were seen as atoning for the sins of the people,[7] and the rabbinic interpretation of the wood for the sacrifice of Isaac as a cross, which I cited above, shows the further connection being made.

In the Cross sayings Jesus both announced his own willingness to be sacrificed for the people's sins like the martyrs before him, and made it a condition of discipleship that the disciples should also be willing, like Isaac, to take the wood of the Cross on their own shoulders.

If I am right, the Cross sayings are not meant to apply to all who believe in Jesus Christ. The sayings are restricted in scope to the small group of martyrs who are to prepare themselves to bear the sins of the people who have broken God's Law and who deserve God's punishment. The martyrs are prepared to die as those who willingly take on themselves the guilt of the people, and who pray to the Father that their sacrifice will be acceptable as an atonement for sin. We remember that the last of the seven brothers prayed,

> 'I, like my brothers, give up body and soul for our fathers' laws, calling on God to show favour to our nation soon, and to make thee

---

[6] Philo, *De Ag.* 97; John 3: 14f; Barnabas 12.7.

[7] 2 Maccabees 7; 4 Macc. 1.11; 6.27–9; 17.21f; Test. Jos. 19.11; Test. Ben. 3.1, 6–8; the story of the seething blood that flowed from the threshold of the Temple, Gittin 57*b*; Babli Sanh. 96*b*; Jerus. Taanith 69*a*; the traditions of the binding of Isaac, Frag. Tg. and Neofiti Gen. 22; 1QS 8.6, 10; 9.4; CD 14.19; Apoc. Elij. 3.33; Josephus, *B.J.* v. 9.4 (419) of his family and of himself; and many other passages.

(the persecutor) acknowledge, in (our) torments and plagues, that he alone is God, and to let the Almighty's wrath, justly fallen on the whole of our nation, end in me and my brothers' (2 Maccabees 7: 37f, Moffatt's translation).

Once we anchor Jesus' Cross sayings firmly in the history of his times, we can no longer interpret them as applying to all believers; they must be restricted to a few.

Of course the sayings were soon generalised by being applied spiritually to all Christians. Some manuscripts of Luke 9: 23 talk about taking up the Cross every day ($\mathfrak{p}^{75}$ $\aleph^*$ B etc.), and Mark 8: 34 adds that the saying was given to the crowd as well as to the disciples. Other more general statements about losing one's life in order to save it are regularly inserted into the context of the Cross sayings, but that, too, represents secondary editorial interpretation. The original idea of the Cross sayings was intended by Jesus to apply to his immediate disciples who were to pledge themselves to the possibility of martyrdom as a condition of following him. Jesus' mission was to all Israel, and he would never have envisaged that all Israel should be martyrs; his own martyrdom and that of his brothers was for the sake of many.

Israel was faced with the prospect of terrible suffering, which Jesus saw as largely deserved, for Jerusalem kept on killing the prophets and stoning those sent to her. The righteous in Israel would suffer with the guilty, and of them it could well be said that for God's sake they were killed all the day long and counted as sheep for the slaughter (Psalm 44: 22), but the point of explicitly preparing disciples in advance to suffer was to prepare them to be the martyrs who would shorten the sufferings of the righteous and turn back the hearts of the unrighteous to God.

Although the generalisation of the sayings in the Gospels, by which they were applied spiritually to all, is secondary, it is not to be regarded as illegitimate. On the contrary, all Jewish martyrs in the documents of the time wished their martyrdoms to be brought to God's remembrance by their fellow-Israelites. The proper response of Israel to the martyrdoms was the spiritual appropriation of the martyrs' death, a making of the martyrs' sacrifice the nation's sacrifice to God. In appropriating the martyrs' actual sacrifice, the later worshippers were themselves making a spiritual sacrifice.

There is another saying of Jesus that mentions the possible death of his followers, which deserves to be considered beside the two forms of the Cross saying, namely, the saying about those who will not taste death before the coming of the Kingdom.

Matthew 16: 28 reads: 'Amen I say to you that there are some standing here who will not taste death before they see a son of man coming in his Kingdom'; for which Mark has: 'Amen I say to you that there are some here standing who will not taste death before they see the Kingdom of God come in power' (9: 1); and Luke: 'I say to you in truth, there are some standing here who will not taste death before they see the Kingdom of God' (9: 27).

In its present form this saying appears to state nothing more than that the Kingdom of God would come before all standing there had died. It is as banal as that. If we knew the age of the youngest in Jesus' audience, and if we knew the generally expected life-span at the time, we could calculate when Jesus expected the Kingdom to come. This sort of reflection has led scholars like Günther Bornkamm to suppose that the saying was inauthentic, and that it was made up by early Christians who were dismayed at the delay of the parousia and who comforted themselves with the conjecture that Jesus could not have meant the delay to be quite as long as one generation.[8] Then we would have to ask ourselves why the authority of this recent conjecture was strong enough to preserve the saying when that first generation had indeed passed without the coming of the Kingdom. Bornkamm's line of reasoning does not really provide a satisfactory solution.

Another approach is to identify the coming of the Kingdom with something other than the patent overthrow of God's enemies – perhaps with Pentecost. But that approach raises fresh difficulties, for there seems no reason for Jesus to emphasise that any of his hearers would die before then. The death of many of his hearers, but not all, must be connected in some vital way with the Kingdom's coming.

I should like to propose for consideration another explanation of the saying. I suggest that a tiny, but understandable, corruption has crept into the text of all three versions of the saying, and that originally Jesus spoke not of those standing 'here', but simply of those standing. The little word 'here' was added by scribes who could make no sense of those standing.

The textual evidence for this conjecture is as follows.

Matthew 16: 28:

των ωδε εστωτων ℵ B D etc.

---

[8] Günther Bornkamm, 'Die Verzögerung der Parusie: Exegetische Bemerkungen zu zwei synoptischen Texten [Markus 9.1; Matthäus 25.1–13]' in Werner Schmauch (ed.), *In Memoriam Ernst Lohmeyer* (Stuttgart, 1951), pp. 116–26 at pp. 116–19. Bornkamm is following Wellhausen, Bultmann and Sundwall.

ωδε εστωτες   E F G H W *ΓΔΦ* etc.

των εστωτων ωδε   Origen 3.550; 4.366

των εστωτων   ff² Hilary [bis]

Mark 9: 1:

ωδε των εστηκοτων   B etc.

των ωδε εστηκοτων   A W Θ etc.

των εστηκοτων ωδε   p⁴⁵ (1) syᵖ etc.

των εστηκοτων   i r

Luke 9: 27:

των αυτου εστηκοτων   א B etc.

των ωδε εστηκοτων   A C D W Θ etc.

των εστηκοτων   1355

In each case the position of the word 'here' is uncertain, and in each case there is some evidence that the word was not found.

Certainly, a reading without 'here' is hard – so hard that it would, if it were original, have almost inevitably attracted the addition of 'here' to make it easier to understand. If we could make sense of this shorter text, we should have good reason to accept it.

The solution seems to be that those who stand means those who withstand persecution. The verb is in fact used absolutely with just this sense. In Ephesians 6: 11, 13, 14 'to stand' means to stand fast in the battle against the powers of evil, and in Revelation 6: 17 the Seer says, 'For the great day of their wrath is come, and who can stand?' The same verb is used absolutely of withstanding God's judgement in Psalm 130: 3.[9]

Jesus would then be prophesying and saying, 'There are some who withstand who will not taste death before the Kingdom of God is come with power.' This implies that he will himself die and that many of his circle will die in persecution but, if they all stand firm, some will not need to die as martyrs before the Kingdom comes. Jesus is comforting the apostles. Like all prophecy, this prophecy is conditional, conditional on the faithful performance of the things God requires from mankind before he brings in the Kingdom. None of Jesus' hearers nor those who followed after them would disbelieve the prophecy simply because it was not fulfilled; rather, they would understand that mankind had failed to fulfil the conditions under which God had promised to act.

If I am right, this saying supplements the Cross sayings I discussed earlier. Both the Cross sayings and the saying about tasting death show

[9] I owe this reference to Dr Horbury.

that Jesus expected the small circle of disciples to prepare themselves for martyrdom. The saying about being prepared to taste death connects this preparedness with the coming of the Kingdom. The coming of the Kingdom in Jewish thought required the repentance of Israel, so the conclusion lies to hand that the readiness for martyrdom of Jesus' close disciples was not for its own sake but for the sake of the people. By their readiness to die like their Lord, they would awaken in the people a consciousness of sin and so produce the fruits of repentance. By dying, the disciples would show the people what they all deserved from God for their sins; their death, like the supreme death of their Lord, the Messiah, would help to achieve the reconciliation God so desired with his sinful children.

All the sayings imply that the sole purpose of the death of the martyrs is to atone for the sins of many. Jesus' purpose in dying was not to provide a model for all but a sacrifice for all. Insofar as he taught that his death was a model, it was a model only for those relatively few close disciples who were called to take a share in his atoning work. His work and their work shared the characteristic of being for others, which is not to deny that his work was distinct from their work. For he saw himself as the Son of God, the Messiah.[10] His death was as distinct from the death of his subordinates as the death of the son in the parable was distinct from the death of the previous messengers (Matthew 21: 33–46; Mark 12: 1–12; Luke 20: 9–19). The Son's death in sacrifice is, by definition, unlimited in scope, reaching even to the salvation of the Gentiles, so that all the nations God has made would come and worship before him (Psalm 86: 9); and it is unsurpassable as sacrifice. But the Son's sacrifice does not deny the value of the sacrifice of those who sacrificed themselves before he came nor, as I shall now argue a little more fully, of the sacrifice of those who would offer themselves after his crucifixion.

The best proof that Jesus specifically prepared a few to suffer for many lies in the fact that these few are those who were called to rule over many. This can most easily be shown by a calm consideration of Jesus' sayings about service. It is commonly assumed that these sayings teach that everyone who believes in Jesus Christ should be 'last of all and servant of all' (Mark 9: 35); Jesus is holding up service to others as the true hallmark of all his followers. I want to argue, on the contrary, that the servant sayings were not meant to apply to everybody, but only

[10] I have discussed this and related questions in the Cunningham Lectures for 1975–6, published as *Messiah: Six Lectures on the Ministry of Jesus* (Cambridge: Cochrane Press, 1980).

to Jesus' few specially chosen followers who were destined to rule in Israel.

My case rests on the simple observation that every saying about service in the Synoptic Gospels in which it is possible to determine the scope of the audience Jesus had in mind refers solely to the inner group of disciples. There are, of course, sayings that do not indicate their scope, and Jesus could have meant them for the crowds, but it is noteworthy that each of the three Synoptic Evangelists thought the sayings were restricted to the Twelve. Only John's Gospel, in the account of the washing of the disciples' feet, gives evidence that the ideal of service was recommended to all who follow Christ – and even that evidence is doubtful (John 13: 14).

My case is open to the objection that every restriction of the duty of service to the Twelve is a distortion of Jesus' teaching by a Church that had become interested in church order (assuming, of course, that Jesus was not).[11]

I have three answers. First, the general historical probabilities strongly favour the assumption that Jesus would have been concerned about who should rule in Israel and how they should rule. The Old Testament and almost every Jewish document we know that was read and cherished by every Jewish group at the time was concerned with this question; the Qumran documents merely serve to confirm what we already knew. If Jesus had wished to challenge the assumption that who should rule and how they should rule was a vital issue, he would have had to say so very clearly and explicitly if he were to be understood. We possess no such clear and unequivocal teaching.

The case for saying that Jesus was just pretending to agree with the Jewish love for order and hierarchy and organisation would need to be argued. 'The Kingdom of God is within you' (Luke 17: 21) is a defensible translation of that much-disputed saying, I grant; but one verse is far too slender a basis for a wholesale reinterpretation of all the rest of Jesus' teaching, and in the end this verse can itself be shown to mean something quite different.[12]

Second, the broad and undisputed facts about the shape of Jesus' ministry confirm that he assumed there was order and hierarchy among his followers. He himself took the lead; he collected a defined group around him; he singled out Peter and gave Peter and James and John a special position within that group; and he seemed also to have recognised

---

[11] E.g. Eduard Schweizer, *Das Evangelium nach Markus* (Göttingen, 1967), p. 126 on Mark 10: 43.
[12] See *Messiah*, Lecture 2, 'The Kingdom'.

wider groups like the seventy and the women, groups that were distinguished from the crowd. He never challenged the authority of the generally recognised leaders of Israel, only their misuse of their authority.

Thirdly, when we can put alongside one another sayings or terms with a restricted application and the same sayings or terms with a general and universal application, the evidence favours the hypothesis that the generalised applications are secondary and later rather than primary and earlier. For example, the term 'disciple' is restricted to the inner group in the earlier strata of tradition, and widened to apply to all Christians in the later strata (e.g. in the Book of Acts).[13] This is not at all surprising. Every scrap of Jesus' teaching was so precious to the early Church that preachers would naturally apply sayings originally restricted to everyone, as we still do. There is little harm in doing so, as long as this homiletic application of the texts is not used to destroy the ministry that Jesus established.

The first servant passage to be considered is the account of the request that the sons of Zebedee should be given positions at the right hand and the left hand (Matthew 20: 20–3; Mark 10: 35–40). Jesus' answer is that the condition for receiving such positions is their readiness to drink the cup he must drink, that is, to prepare to be martyred. He also says that he is not able to assign those positions; for the simple reason, I believe, that he could not claim to be Messiah until the Father had vindicated and enthroned him. Jesus clearly assumes that the Messiah would be proclaimed by the Father, and that the Messiah would then be flanked by a court in which some will have positions of special authority. Nothing he says contradicts that assumption, and the whole incident depends on that assumption's being true.

Matthew and Mark append to that incident a saying about the nature of such authority, and Luke independently gives a similar saying (Matthew 20: 24–7; Mark 10: 41–4; Luke 22: 24–7). Luke's saying continues with one more verse (22: 28), and he then adds another saying about the rule of the disciples on thrones, which Matthew gives in another form in another place (Luke 22: 29f; Matthew 19: 28). Finally, Mark alone in another context gives a short and general saying bearing on the same point (Mark 9: 35), which may be compared with two further sayings, each slightly different from the other, in Matthew and Luke (Matthew 23: 11; Luke 9: 48).

I shall restrict myself to a discussion of the saying about the rulers of

---

[13] This hypothesis needs further discussion, but notice that John's disciples are also clearly distinguished from those he baptised.

the Gentiles (Matthew 20: 25–7; Mark 10: 42–4; Luke 22: 25–6), while noting again that, in all the other cases in which we can discern the scope of Jesus' teaching that his disciples should be servants, the disciples who are meant are the members of the inner circle and they alone.

The scope of the saying about the rulers of the Gentiles is emphatically the problem of how authority is to be exercised, and the authority is authority over those who are ruled.

However, when we look closely at the wording, this general impression is blurred. If we take the words literally, Jesus seems to be saying that any particular member of the group to which he is talking is to be servant of the group itself. We should expect, from general considerations, that Jesus was telling aspiring rulers how to rule others; but the actual saying seems to tell rulers how to behave to their fellow-rulers.

The clearest explanation of this blurring is that a saying addressed to rulers has been taken to refer to the whole Church: those who aspire to rule among you Christians should become servants of all you Christians. Jesus himself is unlikely to have generalised the saying in this way, but it is perfectly understandable that later preachers, addressing the assembled Church, would extend the application. The preaching point would be that any candidates for the ministry should realise that their exercise of authority should be in the form of service. Even so, the saying is restricted to those who aspire to the ministry. Nevertheless, it could be that every Christian was meant to aspire to rule, and we must return to the saying itself to see if that was what Jesus meant.

The textual tradition of both the Matthaean saying and the Marcan saying is very complicated, but this I take to be a sure sign that an original wording has been altered in the transmission by scribes who wished to extend its scope.

Here is a simplified table of the evidence.

Matthew 20: 26:
   (i) $\epsilon\nu$ $\upsilon\mu\iota\nu$ $\mu\epsilon\gamma\alpha\varsigma$ $\gamma\epsilon\nu\epsilon\sigma\theta\alpha\iota$ $\aleph$ etc.
   $\upsilon\mu\omega\nu$ $\mu\epsilon\gamma\alpha\varsigma$ $\gamma\epsilon\nu\epsilon\sigma\theta\alpha\iota$ L 2892
   $\mu\epsilon\gamma\alpha\varsigma$ $\epsilon\nu$ $\upsilon\mu\iota\nu$ $\gamma\epsilon\nu\epsilon\sigma\theta\alpha\iota$ B etc.
   $\mu\epsilon\gamma\alpha\varsigma$ $\gamma\epsilon\nu\epsilon\sigma\theta\alpha\iota$ $\epsilon\nu$ $\upsilon\mu\iota\nu$ C etc.
   $\epsilon\nu$ $\upsilon\mu\iota\nu$ $\gamma\epsilon\nu\epsilon\sigma\theta\alpha\iota$ $\mu\epsilon\gamma\alpha\varsigma$ 440 443 713 1574
   $\epsilon\nu$ $\upsilon\mu\iota\nu$ $\gamma\epsilon\nu\epsilon\sigma\theta\alpha\iota$ 71
   $\mu\epsilon\gamma\alpha\varsigma$ $\gamma\epsilon\nu\epsilon\sigma\theta\alpha\iota$ 440
   (ii) $\upsilon\mu\omega\nu$ $\delta\iota\alpha\kappa\sigma\nu\sigma\varsigma$
   $\upsilon\mu\iota\nu$ $\delta\iota\alpha\kappa\sigma\nu\sigma\varsigma$ sy[s]

Matthew 20: 27:

(i) εν υμιν ειναι πρωτος   ℵ

    ειναι υμων πρωτος   B

    υμων εν υμιν ειναι πρωτος   X 085

(ii) υμων δουλος

    παντων δουλος   M 348 1574 Origen

Mark 10: 43:

(i) μεγας γενεσθαι εν υμιν   ℵ B

    μεγας εν υμιν ειναι   D

    εν υμιν μεγας γενεσθαι   W 565 700

    μεγας γενεσθαι ημων   *l*181

(ii) υμων διακονος   ℵ B

    διακονος υμων   372

    παντων δουλος   Θ

Mark 10: 44:

(i) εν υμιν ειναι πρωτος   B

    εν υμιν πρωτος ειναι   Δ

    υμων ειναι πρωτος   D W fam1

    υμων γενεσθαι πρωτος   A fam13

(ii) παντων δουλος   ℵ B

    υμων δουλος   D

We notice that each word or phrase is suspect that makes the sayings refer to the group addressed as those who both rule and are ruled: whoever 'among you' and 'your' servant. These expressions are all varied in different manuscript traditions, both in order and in wording. Once (440 in Matthew 20: 26) the tell-tale word is not found. The story that best explains these variants is that the original saying was: 'Whoever wants to be great must be a servant, and whoever wants to be first must be the slave of all'. Thus read, the saying applies only to the inner circle and tells them how to exercise their authority over Israel and the Gentiles. A close examination of the texts confirms the overall impression, that Jesus originally addressed the future leaders of Israel and contrasted the way they should rule with the way Gentile rulers behaved.

Jesus is not, however, theorising about the nature of true leadership. He addresses men who are not yet leaders in Israel but who want to rule. The service or slavery is not a general mode of behaviour but a specific well-understood role in Judaism, the role of offering one's life to God as a sacrifice for the sins of the people. Jewish literature of the time is full of the stories of men and women who sacrificed their lives in obeying God's Law, with the clear intention of announcing that the people deserved to die for their sins – 'we suffer these things for our own doings, as sinning against our own God' (2 Maccabees 7: 18) – and with the prayer that God would receive their death as an atoning sacrifice for those sins. This is the service Jesus laid on the future rulers of Israel, his disciples.

Finally, what should I say about the famous ransom saying, which should perhaps provide the final proof of my thesis but is widely regarded as inauthentic? The saying occurs in Matthew 20: 28 and Mark 10: 45, and Luke has a partial parallel to the first half: 'I am in the midst of you ['of them', 1200] as he who serves' (22: 27).

The first half of the saying is almost certainly genuine, since the early Church is unlikely to have coined a phrase in which Jesus would be made to say, 'I have not come to be served.'

The second half raises greater difficulties. The idea itself is well-attested in Judaism: the Maccabaean martyrs gave their lives as a ransom for the people (4 Macc. 6.29; 17.21). True, the word λύτρον is found nowhere else in the New Testament, although ἀντίλυτρον appears in 1 Timothy 2: 6, but in itself the use of a rare word cannot condemn a passage, provided the idea is found elsewhere. None of these factors is decisive, and yet commentators are right to feel uneasy about the statement on the lips of Jesus.

There are two substantial reasons for disquiet. The first is that although Jesus prophesies that he will die, he is in general very reticent about the purpose of his death. We do not expect such an explicit and detailed doctrinal affirmation.

The second reason for disquiet is put, with customary acumen, by Wellhausen. 'The words in fact do not correspond to διακονῆσαι, for that means "serve, wait on table". The step from serving to giving of life as a ransom is a μετάβασις εἰς ἄλλο γένος.'[14]

Wellhausen explained this unlikely conjunction of ideas by supposing that table-service in the authentic first half of the saying suggested the Lord's Table to the early Church, which in turn suggested Jesus' sacrifice of himself for others.[15] This is not very likely. The Last Supper is the occasion on which Jesus presided at table, and Wellhausen's explanation would only become plausible if the saying were enlarged under the influence of the Johannine Last Supper scene. But the Johannine scene uses the sign of washing, not the image of ransom.

---

[14] *Das Evangelium Marci*, 2nd ed. (Berlin, 1909), pp. 84f.

[15] This hypothesis has been recently restated by Jürgen Roloff, 'Anfänge der soteriologischen Deutung des Todes Jesu (Mk. x.45 und Lk. xxii.27)', *NTS* 19 (1972–3), 38–64 (50ff).

Yet Wellhausen has put his finger on the strangest feature of the saying, and has shown that, as it stands, it cannot be authentic. But the inauthentic feature can be avoided, for one very important uncial manuscript, the Washington Codex of Mark, offers us a reading that does not have the difficulty, and is likely to be right. Manuscript W reads λουτρόν instead of λύτρον: 'For a son of man[16] also has not come to be served but to serve, and to give his life as purification for many.' A servant's job was to wash the feet of guests, and service and purification are naturally-related ideas.

Although the reading 'purification' fits far better than the usual 'ransom', can it be original? There is one very searching test that the reading 'purification' passes with flying colours: it provides a very simple explanation for the adoption of the false reading 'ransom'. You will recall that Wellhausen's theory failed this test: he spotted the anomaly 'ransom' but could offer no very convincing reason how it was falsely introduced into the text. But if there existed an original text λουτρὸν ἀντὶ πολλῶν, it is easy to see how the false reading λύτρον ἀντὶ πολλῶν came into existence. Scribes would almost inevitably change λουτρόν to λύτρον because of the next word ἀντί, for getting that ἀντί could mean 'on behalf of' as well as 'in place of, instead of' (e.g. Matthew 17: 27). Their theology of Jesus' death as a ransom in place of many made them write λύτρον ἀντὶ πολλῶν instead of λουτρὸν ἀντὶ πολλῶν.[17]

It will be objected that one manuscript is too little evidence. Not at all. First, the pressure on scribes to conform to the generally accepted reading would be immense; once the theologically charged λύτρον had replaced λουτρόν, it would quickly sweep away the less striking word, especially since the two words were so very similar. Secondly, readings supported only by the Codex Vaticanus are accepted as genuine, and there does not seem to be any reason in principle for not considering single readings in other good manuscripts.[18] Thirdly, the text of the Washington Codex in this section of Mark is 'Caesarean, akin to

[16] At Mark 10: 45 the minuscule 826 reads υιος for ο υιος, and this is likely to be correct. See 'The Silence of Jesus and The Son of Man', *Messiah*, Appendix II.

[17] It is arguable that much the same thing happened in Revelation 1: 5 and that 'washed in his blood' (P 046 82 2059 *g* vulgate coptic) was changed to 'freed by his blood' (𝔭[18] ℵ A C *h* syriac). Professor Moule reminded me of this variant reading.

[18] Westcott and Hort said, 'Even when B stands quite alone, its readings must never be lightly rejected...', in their 'brief and general explanation...appended to the Greek text itself' in the 1881 edition; *The New Testament in the Original Greek* (London, 1885), p. 560.

p⁴⁵'.[19] Finally, there is a curious piece of evidence that supports W's reading at Mark 10: 45. Two minuscules, 828 at Matthew 20: 28 and 346 at Mark 10: 45 read λυτρῶν. The participle of the verb λυτροῦν is an intrinsically unlikely reading; so we must ask, How did it arise? I suggest that a scribe who wanted to read the idea λυτροῦν ἀντί into a text that originally had λουτρὸν ἀντί adopted the participle λυτρῶν rather than the noun λύτρον because the accent of the participle was on the same syllable as the accent of the noun λουτρόν. The verse then sounded much the same in Greek. With caution, these two minuscules may be cited in support of W at Mark 10: 45.

If this reading be accepted, I have removed much of the strangeness of the passage. What I have not removed, and cannot remove, is the idea that Jesus saw his own death as cleansing and atoning. He too was to die in order to make many turn from their sins and be reconciled to the Father (and not alone; note Matthew's ὥσπερ and Mark's initial καί). He too offered his life so that many would turn back to God and ask God to remember his sacrifice as their sacrifice. 'Many shall see it, and fear, and shall trust in the Lord' (Psalm 40: 3). That is the only conclusion a study of Jewish theology will support. Attempts to supplant this theology in favour of a theology in which Jesus' death serves as a model of self-giving love for all mankind founder on the great objection it has been the purpose of this paper to argue. Whenever Jesus does speak of his service as the pattern for the service of others, he is speaking specifically to his close disciples. They are to join with him in his sufferings on behalf of others, and there is no evidence that suffering as such is the expected pattern of life for all who believe in Jesus Christ. Rather, all who believe in Jesus Christ must spiritually appropriate the suffering of Jesus Christ and the martyrs by being sincere worshippers who offer sacrifice for their sins. The sincerity of their worship is tested by their repentance from sin, their turning away from evil, and their making all possible restitution for wrong done. They need the sacrifice of Christ to move them at every step, to empower every response, and to represent their spiritual self-offering to God and their thanksgiving for deliverance. They do not need to become martyrs themselves, unless that is their vocation.

Nothing I have said detracts from the all-sufficiency of Jesus' death, and none of the countless martyrs in the history of the Church who literally followed their Lord to death have ever thought they took away from the necessity of Calvary. Yet their deaths have had atoning power, in that they witnessed to the sin that still holds men captive, and helped

[19] B. M. Metzger, *The Text of the New Testament*, 2nd ed. (Oxford, 1968), p. 57.

to turn sinners back from their wickedness to receive mercy. The martyrs died in order to proclaim Christ's death and to bring sinners to take the benefits of his sacrifice.

There are many more sayings of Jesus that bear on our theme, but even this relatively small sample yields a significant result. The Cross sayings and the servant sayings provide no support for the view that Jesus expected all who believed in him to bear the Cross or to be suffering servants. On the contrary, these sayings show him as the Messiah prepared to die for the world as a sacrifice for sin. But not alone. He chose a small group of men to be members of his messianic court, to occupy positions of authority in the Kingdom. They could not inherit these positions unless they too were willing to die for the people. Jesus established the ministry by appointing apostles, and, until the Kingdom comes, their successors will have to stand firm and be prepared to die for others, as their Lord commanded. That follows from who he is.[20]

[20] I have been greatly helped in revising this paper by comments on the first draft from each of the editors, from Professor Moule, and from Dr Nicholas Boyle.

'Imitatio Christi' and the Lucan Passion narrative

BRIAN E. BECK

Since Martin Dibelius interpreters have often seen Luke's Passion narrative as an attempt to portray Jesus' death as a martyrdom, or at least to interweave the theme of martyrdom with other emphases.[1] His words have been often quoted: 'For Luke the suffering Saviour is the Man of God who is attacked by evil powers and who, with his patience and forgiveness, is a model of innocent suffering...a saintly man closely united with God'.[2] On the other hand this view has not been widely taken up by writers of English commentaries.[3] The purpose of this article is to assess the principal evidence presented by Dibelius and his followers, and draw attention to what may be a largely neglected element in the background of Luke's thought.

Three general considerations may predispose us to look for martyrological motifs in Luke's Passion narrative.

(1) There are the parallels that may be traced between his portrayal of Jesus in the Gospel and both Stephen and Paul in Acts, both of whom are depicted as bearing witness through suffering and death, although in Paul's case the death is prospective only. These parallels are familiar

---

[1] See, e.g., J. Ernst, *Das Evangelium nach Lukas* (Regensburg, 1977), esp. pp. 643ff; W. Grundmann, *Das Evangelium nach Lukas* (Berlin, 1964), esp. pp. 387ff; M.-J. Lagrange, *Évangile selon Saint Luc* (Paris, 1927), p. 593; H. Conzelmann, *The Theology of St. Luke* (London, 1960), pp. 83ff; H.-W. Surkau, *Martyrien in jüdischer und frühchristlicher Zeit* (Göttingen, 1938), pp. 90ff; A. Stöger, 'Eigenart und Botschaft der lukanischen Passionsgeschichte', *Bibel und Kirche* 24.1 (1969), 4–8.

[2] M. Dibelius, *From Tradition to Gospel* (London, 1934), p. 201; cf. *idem*, *Gospel Criticism and Christology* (London, 1935), pp. 51ff. Not all would accept his view that Luke was the first to introduce martyrological motifs. See, e.g., Surkau, *Martyrien*, p. 100, and J. Pobee, 'The Cry of the Centurion - a Cry of Defeat', in E. Bammel (ed.), *The Trial of Jesus* (London, 1970), pp. 91–102.

[3] See E. J. Tinsley, *The Gospel according to Luke* (Cambridge University Press, 1965); I. H. Marshall, *The Gospel of Luke* (Exeter, 1978).

28

and need not be argued in detail.[4] They include structural elements, such as Jesus' and Paul's journeys to Jerusalem, and numerous co-incidences of language and subject matter. Both Stephen and Paul are referred to in Acts by the term, μάρτυς.[5] While the parallels are not exact, and might from a historical point of view be more suspect if they were, they are close enough to suggest that Luke intended his readers to see analogies between Jesus and Paul. It is no great step to suggest that the portrayal of Jesus in the Gospel may have been designed to facilitate the comparison.

(2) A distinctive feature of Luke's christology is the emphasis upon Jesus as a prophet.[6] The belief that the prophets suffered martyrdom had already developed in Judaism (Nehemiah 9: 26) and is attested by Luke himself (Luke 4: 24; 6: 23; 11: 47ff; 13: 33f; Acts 7: 52). He sets Jesus within that tradition. We should therefore expect him to depict Jesus' death as a martyrdom also.

(3) Luke shows himself to be acquainted with some at least of the literature in which martyrdom is devoloped as a narrative form. His acquaintance with Daniel needs no proof. More important is the likeli-hood that he knew 2 Maccabees. This is evident in his description of the death of Herod in Acts 12: 23. While the sudden and humiliating death of a tyrant is a widespread theme, there are particular parallels with the death of Antiochus in 2 Maccabees 9: 5ff; note especially ἐπάταξεν, verse 5, σκώληκας, verse 9, and δίκαιον ὑποτάσσεσθαι τῷ θεῷ καὶ μὴ θνητὸν ὄντα ἰσόθεα φρονεῖν, of Antiochus' confession, verse 12. The reading of D, ἐτὶ ζῶν, in Acts 12: 23, if not original, suggests a scribe who was aware of the parallel (2 Maccabees 9: 9, ζῶντος). It is therefore not fanciful to suggest, if parallels in Luke with earlier martyr-literature can be found, that Luke was aware of their significance.

The case must rest however on the parallels themselves. Here a pre-liminary warning is in order. Reference was made in the previous para-graph to literature in which martyrdom is developed as a narrative form. There is an obvious difference between a bare statement, such as Acts 12: 2, that Herod did away with James the brother of John, and a nar-rative, whether in the rudimentary form of 2 Chronicles 24: 20–2, or in

---

[4] See R. Pesch, 'Der Christ als Nachahmer Christi', *Bibel und Kirche* 24.1 (1969), 10f; A. J. Mattill, Jr., 'The Jesus–Paul Parallels and the Purpose of Luke–Acts', *NovT* 17.1 (1975), 15–46.

[5] Acts 22: 15, 20. The correct translation is, of course, 'witness' not 'martyr', but cf. H. Strathmann, *TDNT*, IV, 493f.

[6] Luke 4: 24; 7: 16; 13: 33; 24: 19; Acts 3: 22f; 7: 37; cf. Luke 7: 39; 22: 64. There is no evidence that Luke regarded this as an inadequate view to be super-seded by 'higher' christological categories.

the fuller versions of Daniel 3 and 6, 2 Maccabees 6: 12 – 7: 42, 4 Maccabees, or the Martyrdom of Isaiah, which dwell on the circumstances of the martyr's sufferings and his bearing under them. It is clear that the latter examples bear witness to a growing tradition, of which the later stages may be traced in rabbinical literature and the martyrologies of the Church. There are similarities in this tradition to motifs in pagan narratives of the defiant deaths of philosophers and other heroes. All these parallels are freely cited by proponents of the martyrological interpretation of Luke. But how far the later literature may be taken as representing the belated transcription of much earlier ideas that might have influenced Luke, is a subject for debate.[7] In what follows we shall err on the side of caution. In listing briefly those aspects of Luke's Passion narrative for which parallels in the literature of martyrdom are claimed, we shall generally restrict our references to the earlier literature, and reserve comment until we consider the objections to Dibelius' theory in general.

(I) CONFLICT

4 Macc. 17. 11–16 presents the deaths of Eleazar and the seven brothers with their mother as a contest, an $\dot{\alpha}\gamma\dot{\omega}\nu$ $\theta\epsilon\hat{\imath}os$, between them and Antiochus, in which, before the world as the spectators in the games, their virtue is tested by endurance and wins the prize of immortality. In putting them to death the tyrant is himself defeated (cf. 1 . 11). In other writings the conflict is given a supernatural setting. Light is in conflict with darkness; the martyr pits his strength against Satan (cf. Mart. Isa. 4. 11f). There are traces of this supernatural conflict at various points in Luke. The narrative begins with Satan taking possession of Judas (22: 3). The arrest is marked by Jesus declaring $\alpha\ddot{\upsilon}\tau\eta$ $\dot{\epsilon}\sigma\tau\grave{\iota}\nu$ . . . $\dot{\eta}$ $\dot{\epsilon}\xi ov\sigma\acute{\iota}\alpha$ $\tauo\hat{\upsilon}$ $\sigma\kappa\acute{o}\tauov s$ (22: 53); perhaps the three hours of darkness at the crucifixion, attributed by Luke to an eclipse, are intended to be symbolic of this (23: 44f). Ahead of the disciples is a period of $\pi\epsilon\iota\rho\alpha\sigma\mu\acute{o}s$, which they are to pray not to enter (22: 40, 46): Satan has been granted his request to sift them like wheat (22: 31). Jesus' prayer on the Mount of Olives (22: 41–4) shows that he too is preparing himself for $\pi\epsilon\iota\rho\alpha\sigma\mu\acute{o}s$, which in the light of 4: 1–13 must be seen as a contest with Satan. The saying about the purchase of swords (22: 36), a well-known *crux*, must be interpreted as an urgent warning in metaphorical terms to be equipped

---

[7] It is the weakness of the Appendix, often cited, in E. Stauffer, *New Testament Theology*, ET (London, 1955), pp. 331–4, that it assumes that there was a unitary 'old biblical theology of martyrdom'. See below, p. 37, n. 24.

for the spiritual warfare about to begin. We note the use of the word ἀγωνία in 23 : 44, which is interpreted to mean 'decisive battle',[8] analogous to the ἀγών of 4 Maccabees. In the course of it Jesus' sweat appears like blood (cf. 4 Macc. 6.10f).

If the martyr must fight against the powers of darkness, he has God on his side. The form that divine help takes may be represented as rescue from threatened suffering, as in the series of miraculous deliverances described in 3 Maccabees, or as protection from its effects, as in the case of the three men in the furnace in Daniel 3 or Daniel himself in the lions' den (Daniel 6), or as resurrection from the dead after suffering faithfully borne, as in 2 Maccabees 7: 9ff. Angels may appear to support the martyr or fight on his behalf (Daniel 3: 25; 3 Macc. 6.18). The moment of death may be marked by supernatural signs (Josephus, *A.J.* XVII. 6.4 (167)). In this context it is natural that the efficacy of prayer in achieving victory should be stressed (cf. 3 Macc. 5.6ff, 25, 50f; 6.1ff; Mart. Isa. 5.6f). In Luke we find Jesus preparing for his ordeal by prayer and being strengthened by an angel (22: 41–4), confident to the last in God and sure of entry to paradise (23: 43, 46). His death is marked by an eclipse and the tearing of the Temple veil (23: 44f).

(2) INNOCENCE

A striking feature of Luke's narrative is the emphasis placed on the fact that Jesus is innocent of the charges brought against him by the Jews before Pilate. They present a picture of him as a political agitator (23: 2) but three times Pilate declares him innocent of this charge, a verdict confirmed by Herod (23: 4; 14f, 22). His innocence is also attested by one of the convicts crucified with him (23: 41) and (on one interpretation at least) by the centurion (23: 47). Different assessments may be made of this fact, which are discussed below. It is a natural feature of the literature of martyrdom to insist that the victims are innocent of any real crimes and are being punished only for their religious loyalty or because their persecutors are activated by supernatural malice (cf. Daniel 6: 4f; 3 Macc. 3.1–10; 1 Peter 2: 19f).

(3) THE ATTITUDE OF BYSTANDERS

As Stöger remarks, a martyrdom is an exhibition, θεωρία (cf. 3 Macc. 5.24).[9] In some descriptions of martyrdom the sufferings of the victim

[8] Cf. Stöger, 'Eigenart und Botschaft', p. 6.
[9] *Ibid.* p. 8.

are described in horrific detail; his endurance is thereby emphasised and its effect on his persecutors and onlookers is noted. They are amazed at his courage, and (in the later literature, at least) may even be provoked to remorse. They may try to dissuade him from his course out of pity, although he sees their suggestions as a temptation to betray the cause. On the other hand persecutors or onlookers may intensify the martyr's sufferings by mocking his plight (cf. e.g. 2 Maccabees 6: 18 – 7: 41; 4 Maccabees *passim*; Mart. Isa. 5.1ff). There is relatively little about Jesus' physical suffering in Luke, although we have already referred to his blood-like sweat (22: 44). But he is mocked by his guards (22: 63–5), and by Herod and his troops (23: 11) and taunted by the Jewish authorities, the execution party and one of the convicts crucified with him (23: 35–9). The attitude of the crowd is ambiguous, as it depends on whether θεωρῶν in 23: 35 is intended (as an echo of Psalm 22: 8) in a hostile sense, or to be distinguished from the mockery of the leaders. In the former case 23:48 describes a change of heart, which may amount to repentance. It is possible that there is in the σῶσον σεαυτόν of 23: 39 an echo of the exhortation to the martyr to avoid further suffering by recanting, or appearing to do so by adopting some subterfuge.[10] Luke refers to Jesus' death as a θεωρία (23: 48).

(4) THE CONDUCT OF JESUS

Naturally the bearing of the sufferer is the central point of interest in any description of martyrdom. He is not a casual victim of random violence, but suffers for a cause.[11] His loyalty to the cause, his endurance of suffering, and the expression he gives of the truths for which he stands, are all important for the reader. Dying words often occupy a disproportionate amount of space in the narrative (cf. 4 Maccabees *passim*). In this respect Luke's Jesus conforms to the pattern. As in all the Gospels, but with a greater frequency of the verb δεῖ, the divine necessity of his suffering is stressed. As in Mart. Isa. 5.13, his suffering is a cup he must receive from God (22: 42). The element of resistance to God's will in Jesus' prayer before his arrest seems softened in Luke (22: 42; cf. Mark 14: 36; Matthew 26: 39). The cry of dereliction is omitted and in its place occurs the trusting quotation from Psalm 31: 6 (23: 46). Thus Jesus dies willingly and with composure. We are also given a wider selection of last words and deeds. Jesus shows compassion

[10] Cf. 2 Maccabees 6: 21f; 7:24f (σωτηρία).

[11] In this respect Simon of Cyrene (see next paragraph) is only a symbol of martyrdom.

to those who arrest him, healing the injured servant's ear (22: 51), and prays for his persecutors (23: 34). In his last hours he can still respond to the appeal of the penitent (23: 42f). On the way to the Cross he witnesses to the impending judgement of God (23: 27–31). The Lucan narrative of the trial brings out Jesus' fearless acknowledgement of the truth, even though his judges are incapable of apprehending it, and it will lead directly to his condemnation (22: 66–71).

(5) FOLLOWING JESUS

In standing before Jewish and Gentile rulers, Jesus suffers the fate he has already predicted for his followers (21: 12). Luke has already stressed earlier in the Gospel that discipleship involves taking up the Cross and following Jesus (9: 23; 14: 27), and this language is echoed in his description of Simon of Cyrene (23: 26; cf. Mark 15: 21). By the use of the words τὸν σταυρὸν φέρειν ὄπισθεν τοῦ 'Ιησοῦ the reader is reminded of the implications for others of what happens to Jesus. At other points the necessity to imitate Jesus is stressed. His prayer on the Mount of Olives is framed by two appeals to the disciples to pray. Simon's promise to follow, and failure to do so, are set in contrast to Jesus' bearing of abuse (22: 33f, 54–65). His denial of Jesus takes place in his presence and its significance is underlined by Jesus looking at him (22: 61). In particular the discourse at the Supper, 22: 14–38, whether it is to be regarded as a traditional section that Luke has included at this point or his own editorial compilation, is dominated not only by the thought of Jesus' impending suffering, but by the idea of the testing of the disciples, which holds the various pieces together. The betrayer has already succumbed to Satan (verses 21–3), who is about to attack the rest (verse 31): Peter will soon deny Jesus (verse 34). A bitter conflict awaits them, such as they have not known before (verses 35f), and they will no longer have Jesus with them because his time has come (verse 37; cf. 12: 50; 13: 32). In the past they have stood by Jesus,[12] and he has prayed for their future survival (verses 28, 32). Lordship is promised to them in the coming Kingdom, as to Jesus himself (verses 29f), but this lordship is to be defined, not in the world's terms, but in terms of the service that Jesus gives (verses 24–7). The test that awaits the disciples is thus both internal and external. Disunity is akin to betrayal (verses 23f). To be like Jesus is sufficient guidance.

---

[12] It is a weakness of S. Brown's work, *Apostasy and Perseverance in the Theology of Luke* (Rome, 1969), that he regards πειρασμοί in 22: 28 as different in kind from the πειρασμός of 4: 13 and 22: 40, 46. Cf. esp. pp. 6–19.

(6) REDEMPTIVE DEATH

It is often observed that the redemptive significance of Jesus' death in terms of expiation of sins receives little attention in the two volumes of Luke. The main stress is on the necessity of death as a prelude to resurrection. The saying in Mark 10: 45 is omitted by Luke, even though at 22: 27 he includes a similar tradition to which he could have appended it. The idea of expiatory death is absent from the missionary sermons in Acts, and strikingly omitted from the quotation in Acts 8: 32f. Only in Acts 20: 28 and the longer text of Luke 22: 19f do we encounter anything approaching it. Neither passage contains a reference to sin. Nevertheless the sayings over the bread and cup at the Supper have been regarded as further evidence that Luke saw Jesus' death in terms of martyrdom in view of the expiatory language of 4 Macc. 6.28f; 17.21f.[13]

Taken together with the general considerations with which we began, these detailed parallels, so many of them peculiar to Luke,[14] add up to a strong argument for the view that Luke presents the death of Jesus as a martyrdom and an example for others to follow. But it is pertinent to ask whether the argument is conclusive.

(1) There is the general question how far the expectation of martyrdom for Christians as a matter of course does in fact belong to Luke's outlook. On the one hand we may cite Acts 14: 22; although πολλαὶ θλίψεις might be taken as a general phrase (cf. Acts 7: 10f), Acts 11: 19; 20: 23 on the contrary suggest persecution, if not actual death. On the other hand there are signs that Luke has sometimes softened the references to persecution found in his sources.[15] Mark 8: 34 has become a call to take up the Cross καθ᾽ ἡμέραν (Luke 9: 23); while it would be going too far to say that Luke has trivialised the Cross, he has undoubtedly broadened the reference, so that we no longer have a sharp summons to make the ultimate sacrifice. His version of the final beatitude avoids the technical word διώκειν (Matthew 5: 11) in favour of μισεῖν, ἀφορίζειν, ὀνειδίζειν, ἐκβάλλειν τὸ ὄνομα ὡς πονηρόν (Luke 6: 22). While the reference to death is retained in 12: 4f, and διώκειν is introduced into the Marcan material at 21: 12 (cf. Mark 13: 9), 21: 16 predicts the death only of some (cf. Mark 13: 12). The disaster that is to overtake Jerusalem is not considered as a threat to disciples (21: 20-4;

---

[13] Cf. Ernst, *Das Evangelium nach Lukas*, p. 588.

[14] The view adopted here is that Luke's Passion narrative is based on Mark, although other traditions are incorporated and the whole has been welded together by Luke's editorial work. The view taken of sources, however, does not radically affect our assessment of the overall impact of the narrative and its affinities.

[15] Cf. Brown, *Apostasy and Perseverance*, pp. 49, 122.

cf. Mark 13: 14–20) but an occurrence that they will observe. It is difficult to form a clear impression of all this,[16] but it is probably true to say that, while Luke saw Stephen and Paul as martyrs (in the later technical sense of the word) and expected that some Christians might undergo a similar fate, he thought of most of his readers as likely to be exposed to less violent forms of social pressure and popular hostility. To the extent that this is true, it is the less probable that the sufferings and death of Jesus were understood by him as a paradigm for all Christians.

(2) We have also to do justice to the fact that, whatever parallels to the literature of martyrdom there may be in Luke, there are many features of that literature that are absent.[17] The aggressiveness of the martyr, seen in his condemnation of his persecutors (cf. e.g. 2 Maccabees 7: 14, 17, 19, 31–5), is absent from Luke, unless it is to be seen in the somewhat gentler words of 23: 28–31. Instead we have, in the longer text of 23: 34, a prayer for their forgiveness. The taunting of persecutors to get on with their work (e.g. 2 Maccabees 7: 30) is absent, unless the tone of 22: 68f is to be taken as truculent. There is, as we have already observed, relatively little stress on physical pain, and correspondingly less scope for showing Jesus' physical endurance. The mockery of Jesus is lightly described by comparison with Mark, there is no reference to the crown of thorns, no spitting and no scourging; instead Pilate offers merely to beat him (παιδεύσας, 23: 22). Also absent from Luke's presentation is any suggestion that the martyr's suffering has disciplinary or educative value for the sufferer (cf. 2 Maccabees 6: 12ff; 7: 18f, 32), or (unless at 22: 19f, which is considered below) any expiatory value for others. What J. Pobee refers to as 'stock martyrological proof-texts'[18] particularly Psalm 22, are less prominent in Luke. There is above all no clearly defined cause such as the Law or a particular commandment such as the prohibition of unclean food for which the martyr dies and which emerges as the issue in debate between him and his persecutors. It is less easy to see how Jesus could have defected, in the way that, e.g., Eleazar could have done simply by eating pork (2 Maccabees 6: 18–20), or, in the later martyrologies, Christians by a token of emperor worship.

[16] Still less of Luke 8: 13, although, against Brown, *ibid.* p. 14, Luke's alteration of Mark's θλίψεως ἢ διωγμοῦ διὰ τὸν λόγον to the simple πειρασμοῦ is probably to be seen, not as the result of reserving πειρασμός for testing that results in apostasy, but as an attempt to broaden the reference to a wider range of stresses than Mark's more limited persecution for the Gospel.

[17] For some of the points that follow I am grateful for some unpublished comments of Professor C. F. D. Moule presented to the New Testament Seminar on 11 May 1976, the minutes of which he kindly allowed me to consult.

[18] 'Cry of the Centurion', pp. 9of. For Luke, cf. 23: 34–6.

(3) Along with this must go the recognition that if martyrdom is a theme in Luke's narrative it is not the only one. The key, as he himself provides it, is to be found in the Messiahship of Jesus and the scriptural necessity that as such he must suffer (cf. 24: 7, 25–7, 44–9). For the claim to be Messiah, the Son of Man and Son of God, titles that in Luke are virtually equivalent and mutually defining, Jesus is condemned by the Jews; in a politicised form the same charge is brought against him before Pilate, in language intelligible to Gentiles, as King of the Jews (22: 66–71; 23: 2ff). The same terms are used by those who mock him on the Cross, Jews as Messiah, Gentiles as King.[19] As messianic saviour he is taunted on the Cross, and responds to the penitent convict. Whatever echo there may be of the martyr literature in σῶσον σεαυτόν in 23: 39 is effectively drowned by the dominant significance of the salvation theme in Luke's theology as a whole.[20] This alone makes sense of the irony, ἄλλους ἔσωσεν, σωσάτω ἑαυτόν (23: 35). The obedience of Jesus to the will of God laid down in scripture is thus not just the obedience of one martyr among many to some ill-defined holy cause, a Man of God (in Dibelius' phrase) who is of interest primarily as a typical human being; it is primarily the assent of the Messiah, the elect one (23: 35), to a specific vocation laid down in scripture for him as for no other.

(4) In the preceding paragraph we have already touched on the interpretation of some of the passages adduced previously as parallels to the literature of martyrdom. It would be out of place in this essay to attempt a discussion of the exegesis of every passage. For this, reference must be had to the commentaries. It is however important to stress that in some cases at least the interpretation placed on the passages by the followers of Dibelius is not the only one possible. For example, Satan has such an established function as an inciter to evil and adversary of God in the biblical literature where eschatological or martyrological categories do not apply[21] that his introduction at 22: 3 does not by itself prove that we are about to read an account of a martyrdom. Or we might ask whether the enigmatic saying about the swords in 22: 35f is really concerned with the disciples' preparedness for imminent martyr-

---

[19] Luke is careful throughout chapter 23 to keep the title appropriate to the speaker. This in itself proves false the often repeated claim that Luke represents the Jews as carrying out the execution of Jesus (cf. 23: 25). The soldiers at verse 37 are Gentiles, as the use of βασιλεύς proves; contrast verses 35, 39.

[20] Cf. I. H. Marshall, *Luke, Historian and Theologian* (Exeter, 1970), pp. 77ff.

[21] Cf. 1 Chronicles 21: 1; Zechariah 3: 1; Mark 3: 23, 26//Luke 10: 18; 13: 16, and the fact that in the interpretation of the parable of the Sower Satan takes away the seed before faith occurs (Mark 4: 15//).

dom or more broadly with their vulnerability in mission in the time of the Church beyond the Passion of Jesus. Exegesis of this passage is too often dominated by Conzelmann's view that the period of Jesus' ministry was Satan-free.[22] The turning-point between 22: 35 and 36 is due, not to the re-entry of Satan in 22: 3 but to the death of Jesus in accordance with God's design (cf. verse 37). Particularly insecure is the attempt to link 22: 19f, the words over the cup and bread, with the expiatory blood of the martyrs. The text is disputed, although recent opinion has tended to accept the longer text as genuine.[23] Of greater importance are the arguments of S. K. Williams, that substitutionary expiatory language is not in fact used of the death of martyrs in early works with the exception of one, 4 Maccabees, and there only for special reasons.[24] In view of this we should look for more precise parallels with 4 Macc. 6. 28f; 17. 21f than we actually have. 4 Maccabees does not refer to the covenant, nor Luke to sin or ἀντίψυχον. The evidence suggests that we should assign 22: 19f to one of the other elements in Luke's total picture rather than to the martyr theme, and, in view of his overall treatment of the death of Jesus, perhaps regard this passage, along with the less precise Acts 20: 28, as unassimilated fragments of pre-Lucan tradition, or at least subsidiary strands in his thought, rather than conscious formulations intended to be regulative of the whole narrative.[25]

The evidence of parallels must be cumulative, and some examples at least need to be unambiguous. The passage that is probably decisive in tipping the balance one way or other is the prayer of Jesus and his disciples in 22: 39–46, for here there are notable differences from Mark, and a rich accumulation of parallels. Unfortunately the text is in dispute,[26] and it is easier to point to parallels that suggest the martyr theme than to say precisely what they mean. In particular, does ἀγωνία refer

[22] Conzelmann, *Theology of St. Luke*, pp. 16, 28f, Stöger, 'Eigenart und Botschaft', p. 5. This view ignores 10: 18; 11: 18; 13: 16; 22: 28.

[23] Marshall, *Gospel of Luke*, pp. 799f; B. M. Metzger, *A Textual Commentary on the Greek N.T.* (London, 1971), pp. 173–7.

[24] S. K. Williams, *Jesus' Death as Saving Event, the Background and Origin of a Concept* (Missoula, 1975). Whether he is equally right in his account of the origins of the NT concepts, or has fully explicated the ideas of 4 Maccabees itself is another question.

[25] Cf., for discussions of this problem, E. Lohse, *Märtyrer und Gottesknecht* (Göttingen, 1955), pp. 187ff; A. George, 'Le sens de la mort de Jésus pour Luc', *RevBibl* 80 (1973), 186ff; R. Zehnle, 'The Salvific Character of Jesus' Death in Lucan Soteriology', *ThS* 30 (1969), 420ff.

[26] Followers of Dibelius regard verses 43f as genuine on internal grounds, while textual critics tend to reject them. Cf. Dibelius, *Tradition to Gospel*, p. 201, n. 1.; Surkau, *Martyrien*, p. 93; Metzger, *Textual Commentary on Greek NT*, p. 177.

to an external struggle against an adversary or an inner distress of mind?[27]

If we assume for a moment that verses 43f are genuine, it is important to grasp firmly the clues offered by the text itself for its interpretation. (*a*) Jesus is engaged in prayer to God. The result of the angel's assistance is to enable him to pray more strenuously, ἐκτενέστερον, of which his sweat is evidence. This prayer is a struggle. Surkau and others think that Jesus is strengthened by receiving from the angel a revelation of his coming suffering (cf. Daniel 10: 18f),[28] but this is surely reading too much into the text. A closer analogy must be the guardian angel who fights on behalf of the faithful (cf. Daniel 3: 25; 10: 20 –11: 1; 12: 1). (*b*) The angel is sent from heaven, that is, from God. The exertions of Jesus can therefore hardly be a wrestling with God himself, after the fashion of Jacob at Peniel (Genesis 32: 24–32). (*c*) The disciples are bidden to pray μὴ εἰσελθεῖν εἰς πειρασμόν, for which we may compare the clause in the Lord's Prayer, μὴ εἰσενέγκῃς εἰς πειρασμόν (11: 4). It is natural to think that Jesus is doing the same. In that case his prayer is not itself the moment of testing but preparatory to it, a request to God to grant the right outcome.[29] (*d*) The words of Jesus' prayer should be interpreted in the light of this. He is not in conflict with himself. This is not an act of self-inducement to accept the cup of suffering but a request to God that Jesus may not fail. As in the comparable Matthaean clause in the Lord's Prayer (6: 10), τὸ θέλημα τὸ σὸν γινέσθω is a prayer to God to act.

In 22: 31f reference is also made to Jesus' praying in a way that illuminates the present passage. That saying describes Satan and Jesus presenting competing petitions before God on behalf of the disciples. ὁ σατανᾶς ἐξῃτήσατο ὑμᾶς suggests the heavenly court-scenes of Job 1: 6 – 2: 10; Zechariah 3: 1–5.[30] In one respect at least Jesus has prevailed with God against Satan, ἵνα μὴ ἐκλίπῃ ἡ πίστις σου. This setting is what we require for verses 40–6. We are shown one side of a conflict of advocates before God. A time of testing is coming for both Jesus and the disciples; its outcome will be determined by God, but that decision

---

[27] Cf. for the one view, Stöger, 'Eigenart und Botschaft', p. 6, for the other, E. Stauffer *TDNT*, I, 140; Grundmann, *Das Evangelium nach Lukas*, p. 412.

[28] Note the use of ἐνισχύω in Theodotion. Cf. Surkau, *Martyrien*, p. 94; Grundmann, *Das Evangelium nach Lukas*, p. 412.

[29] It is difficult to endorse Brown's view (*Apostasy and Perseverance*, pp. 15f) that πειρασμός by itself virtually means 'apostasy'; the phrase εἰσελθεῖν εἰς πειρασμόν should probably be translated 'succumb to temptation'. Cf. Marshall, *Gospel of Luke*, pp. 461f, quoting J. Carmignac, *Recherches sur le 'Notre Père'* (Paris, 1969), pp. 236–304, 437–45 (cf. esp. pp. 271–4).

[30] Cf. Surkau, *Martyrien*, p. 92.

can be influenced beforehand by petition. Satan is renewing his claim now, not only for the disciples, but for Jesus. In the case of the disciples this will mean their losing faith and falling away; in Jesus' case it will mean his failure to carry out the will of God that the Messiah should suffer and thereby enter his glory (24: 26). Satan's petition must be resisted by counter-petition, the disciples praying not to succumb, Jesus, that he should accept the cup. Strenuousness in prayer is demanded by the energy with which Satan is pressing his suit. While God, in sending the angel, shows favour to Jesus, this does not render the contest unnecessary. It is a decisive contest in that its outcome will be God's verdict on how the subsequent events, the actual time of testing, will go.[31] If Luke saw the episode in these terms, it explains the relative calm of the rest of the Passion narrative. From this moment events will take their predetermined course, both in crucifixion and resurrection (cf. Acts 2: 23–8), much as they do in the Johannine narrative, only there the issue is settled much further back in time (cf. John 10: 18; 14: 30f).

This line of interpretation does not settle the meaning of ἀγωνία or resolve the textual problem, but both are clarified by the reference to the λύπη of the disciples in verse 45. This is usually translated 'grief' and cited as evidence of Luke's psychologising tendencies and desire to exonerate the disciples for sleeping. At the same time commentators note that grief commonly leads to insomnia! But the real incongruity lies elsewhere: Luke has given no reason for such grief. Grief implies expectation of bereavement, but there is no such expectation in Luke at this stage. Consistently, often by additions to his Marcan source, he emphasises that the disciples did not comprehend the necessity for Jesus to suffer (cf. esp. 9: 45; 18: 34; cf. 24: 35 and their action with the swords, 22: 49ff).[32] On the other hand he differs from Mark in that all the disciples (not just three) are associated with Jesus in his prayer, and bidden to pray at the outset (cf. verses 40, 46 with Mark 14: 32, 34, 38). It seems that, for all their failure to understand, Luke wishes to associate the disciples as fully as possible with what Jesus endures; in his Gospel they do not run away at the arrest but, apparently, remain as spectators to the end (cf. 23: 49).[33] We should therefore see the λύπη of the disciples as a counterpart to the ἀγωνία of Jesus, both terms referring not to actual conflict, but to inner states associated with it. λύπη is not con-

[31] This view of prayer as actually affecting the outcome of events is reflected in 3 Maccabees, but is widespread in the OT.
[32] Cf. Brown, *Apostasy and Perseverance*, pp. 60–2, 69.
[33] οἱ γνωστοί 23: 49; cf. the similarly vague οἱ περὶ αὐτόν 22: 49. Conzelmann, *Theology of St. Luke*, p. 200.

39

fined in its meaning to grief or mourning; it can refer to other states of mental distress.[34] If Luke represents the disciples as trying, within their limits, to be obedient to Jesus, and carrying out the command to pray, he may have considered that, if the demands of prayer were such that even Jesus sustained them only with difficulty and by angelic help, the disciples would have been totally exhausted by them.[35] λύπη may then be rendered 'stress', and γενόμενος ἐν ἀγωνίᾳ, 'becoming profoundly disturbed'.

If this interpretation is allowed, it gives us a decisive reason for regarding Luke 22: 43f as genuine. The textual evidence is evenly divided,[36] the style and language are consistent with Lucan authorship, and the angel and the reference to sweat accord with his interests elsewhere.[37] But without ἀγωνία in verse 44, λύπη in verse 45 remains problematic. Only when it was read in the light of John 16: 6 could it be understood as 'grief', and the excision of verses 43f, presumably because the humanity of Jesus was accentuated too much for later susceptibilities, became possible.

The importance of the above paragraphs is easy to see. If 22: 43f are genuine we have a strong case for a martyrological interpretation of Luke's Passion narrative. It is difficult to interpret these verses in messianic terms. πειρασμός, lacking the definite article, can hardly refer simply to the final eschatological test. The idea of Jesus as an example is strongly emphasised. Yet it remains true that it is difficult to specify the cause for which Jesus dies, that martyrdom is only one of the motifs that Luke employs and that with regard to Christians his allusions to martyrdom seem to be muted.

We can make progress with these problems by considering the cen-

---

34 See especially 1 Peter 1: 6; 2: 19. That most of the occurrences of λύπη/λυπεῖσθαι in the NT are in John and Paul where 'grief' predominates, should not determine the meaning of the single occurrence in Luke. Cf. R. Bultmann, *TDNT*, IV, 313, 317f; W. F. Arndt, F. W. Gingrich, *A Greek–English Lexicon of the NT*, 2nd ed. (Chicago, 1979), p. 482 (but translating 'sorrow' here). In Luke 18: 23 περίλυπος indicates disappointment or perhaps even frustration, rather than the grief of bereavement.
35 Perhaps λύπη reflects περίλυπος in Mark 14: 34 (echoing Psalm 42(41): 6, 12), and γενόμενος ἐν ἀγωνίᾳ represents ἤρξατο ἐκθαμβεῖσθαι καὶ ἀδημονεῖν (Mark 14: 33; cf. Matthew 26: 37, ἤρξατο λυπεῖσθαι, κτλ). In that case λύπη and ἀγωνία are not far apart in meaning.
36 Metzger, *Textual Commentary on Greek NT*, p. 177, summarises the evidence.
37 ὤφθη occurs more often in Luke–Acts than elsewhere in NT; ὤφθη ἄγγελος, cf. Luke 1: 11; Acts 7: 30; ἀπό with οὐρανοῦ is much rarer than ἐκ, but cf. Luke 9: 54; 17: 29; 21: 11; ἐνισχύω only here and Acts 9: 19; γενόμενος ἐν, cf. Acts 12: 11; ἐκτενής, cf. the adverb in Acts 12: 5, the noun in Acts 26: 7; ὡσεί is a favourite Lucan word. For angels cf. Luke 1: 11, 26; 2: 9, 13; 24: 23; Acts 5: 19; 8: 26; 10: 3; 12: 7, 23; 27: 23; for his interest in physical manifestations accompanying inner events cf. Luke 1: 20; 3: 22; 24: 39–43; Acts 2: 2; 9: 18.

turion's confession in 23: 47, ὄντως ὁ ἄνθρωπος οὗτος δίκαιος ἦν. Here, as is well known, Luke differs from Mark 15: 39, although the reason is not clear. One point however should be obvious: whether his version is editorial or derives from a source, Luke could hardly have abandoned Mark's very positive formulation unless he intended at this point to say something equally positive. What this was depends on the meaning of δίκαιος, which has been variously translated as 'just', 'perfect', 'righteous', 'good', 'great and good', 'upright' or 'innocent'.[38] The modern tendency is to opt for 'innocent', for a variety of reasons. (*a*) It is historically more appropriate to a pagan bystander. (*b*) It continues the emphasis in Luke's narrative on the innocence of Jesus (23: 4, 14f, 22, 41). (*c*) Luke–Acts has an apologetic purpose, Luke wishing to reassure the Roman state or the Jews or Christians (here the proponents of the theory begin to subdivide) that neither Jesus nor the Christians are politically subversive or morally reprehensible.

But it is very questionable whether this translation can be upheld. (*a*) The question is, not what the centurion might actually have said, but what Luke would have represented him as saying. The remarks of his characters are often in keeping with the situation.[39] On the other hand the question of the jailer at Philippi has a distinctly Christian ring (Acts 16: 30f). If Luke intended to suggest that the centurion underwent conversion at the Cross (or took a step towards it), he could have made him speak in Christian terms. (*b*) While the innocence of Jesus is emphasised in chapter 23, is this the point being made at verse 47, which must mark the climax of the chapter? In view of his use of more distinctly christological themes, is this the best Luke can do to sum up? (*c*) Is it really true to say that Luke's purpose in the Passion narrative is apologetic? Due weight must be given to P. W. Walaskay's argument that any Roman reader would have to conclude that Roman justice had miscarried and would hardly see Pilate's verdict as independent attestation of Jesus' innocence.[40] The real significance of the testimonies to Jesus' innocence does not lie in the identity of the persons who give them (what weight would a convict's word carry?). With the rest of the

---

[38] E. J. Goodspeed, *Problems of NT Translation* (Chicago, 1945), pp. 90f. 'Innocent' is also preferred by RSV and NEB, 'great and good' by JB, 'a good man' by Phillips and TEV. Ancient commentators are little help. For the most part they are concerned with reconciling Luke with Matthew and Mark, e.g. Augustine, *De Cons. Evang.* III.20.57 (*PL* XXXIV, 1193f).

[39] Cf. Festus' reference to δεισιδαιμονία in Acts 25: 19 and the χριστός/βασιλεύς distinction in Luke 23 (p. 36, n. 19).

[40] P. W. Walaskay, 'The Trial and Death of Jesus in the Gospel of Luke', *JBL* 94.1 (1975), 81ff. Cf. also C. K. Barrett, *Luke the Historian in Recent Study* (London, 1961), p. 63.

41

Gospel before us we hardly need reassurance that Jesus was innocent. These testimonies emphasise that his sufferings were maliciously caused: the Jews who charged Jesus with sedition called instead for the release of Barabbas, imprisoned for στάσις and φόνος (repeated, 23: 19, 25), and the Romans (albeit reluctantly) connived. In other words the condemnation of Jesus was an act of blatant persecution. This is not good apologetic for Romans or Jews, but would encourage hard-pressed Christians to see Jesus as a pattern for themselves.[41] (*d*) There is also the linguistic question, can δίκαιος mean 'innocent'? G. D. Kilpatrick's arguments, that it can, have been well answered by R. P. C. Hanson.[42] Kilpatrick's case is only partly linguistic anyway, but the decisive question is not the usage of the LXX in the passages he quotes, but the usage of Luke. In no other instance in the Gospel or Acts can δίκαιος or its cognates be restricted to 'innocent'. In view of δικαίως in 23: 41 and δίκαιος of Joseph of Arimathea in 23: 50 it is difficult to see how Luke could suddenly have narrowed the meaning of the word in verse 47. (*e*) Finally, we are left with the difficulty of ἐδόξαζεν (or ἐδόξασεν).[43] If the centurion is merely remarking on the innocence of Jesus, this verb must be given a reduced sense, 'his remark unconsciously acknowledged God's glory'. How could he consciously praise God for the execution of the innocent? This meaning is not impossible here (at least if the aorist is read), or in some other passages (e.g. Luke 7: 16; Acts 11: 18), but it is nowhere required (except possibly in the odd phrase ἐδόξαζον τὸν λόγον τοῦ θεοῦ (Acts 13: 48)) and is sometimes plainly impossible (e.g. Luke 2: 20). The best interpretation of the evidence is that Luke normally uses the verb to mean 'gave conscious praise to God'. If this is so, δίκαιος cannot mean 'innocent'. Luke can hardly depart from his normal usage twice in one sentence.

We are therefore driven to translate δίκαιος as 'righteous' in some sense. It will, of course, include the notion of innocence, but imply

---

[41] It is possible that by using the word κακοῦργοι at 23: 32f, 39, instead of λῃσταί (Mark 15: 27), Luke intends to suggest that the issue is not narrowly political. Jesus as δίκαιος is to be contrasted with all κακουργία. Cf. the interesting parallel (noteworthy because κακοῦργος and cognates are rare in LXX) to the use of these terms in the LXX additions to Esther (16: 15 = 8: 12 p in A. Rahlfs, *Septuaginta*, 5th ed. (2 vols., Stuttgart, 1952), i, 968). Cf. Josephus' interpretation of the passage in *A.J.* XI. 6. 12 (279). δίκαιος here cannot mean 'innocent'.

[42] G. D. Kilpatrick, 'A Theme of the Lucan Passion Story and Lk xxiii.47', *JTS* 43 (1942), 34–6; R. P. C. Hanson, 'Does δίκαιος in Luke xxiii.47 Explode the Proto-Luke Hypothesis?', *Hermathena* 60 (1942), 74–8.

[43] The aorist is read by the corrector of 𝔓75, the *Koine* text and a few other manuscripts.

something more positive. Our next task is to determine what this additional content is. It is unlikely that the word is used simply as a technical designation for the Messiah.[44] Of the Lucan examples of the word Acts 22: 14 comes closest to this; while Acts 3: 14; 7: 52 may also illustrate the usage, it is probable that in part the intention is to allude to the character of Jesus as it is attested in Luke 23: 47.[45] In any case the absence of the definite article with δίκαιος in the centurion's confession argues against its being a title.

Some have argued for a reference to the Servant of Deutero-Isaiah.[46] In support of this Luke 22: 37 and Acts 8: 32f can be cited. There is little doubt that Luke saw the death of Jesus as fulfilling certain aspects of the description of the Servant. Two reservations must however be expressed. In the first place, Luke's use of this theme cannot be utilised to argue that he saw atoning significance in Jesus' death. The quotations point only to the circumstances of his death and his bearing under suffering.[47] Luke does not use Isaiah 53 to amplify the idea of martyrdom with notions of expiatory death; on the contrary he sees the Isaianic passages only as descriptions of a martyr. In the second place it must remain open to question whether Luke 23: 47 alludes to the Servant because only once is δίκαιος used of the Servant in the LXX of Isaiah, in 53: 11, and although this is in the context from which Luke 22: 37 quotes, it hardly figures as a technical designation for the Servant.

Instead, we must look elsewhere. It is surprising that, among the surviving early Jewish documents that deal with the sufferings of the righteous, more attention has not been given by commentators to Wisdom 1–5, particularly in view of the parallels contained in these chapters

[44] Against Stöger, 'Eigenart und Botschaft', p. 8.
[45] Cf. E. Haenchen, *The Acts of the Apostles* (Oxford, 1971), pp. 206, 626; G. Schrenk, *TDNT*, II, 188f.
[46] E.g. (tentatively) G. W. H. Lampe in D. E. Nineham (ed.), *Studies in the Gospels* (Oxford, 1955), p. 179. Marshall, *Luke, Historian and Theologian*, p. 172, argues that Isaiah 53: 12 stands behind Luke 23: 34, but if so it is the Massoretic Text (as perhaps in 22: 37), not the LXX. See *idem, Gospel of Luke*, p. 826. The possibility of Isaiah 53: 8 behind Luke 23: 18 (*ibid.* p. 860) seems remote. But for ἐκλεκτός in Luke 23: 35, cf. Isaiah 42: 1.
[47] Cf. George, 'Le sens de la mort de Jésus', pp. 195–8.
[48] The parallels with Matthew are more often noted. For ancient commentators, see Clement of Alexandria, *Strom.* v.14 (*PG* IX, 164), Cyprian, *Test.* 2.14 (*PL* IV, 708), Augustine, *Civ. Dei* XVII.20.1 (*PL* XLI, 554). Most however tend to refer to Isaiah 3: 10 LXX which Wisdom 2: 12 echoes. For moderns, cf. G. Ziener, *Die theologische Begriffssprache im Buch der Weisheit* (Bonn, 1956), pp. 114ff. C. Larcher, *Études sur le livre de la Sagesse* (Paris, 1969), pp. 12ff, plays down the parallels with Wisdom, but is primarily concerned with direct dependence, and does not consider the question in a martyrological context.

to the Passion narratives,[48] especially in the section 1: 16 – 3: 9. These paragraphs depict the persecution of the righteous (ὁ δίκαιος) by the irreligious. The essential point is that the ultimate test of the righteous man is in the way he meets suffering and ignominious death. By his manner of life the righteous man is a rebuke to his oppressors, who have made a pact with death and opted for a life of pleasure; in their resentment they intend to prove false his claim to have God for his father and protector, not recognising that the righteous are in the hands of God beyond death.

There are similarities here to the other literature of martyrdom, but important differences. Righteousness is not primarily defined in terms of loyalty to Torah or to any particular observance such as kosher food, but rather in terms of wisdom and moral virtues (ἀρεταί, cf. 8: 7). While the death of the righteous is described as a sacrificial offering (3: 6), it is not regarded as an expiation for the sins of Israel. In fact, although Wisdom is evidently a Jewish writing, righteousness is denationalised; Solomon appeals to the kings of the earth to pursue wisdom, which is accessible to all seekers.[49] Moreover, while it is made clear that the ungodly will be punished, the righteous sufferer is not depicted as declaring judgement on them or cursing them. He suffers in silence, a remarkable fact since the utterances of the ungodly are given at length. Indeed his ἀνεξικακία and ἐπιείκεια are his positive virtues (2: 19). These differences are striking in their similarity to the differences we noted between Luke and other martyrological writings.[50]

There are interesting parallels of language and ideas between Luke and Wisdom that suggest that Luke may have known the book,[51] but it would be going too far to suggest direct literary indebtedness in his Passion narrative. The differences are important: in Wisdom the suffering of the righteous is educative, a means of their perfecting (3: 5f): man was created immortal while death, the lot of the ungodly, came in φθόνῳ διαβόλου (2: 24); there is no doctrine of bodily resurrection; above all, of course, the book appeals for its readers to embrace wisdom, which is replaced in Luke by his christological and soteriological inter-

---

[49] Cf. J. M. Reese, *Hellenistic Influence on the Book of Wisdom and its Consequences* (Rome, 1970), esp. pp. 109–13.

[50] ὁ δίκαιος in Wisdom is sometimes held to be a technical designation of the Messiah. Cf. Ziener, *Die theologische Begriffssprache*; G. Schrenk, *TDNT*, IV, 187, but the objections of P. Heinisch, *Das Buch der Weisheit* (Münster, 1912), pp. 55ff, do not seem to me to have been answered.

[51] Cf. H. MacLachlan, *St. Luke the Man and his Work* (Manchester, 1920), pp. 244–56, for a list of parallels between Luke and Wisdom.

ests. Nevertheless there are three points that suggest a common background of ideas for Wisdom and Luke in the Passion narrative.

(1) The righteous man boasts that God is his father (Wisdom 2: 13,
16, 18), claiming knowledge of him (2: 13).[52] Jesus is the Son of God for
Luke, and has unique knowledge of him (cf. esp. 10: 21f; 22: 70). While
Luke avoids Mark's υἰὸς θεοῦ in the centurion's confession, he includes
two prayers in the immediate context that begin πάτερ, at 23: 34 and
23: 46. Moreover, in the second prayer Psalm 31(30): 6 is cited. While
commentators observe that this is the prayer of the pious Israelite before
sleeping,[53] it is also, in the context of the entire psalm, a prayer of the
righteous (verse 19, τοῦ δικαίου) for deliverance, which is appropriate
to the context of Wisdom 2. If Luke had the ideas of Wisdom in mind,
this may have been part of the reason for the choice of these particular
words to make up for the omission of the cry of dereliction (Mark 15: 34).

(2) The ungodly consider the death of the righteous to be his end,
but in truth he is with God (Wisdom 3: 2f; 4: 16ff). It is not fully clear
whether deliverance occurs at the moment of death or later (3: 7ff) but
in either case there is a contrast between the plight of the sufferer and
the immortality of which he is assured. A distinctive feature of the Lucan
passion is that Jesus dies in full conviction that he will survive death
(23: 43, σήμερον).

(3) Two issues are put to the test when the righteous man is persecuted: will God deliver him (2: 18), and, can he sustain insult and torture without moral collapse (2: 19)? As to the former, the persecutors
make the mistake of expecting the deliverance, if it is to occur, to come
before death, but the latter is a genuine test. The key words are ἐπιείκεια
and ἀνεξικακία. The righteous man is persecuted because he is unlike
others and shows up their lives as counterfeit (2: 15f). By his constancy
in goodness even under insult and torture he proves himself ἄξιος τοῦ
θεοῦ (3: 5); he vindicates his right to be called δίκαιος. At several
points in the Passion narrative Luke brings out the bearing of Jesus
under testing, and illustrates his consistency of character. His response
to the violence of the disciples is not merely to rebuke, but, as always,[54]
to heal the sufferer (22: 51). When he is crucified he prays for his
enemies (23: 34).[55] On the Cross he continues to save those who repent

---

[52] Cf. a similar association of righteousness with sonship of God in Esther
16: 15f (8: 12 p–q).

[53] H. L. Strack and P. Billerbeck, *Kommentar zum Neuen Testament aus Talmud und
Midrasch* vol. II (Munich, 1924), p. 269. The evidence cited is later than Luke.

[54] Luke 6: 19, πάντας, cf. Mark 3: 10, πολλούς.

[55] The text of 23: 34 is in doubt, but the parallel with the prayer of Stephen, in
view of the many other parallels, makes its genuineness virtually certain.

(23: 43). Although insulted and crucified, and taunted to save himself before he dies, he maintains his character and his trust in God to the end (23: 46). His prayer that he should not succumb to the test (22: 40ff) is granted.

In all this, the tally with the Lucan version of the great sermon should be noted (6: 20–49). Whatever the relation between tradition and redaction in the sermon, the finished product is striking, not only for the extent to which it is dominated by the call for love, but also for the way in which this theme is inseparable from the topic of persecution and response to enemies (6: 22f, 27–9, 31, 35f). It is also noteworthy both for the insistence on obedience to the teaching (6: 41–9) and for the introduction to this: the fully-equipped disciple will be like his teacher (6: 40).[56] What Jesus exemplifies in his Passion is the way of loving and forgiveness of enemies to which he has called his followers; as they are to comport themselves under persecution so has he.[57] It is in this respect, by drawing swords on the arresting party, rather than by running away, that the disciples fail (22: 50f).

The confession of the centurion is thus appropriate to the Lucan context. As the verb ἐδόξαζεν shows, he is converted by Jesus' behaviour in his last hours,[58] and makes a positive, Christian comment upon it. In spite of crucifixion Jesus has not wavered. He is entitled to be called δίκαιος and by recognising it the centurion becomes the first of his adversaries to be conquered by his death. There may even be a particular point in the adverb ὄντως. In more than one place Luke refers caustically to those whose righteousness is feigned or based only on self-esteem (16: 15; 18: 9; 20: 20); in Jesus we see the genuine thing.

I have tried in this essay to evaluate the arguments for regarding Luke's Passion narrative as a martyrdom. We found in the study of 22: 43f a strong argument in favour, but noted that other motifs were also present and that in the Gospel and the Acts the idea of Christians suffering to the death is not accentuated. Of course Luke might have combined martyrdom and messiahship in such a way that Jesus' unique status as

---

[56] It is difficult to see Luke 6: 40; 13: 32, with Mattill, 'Jesus–Paul Parallels', pp. 41ff, as evidence that Luke saw Jesus himself being made perfect through suffering.

[57] Cf. Stöger, 'Eigenart und Botschaft', p. 8, who refers to the persistence of Jesus as prophet, saviour and teacher; but it is primarily in faithfulness to his own teaching that he presents an example that others can follow.

[58] τὸ γενόμενον refers to Jesus' death, and is equivalent to Mark's ἰδὼν ὅτι οὕτως ἐξέπνευσεν. Luke gains succinctness and clarity by moving the reference to the eclipse and the temple veil to a position before the death (cf. Mark 15: 38f). Thus there is no possibility of regarding the centurion as responding to cosmic signs (as in Matthew 27: 54).

Messiah would preclude the necessity for the suffering of others.[59] Yet we noticed an emphasis on following Jesus. The comparison with the suffering righteous in Wisdom has illuminated the background of Luke's thought. It cannot be regarded as the only example of martyrological ideas contributing to his conception, but it has helped to pin-point the cause for which Jesus died and given grounds for thinking that his death is indeed exemplary, for the righteous man of Wisdom 2 is a typical, not a unique, figure. We thus see two strands in Luke's Passion narrative, one unique and messianic, the other typical and exemplary. As a martyr Jesus dies for the cause of his own teaching in obedience to the way of life that he has laid on his disciples. In this he is their pattern. If the physical suffering of Jesus after his arrest is not emphasised it may be because Luke does not wish to over-dramatise the sufferings his readers may expect; on the other hand he does not conceal what may be at stake for some. Two things however are made very clear: such faithfulness in loving enemies may win converts, causing even persecutors to give glory to God; but the test will only be passed, and the faithfulness maintained, if the victory is first won in the strenuousness of prayer.

[59] Cf. George, 'Le sens de la mort de Jésus', pp. 208f.

The persecution of Christians in John 15: 18 – 16: 4a

BARNABAS LINDARS, SSF

The nature of the Johannine community and its historical situation have been the subject of lively debate in recent years.[1] Information may be gleaned from both the Gospel and the Epistles of John, but the relationship between them is still an unsolved problem.[2] The persecution of Christians is one matter in which they presuppose completely different situations. In the Gospel the disciples are warned to expect persecution from the unbelieving Jews outside the Church. In the Epistles, on the other hand, the adversaries are dissident or heretical members within the Johannine community itself. A preliminary solution is to suppose that the persecution of which the Gospel speaks has ceased to be a factor by the time that the Epistles are written. On this showing the Epistles are the final product of the Johannine school, possibly overlapping the last stages of the editing of the Gospel. The Gospel itself, however, has a complex literary history behind it. The references to persecution may be fitted anywhere along that line of development. It will be the aim of this article to analyse John 15: 18 – 16: 4a in such a way as to show the connections between this passage and the literary history of the Gospel, and also to estimate its evidential value for persecution in the Johannine Church.

I

Apart from 15: 20 the verb διώκειν is used only once in the Gospel, and that is with Jesus as object in 5: 16. Thereafter, though the word is not used, the persecution of Jesus is a constant theme, reverberating through

---

[1] Cf. R. Kysar, *The Fourth Evangelist and his Gospel* (Minneapolis, 1975), pp. 83–172; O. Cullmann, *The Johannine Circle* (London, 1976); A. R. Culpepper, *The Johannine School* (Missoula, 1975); R. E. Brown, *The Community of the Beloved Disciple* (London, 1979).

[2] Cf. R. E. Brown, 'The Relationship to the Fourth Gospel shared by the author of I John and by his opponents', in *Text and Interpretation: Studies in the New Testament presented to Matthew Black*, ed. E. Best and R. McL. Wilson (Cambridge University Press, 1979), pp. 57–68.

the Gospel until the climax is reached in the Cross. The persecution of the disciples, however, is not referred to during the ministry of Jesus. But we find a first hint in chapter 9, where the man born blind is cross-examined by the authorities and ejected from the Synagogue (9: 34). J. Louis Martyn has argued that the account reflects conditions in John's milieu, where Jews were subjected to cross-examination if suspected of becoming converts to Christianity.[3] Once this connection is allowed, a great deal of the debate between Jesus and the Jews in the rest of the Gospel may be presumed to reflect the contemporary conflict between Church and Synagogue. In spite of efforts to date John early,[4] the picture that emerges from this interpretation suits best the Jamnia period, when the Pharisees were making strenuous efforts to preserve the purity of the people and the integrity of the Law.[5]

The crucial verse is 9: 22: 'The Jews had already agreed that if anyone should confess him to be the Christ, he was to be put out of the synagogue.' The same word ($\dot{\alpha}\pi o\sigma v\nu\dot{\alpha}\gamma\omega\gamma o\varsigma$) occurs again at 12: 42; 16: 2, and is not found elsewhere in the New Testament. The word itself, of course, cannot decide the issue whether there is here a reference to the *Birkat-ha-Minim*.[6] For the possibility of exclusion from the Synagogue

---

[3] J. L. Martyn, *History and Theology in the Fourth Gospel* (New York and Evanston, 1968), p. 9.

[4] J. A. T. Robinson, *Redating the New Testament* (London, 1976), pp. 254–311.

[5] Cf. S. Pancaro, *The Law in the Fourth Gospel*, Supplements to Novum Testamentum 42 (Leiden, 1975), pp. 492–534.

[6] This is the addition to the Twelfth of the Eighteen Benedictions, which operated as a virtual form of exclusion of Christians and heretical Jews from the Synagogue, because it required them to curse the Nazarenes (*ha-nōṣᵉrim*) and the *Minim* (heretics), and was introduced towards the end of the first century precisely for this reason. A probable form of the Benediction is given by C. K. Barrett, *The New Testament Background: Selected Documents* (London, 1961), pp. 166f, as follows: 'For the renegades let there be no hope, and may the arrogant kingdom soon be rooted out in our days, and the Nazarenes and the *Minim* perish as in a moment and be blotted out from the book of life and with the righteous may they not be inscribed. Blessed art thou, O Lord, who humblest the arrogant.' The addition consists of 'and the Nazareans...inscribed.' For the Hebrew text and discussion of the problems, see W. D. Davies, *The Setting of the Sermon on the Mount* (Cambridge University Press, 1963), pp. 275f. Recent studies express doubt whether there was a direct policy of opposition to Christians in the Jamnia period, or that the addition to the Twelfth Benediction can be dated so early, but this is due to the inadequacy and inconclusive nature of the evidence, not to any fresh information, cf. E. Schürer, G. Vermes, F. Millar and M. Black, *The History of the Jewish People in the Age of Jesus Christ*, vol. II (Edinburgh, 1979), pp. 461–3; P. Schäfer, 'Die sogenannte Synode von Jabne', *Judaica* 31 (1975), 54–64, 116–24. It must be pointed out, however, that the evidence of Justin, *Dial.* 16; 47; 93; 95; 96; 108; 117; 133 is misrepresented in the former (137 is *not* characteristic), and totally disregarded by the latter.

for particular offences was always present, and Jewish persecution of Christians is attested already in 1 Thessalonians 2: 15. But the significant point is the *agreement* mentioned in John 9: 22. This suggests a definite policy, rather than occasional *ad hoc* decisions. Moreover the offence is the *confession of faith* in Jesus as the Messiah. This is the test of membership of the sect of the Nazarenes, against which the *Birkat-ha-Minim* was directed, and no one who confessed this faith could recite it.

Similarly 12: 42 refers to leading Jews who were privately believers, but 'did not confess (Jesus) on account of the Pharisees, lest they should be put out of the synagogue'. Here again all the details fit the situation implied by the addition to the Twelfth Benediction. The Pharisees are the ruling party, the offence is the confession of faith, and the penalty is exclusion from the Synagogue. This verse clearly has a strongly apologetic motive, and indicates that John has reason to believe that there are indeed prominent men who are held back from throwing in their lot with the Christians on account of their position in the Jewish community. The Gospel itself includes two examples of such men in Nicodemus and Joseph of Arimathea. Nicodemus came to Jesus 'by night' (3: 1), thus avoiding public notice, but was accused of being a 'Galilean' when he spoke up for Jesus in the Sanhedrin (7: 50–2). Eventually he assisted Joseph with the burial of Jesus (19: 39). Joseph himself is expressly stated to be a disciple, 'but secretly for fear of the Jews' (19: 38). In calling Joseph a disciple, John is taking up a hint supplied by Matthew (27: 52). But Matthew gives no indication that Joseph had anything to fear from his fellow-countrymen. Thus the description of these two leading Jews fits the situation presupposed by 12: 42. On the other hand the verse cannot be regarded as intended to apply solely to them. It is a general statement, and the bitter comment with which it ends (verse 43) conveys a strong impression of active involvement. It is the way in which John explains *to himself* this tragic failure of the Jews.

The reference to excommunication in 16: 2 will claim our attention below. Though it adds nothing further to what we have already observed, the remainder of the verse goes further in suggesting that the disciples will run the risk, not only of excommunication, but even of death.

What conclusions can be drawn from this scanty evidence? In the first place, it can be asserted that, if a late date is assigned to the Fourth Gospel, a reference to the *Birkat-ha-Minim* is both possible and probable. On the other hand it is unlikely that this happened suddenly, without previous steps in the same direction. The Gospel of John gives evidence only for the circumstances of the Johannine Church. A local decision of the rabbinate is sufficient to account for what is said here. This could have been taken some years earlier. This need not have been the addition of the *Birkat-ha-Minim* as such, and indeed may well have been something more drastic. We have to allow for local variation in the factors that led up to the Jamnia decision. But the persecution envisaged by John appears to be more clearly defined and deliberately organised than that which is implied by Matthew and Mark.[7] Matthew, indeed, reveals a situation that has much in common with John: a Jewish Church recognising the validity of the Gospel to the Gentiles, living in contact with the Synagogue, and claiming to represent the true interpretation of the Law against active hostility from the unbelieving Jews.[8] But in John the struggle is intensified.

II

Though John probably belongs to the Jamnia period, there was certainly persecution much earlier, and it appears in the Gospel traditions that John received. John 15: 18 – 16: 4a is widely recognised to be dependent upon earlier traditions found also in the Synoptic Gospels. The most important passages are the Mission Charge of Matthew 10: 17–25[9] and the Little Apocalypse of Mark 13: 9–13. But these two passages do not represent distinct sources, because most of the Matthaean passage is derived from Mark. Consequently Matthew has reduced this material in his own version of the Little Apocalypse at 24: 9. Luke similarly has the material in both types of context, i.e. Luke 12: 11f and 21: 12–19. In this case we may suspect that Q has contributed to one of the Lucan versions, although the parallel passages cannot be convincingly separated into a Marcan and a Q form.[10]

---

[7] D. R. A. Hare, *The Theme of Jewish Persecution of Christians in the Gospel according to Matthew*, Society for New Testament Studies Monograph Series 6 (Cambridge University Press, 1967), p. 55, attempts to escape this conclusion by assuming that John's anti-semitic tendency has led him to say more than was actually the case. The assumption is left unproved.

[8] Cf. Davies, *Sermon on the Mount*, pp. 256–315; D. Hill, *The Gospel of Matthew*, The New Century Bible (London, 1972), pp. 48ff. H. B. Green, *The Gospel according to Matthew*, The New Clarendon Bible (Oxford University Press, 1975), p. 33, places Matthew later than the *Birkat-ha-Minim*.

[9] See the table of correspondences in R. E. Brown, *The Gospel of John*, The Anchor Bible, vol. II (Garden City, 1971), p. 694.

[10] Cf. I. H. Marshall, *The Gospel of Luke*, The New International Greek Testament Commentary (Exeter, 1978), p. 519. See also H. Schürmann, *Traditionsgeschichtliche Untersuchungen zu den synoptischen Evangelien* (Düsseldorf, 1968), pp. 150–5, who proposes a connection with Matthew 10: 23.

51

The question at once arises to which kind of context this material properly belongs. Even assuming the priority of Mark, it is less likely that Mark has the original setting, because his Little Apocalypse is an artificial compilation, including a number of items on discipleship. Indeed it may be conjectured that he has placed the teaching on persecution here because of the apparent remoteness of the circumstances with which the verses deal.[11] Mark 13 is notable for its ambiguity with regard to the time of the future events. Verse 32 ('no one knows') is 'out of harmony with the trend of 5–31'[12] (cf. verse 30: 'this generation'). At the time when Mark is writing, no actual fulfilment of Jesus' teachings on persecution has been reached. Matthew's transference of them to the Mission Charge is an indication that they have now become relevant to the actual situation of the Church. With his concept of a delay of the parousia, it is necessary for him to distinguish sharply between the contemporary struggle of the Church and the future tribulations. Luke 12 has the same material in a collection of general warnings concerning discipleship, which has parallels not only with the Mission Charge in Matthew, but with Q material elsewhere.[13] But Luke retains the same passage in its Marcan position in the Little Apocalypse (21: 12–17), though with considerable alterations. He does not need to remove it from this context, because he regards the apocalypse as already partially fulfilled, rather than wholly concerned with the future.[14] These con-

---

[11] This is not to deny the widely held view that Mark emphasises the suffering involved in discipleship because of a real threat of persecution; cf. B. M. F. van Iersel, 'The gospel according to St. Mark – written for a persecuted community?', *Nederlands Theologisch Tijdschrift* 34 (1980), 15–36. W. Marxsen, *Mark the Evangelist* (Nashville, 1969), pp. 171ff, has argued that Mark is applying persecution material to the situation facing the Church at the time of the Jewish War of A.D. 66–73. But he notes that Mark 13: 10 – an addition of the Evangelist to his source – changes the meaning of verse 9 from defence before a tribunal to preaching in general. If the 'abomination of desolation' refers to a fear of future action by an emperor, engendered by Caligula's attempt to place a statue of himself in the Temple in A.D. 40, and if the allusion to arraignment before the secular power in verse 9 refers to the reprisals of Nero against the Christians in Rome in A.D. 64, the mounting unrest in Judaea in this period would be sufficient to give rise to anxiety about the future even before the outbreak of war in A.D. 66. By placing this material within the Little Apocalypse, Mark expresses his conviction that the persecution is the prelude to the final woes, which now seem to be imminent. See also G. R. Beasley-Murray, *A Commentary on Mark 13* (London, 1957), pp. 40–53.

[12] V. Taylor, *The Gospel according to Saint Mark* (London, 1963), p. 523.

[13] Luke 12: 2–9 = Matthew 10: 26–33; Luke 12: 10 sides with Matthew 12: 32 against Mark 3: 28f; Luke 12: 22–31 = Matthew 6: 25–33; Luke 12: 33f = Matthew 6: 20f; Luke 12: 39–46 = Matthew 24: 43–51.

[14] In Luke 21: 20 a direct forecast of the destruction of Jerusalem is substituted for the obscure reference to the 'abomination of desolation' in Matthew and

siderations lead to the conclusion that the connection with discipleship is primary.

It is generally agreed that this material goes back ultimately to Jesus himself. Beasley-Murray has argued that it is to be seen in relation to Jesus' teaching on his personal danger at the hands of the Jewish authorities. If so, the warning to the disciples is concerned in the first instance neither with the Church's mission nor with the trials that precede the end time, but with the danger that Jesus himself faces, in which the disciples are necessarily involved.

The transition from discipleship to apocalyptic and back again, which appears in the complex relationships of the Synoptic parallels, is only a part of the tradition-history of this material. It also found its way into the Fourth Gospel. It is not necessary to assume direct dependence on Matthew and Mark, because the traces of a Q version are sufficient to show that this material circulated in more than one form. But, like Matthew, John has used it in its traditional context of discipleship.

In composing the Fourth Gospel, John reserved the teaching on discipleship for the setting of the Last Supper (John 13–17). Within these chapters it is possible to distinguish two stages of composition, inasmuch as 14: 31 should be followed by 18: 1.[15] Our passage on persecution in 15: 18 – 16: 4*a* thus belongs to a later redaction in connection with the special reasons that led to the composition of chapters 15–17.

These new chapters are concerned with particular issues affecting the life of the community. Chapter 17, the prayer of Jesus, shows grave anxiety about the possibility of apostasy (verses 12–19) and the threat of disunity in the Church (verses 20–3). John needs to give special teaching on these matters, and he has done this by composing a fresh discourse in chapters 15–16. For this purpose he has used materials,

Mark. Though the phrases used are drawn from Old Testament prophecy (C. H. Dodd, *More New Testament Essays* (Manchester, 1968), pp. 69–83), and so do not constitute a description of what actually happened (thus allowing for the possibility of an earlier date, Robinson, *Redating the NT*, p. 27), it remains probable that the prophecy is a *vaticinium ex eventu*, and that the reason for Luke's alteration of the tradition is his belief that the fall of Jerusalem is the proper meaning of this item in the Little Apocalypse, cf. Marshall, *Gospel of Luke, ad loc.*

[15] This is not the only solution to this problematical verse, but the theory that chapters 15–17 belong to a later stage of the composition of the Gospel has much to commend it on other grounds; cf. B. Lindars, *Behind the Fourth Gospel* (London, 1971), pp. 75ff; *idem, The Gospel of John*, The New Century Bible (London, 1972), pp. 465ff; R. Schnackenburg, *Das Johannesevangelium*, Herders Theologische Kommentar zum N.T., vol. iii (Freiburg-im-Br., 1975), p. 102; H. Thyen, 'Johannes 13 und die "Kirchliche Redaktion" des vierten Evangeliums', in *Festgabe für K. G. Kuhn* (Göttingen, 1971), p. 356.

including the traditions on persecution, that were doubtless available to him all along, though not required previously. The fact that he now uses the persecution material, underlined by the fears expressed in 17: 12–19, suggests that the relationship between Church and Synagogue has deteriorated since the main part of the Gospel was written. The policy of exclusion from the Synagogue, already mentioned in chapter 9, is still operative, and John fears a more violent form of persecution (16: 2). There is a need to restore the morale of the Christians. We shall not be surprised to find that John's way of doing this is to point to the theological factors that are at stake.

III

We now turn to John 15: 18 – 16: 4*a*, and we shall expect it to be carefully composed to deal with the situation outlined above. From the point of view of literary structure the complete unit extends as far as 16: 15, embracing not only the persecution material but also the work of the Paraclete.[16] Persecution is referred to in 15: 18–25; 16: 1–4*a*, and the work of the Paraclete is dealt with in 15: 26f; 16: 8–16. The necessity for the departure of Jesus, in order that the Paraclete may take over his role through the disciples, is described in 16: 4*b*–7. These verses thus form a transition from the theme of persecution to the theme of the Paraclete. This throws into relief the anticipation of the latter theme, which has already appeared in 15: 26f. The conclusion follows that John has welded together materials that are distinct from a literary point of view, characteristically dovetailing them together by means of some measure of overlapping.[17] Nevertheless, at bottom the persecution material and the Paraclete material come from the same source. This can be seen in the parallel material of the Synoptic Gospels, in which the Holy Spirit inspires the disciples when they have to defend themselves on trial.

It thus comes about that we have here two developments from the persecution traditions, which nevertheless have had a separate history before being brought together again in their present form. This is due simply to John's method of taking up a point from the tradition and developing it into a discourse for a particular purpose. It does not necessarily mean that he was unmindful of the underlying relationship

[16] Cf. R. Bultmann, *The Gospel of John* (Oxford, 1971), p. 547.
[17] Similarly the theme of the disciples' sorrow in 16: 4*b*–7 anticipates the structurally separate section, 16: 16–22; cf. also the overlapping of material in chapter 10, where 10: 19–21 picks up the theme of chapter 9, and 10: 26–9 resumes the Shepherd allegory from 10: 1–18.

between them. In this case he has taken up the theme of persecution in order to expose its theological significance, and he has (presumably on some other occasion originally) taken up the theme of the witness of the Spirit so as to apply it more broadly to the teaching function of the Church.

With these facts borne in mind, it is tempting to seek for two self-contained homilies that have been welded together to form the present unit. Detailed analysis soon shows, however, that the truth is more complex. We shall see that the persecution material is closely integrated into the Gospel as a whole, so that very little underlying material can be extracted from it that might point to an earlier composition. The Paraclete material, however, does depend on previous work, although it is not possible to isolate a continuous discourse by putting together the relevant verses from chapters 14–16.[18] Thus the relationship between the finished result and the source-material is variable.

If we now try to imagine John at work in his study, we must assume that he composes 15: 18 – 16: 15 with the following materials in front of him. He has the Gospel, which he has already written, to which he will refer by means of a quotation in 15: 20. He has his various homilies, of which some have been used for the Gospel, and others are still available for his present task. These include something that he has written on the Paraclete. He also has collections of the sayings of Jesus and other Gospel traditions. We can leave the question open whether he has a copy of Mark, and how much of this traditional material is available to him in written form, and how much he simply carries in his head. With these materials to hand he incorporates into the Gospel an urgent message for the benefit of his fellow-Christians.

Having written 15: 1–17, which may well be one of the available homilies on his desk, he begins to compose his message on persecution. First, 15: 18–25 form an artistic unit specially composed for its present position:

15: 18 (a) If the world hates you,
     (b) know that it has hated me before it hated you.
   19 (a)   If you were of the world,
     (b)   the world would love its own;
     (c)   but because you are not of the world,

---

[18] Bultmann postulates an underlying revelation–discourse, which had three sections, corresponding with 15: 18–20; 15: 21–5; 15: 26 – 16: 11. He omits 15: 27 – 16: 7 as an expansion of the Evangelist, and cuts out portions of the two preceding sections. H. Becker, *Die Reden des Johannesevangeliums und der Stil der gnostischen Offenbarungsrede* (Göttingen, 1956), is even more drastic in his excisions.

    (d)   but I chose you out of the world,
    (e)   therefore the world hates you.
20 (a) Remember the word that I said to you,
    (b) 'A servant is not greater than his master.'
    (c)   If they persecuted me,
    (d)   they will persecute you;
    (e)   if they kept my word,
    (f)   they will keep yours also.
21 (a) But all this they will do to you on my account,
    (b) because they do not know him who sent me.
22 (a) If I had not come and spoken to them,
    (b)   they would not have sin;
    (c) but now they have no excuse
    (d)   for their sin.
23 (a) He who hates me
    (b) hates my Father also.
24 (a) If I had not done among them the works
    (b) which no one else did,
    (c)   they would not have sin;
    (d) but now they have seen and hated
    (e)   both me and my Father.
25 (a) It is to fulfil the word that is written in their law,
    (b) 'They hated me without a cause.'

The artistic balance is gained by alternating statements in prose (for the most part) with more rhythmical conditional sentences. Verse 25 makes an inclusion with verse 18 on account of the word 'hate'. The same word makes two lesser inclusions in such a way as to divide the material into well-defined stanzas. Thus verses 18 and 19 together make the first stanza, beginning and ending with 'the world hates you'. In the same way the final stanza before the conclusion consists of verses 23 and 24, bounded by the idea of hatred of both Jesus and the Father. In all there are four stanzas, each consisting of a prose verse and a rhythmical conditional sentence, plus a prose conclusion (verse 25). Furthermore, the first two stanzas are distinguished in form from the third and fourth, inasmuch as their conditional sentences (verses 19(a)(b)(c)(e), 20(c)–(f)) are in the form of well-balanced short couplets, whereas those of the third and fourth stanzas (verses 22, 24) are unreal past conditions followed by νῦν δέ. Finally the composition is bonded together by the recurrence of the hatred motif in verse 23, thus linking together the first stanza (18–19) and the fourth (23–4); and by the recurrence of the adversative particle ἀλλά in verse 25, thus linking together the opening of the third stanza in verse 21 ἀλλὰ ταῦτα πάντα ποιήσουσιν ...) with the conclusion to the whole piece (ἀλλ' ἵνα πληρωθῇ ...). It will be observed that this artistic connection implies that the contents of verse 21 are to be regarded as the suppressed main clause of verse 25.[19]

A quick glance shows that the argument is contained in the prose verses (18, 20(a)(b), 21, 23, 25), and the conditional sentences develop each point in turn. Thus verse 18 states the world's hatred (18(a)), expounded in verse 19. Verse 20(a)(b) resumes the point of 18(b), i.e. the relation of the world's hatred of the disciples to its hatred of Jesus, and this is expounded in verse 20(c)–(f). The third prose verse (21) introduces a new theme: the persecution of the disciples arises from the nature of Jesus' mission from the Father. Verse 22 describes the mission of Jesus and its effect, so that this verse forms the exposition of verse 21(a). Then, just as before, the point of 21(b) is resumed in the fourth prose verse (23), which briefly reintroduces the connection between Jesus and the Father, and this is expounded in verse 24. Verse 25 rounds off the whole argument by tracing these facts to what has been foretold in scripture.

This well-balanced composition is clearly artificial, and signs of adaptation can be easily detected. Verse 18 is not really prose; omission of 'know that' (γινώσκετε ὅτι) leaves a couplet in the form of a conditional sentence like verses 19 and 20(c)–(f). For this reason Bultmann takes verse 18 to be part of the underlying revelation-discourse. Verse 23 is also not really prose; it belongs to a type of proverbial statement that is common in the sayings-tradition, and indeed appears in the saying referred to in verse 20 (i.e. 13: 16–20). Conversely we also have to reckon with prose elements in the 'poetic' lines. Verse 19(d) is an addition to the original form of the couplet (so Bultmann). It is significant that this line is yet another quotation (cf. 15: 16). The poetical character of verses 22 and 24 is also not assured. They depend more on the repetition of the form of the sentence than on their rhythm for their overall poetic effect. In any case, even if verse 22 is regarded as a poetic fragment, verse 24 is overloaded. Omission of 24(b) helps (Bultmann), but still leaves the imbalance between the νῦν δέ clauses of the two verses.

Two conclusions already emerge from these observations. First, the

---

[19] Cf. C. F. D. Moule, *An Idiom Book of New Testament Greek* (Cambridge University Press, 1959), pp. 144f, for the view of Cadoux that ἵνα here is imperatival, so that the phrase means, 'the word...had to be fulfilled' (cf. NEB margin). BDF §448 (7) regards it as elliptical. The connection with verse 21 supports the translation 'it is to fulfil' (RSV, cf. AV, RV, against NEB text, JB).

additions to verses 18 and 19, and the lack of balance in verses 22 and 24, show that John is adapting miscellaneous material, which did not make a coherent sequence previously. Secondly, the prose lines, including 19(d), are remarkable for their allusions to other parts of the Gospel, and suggest that John has written this composition in full view of his work already contained in the Gospel. Hence this is a new composition, and it is legitimate to expect that it will provide information concerning the situation in which it was written.

We turn now to more detailed analysis.

Verse 18 has been adapted to form the opening of the whole piece, and so announces the theme of the hatred of the world. Two things need to be said about this, Firstly, verses 18 and 19, without the additions, make a well-rounded small unit, the first line being reproduced as the last line in chiastic order (εἰ ὁ κόσμος ὑμᾶς μισεῖ...διὰ τοῦτο μισεῖ ὑμᾶς ὁ κόσμος). It is true that the hatred of Jesus, referred to in 18(b), is not taken up in verse 19, but it is presupposed, seeing that the disciples belong to Jesus. John has felt it necessary to clarify this point by his insertion of 19(d). It thus seems probable that John is here using an item that was complete in itself, and it may be regarded as an example of the 'maxims' of the Johannine Church.[20] It is not necessary to assume that it is a fragment of a longer, sustained composition or revelation-discourse.

Secondly, the 'maxim' depends in the first instance on the tradition of the sayings of Jesus. Thus it echoes Matthew 10: 22//Mark 13: 13: 'You will be hated by all for my name's sake.' From this point of view verse 18(b) could be regarded as an explication of 'for my name's sake' in the underlying tradition. The hatred of the world is also a feature of the Sermon on the Plain (Luke 6: 22, 27; cf. Matthew 5: 11, 44).[21] This is a context of discipleship that has not been adapted for the apocalyptic discourse. Jeremias draws attention to this fact as an indication that this is a survival of tradition virtually unaltered.[22]

No reason is given for the world's hatred in verse 18, but this appears

---

[20] The Johannine writings contain certain statements of a proverbial type, which function in a similar way to the sayings of Jesus, but are not actually derived from the sayings-tradition, and these can be conveniently styled 'maxims of the Johannine Church'. Examples include the testimony-formula that lies behind John 3: 11; 19: 35; 21: 24; 1 John 1: 1–3; 3 John 12, and the invitation to drink in John 4: 14; 7: 37f; Revelation 21: 6; 22: 17. I hope to publish a study of these maxims on another occasion.

[21] For the originality of Luke's form against Matthew, cf. Marshall, *Gospel of Luke*, p. 253; H. Schürmann, *Das Lukasevangelium*, Herders Theologische Kommentar zum N.T., vol I (Freiburg-im-Br. 1969), pp. 345f.

[22] *New Testament Theology I* (London, 1971), p. 240.

in the remainder of the maxim in verse 19. It is because the disciples, as followers of Jesus (18(b)), are 'not of the world', i.e. do not belong to the world or derive their moral position from it.[23] The reason for this is that the proclamation of Jesus and the disciples has the effect of exposing the evil of the world (cf. 3: 20; 7: 7). This point (not stated here) will be taken up in verses 22 and 24, where the teaching and acts of Jesus himself expose the world's sin; and, because they are the works of God, the hatred accorded to Jesus is directed against him also. Similarly the disciples, who continue the work of Jesus, are his delegates to convey the divine judgement, and thereby incur the hatred of the world. It will be observed that the principles that lie behind John's maxim here agree with the implications of the Synoptic tradition with regard to the apostolic mission.

Before I leave the first stanza, it may be noted that the additional words in 19(d) refer not only to 15: 16, but behind this to 13: 18 (cf. also 6: 70). This is another indication that John is working on the basis of his Last Supper account in composing the present passage. When we add to this the underlying debt to the tradition in Matthew 10: 22, we begin to see that there is a kind of triangular relationship between the Mission Charge of Matthew 10, John's Last Supper account where sayings on discipleship are introduced (John 13: 16–20) and the present passage. This will appear more clearly in the next verse.

The second stanza (verse 20) begins with an acknowledged quotation of 13: 16(a). This is one of the clearest indications that we are here dealing with material that belongs to a later stage of redaction. But it is a necessary element in the argument. John wishes his readers to recall the whole of 13: 16, together with the context in which it is spoken. Moreover this is another instance of a saying that has its closest Synoptic parallel in the Mission Charge, Matthew 10: 24. John reminds his readers of this teaching because it is the foundation of the meaning of apostleship. John is fully aware of the principles of agency on which this is based.[24] As Jesus' accredited agents, the disciples will suffer the same treatment as Jesus himself. This was not mentioned in 13: 16–20. But it was present in the tradition, as we see from the continuation in Matthew 10: 25: 'It is enough for the disciple to be like his teacher, and the servant like his master. If they have called the master of the house

---

[23] For John's use of ἐκ, cf. R. Schnackenburg, *Die Johannesbriefe*, Herders Theologische Kommentar zum N.T. (1953), pp. 114f. The clearest example of the present usage occurs in John 18: 37, ὁ ὢν ἐκ τῆς ἀληθείας.

[24] Cf. P. Borgen, 'God's Agent in the Fourth Gospel', in *Religions in Antiquity: essays in memory of E. R. Goodenough*, ed. J. Neusner (Leiden, 1968), pp. 137–48; K. H. Rengstorf, *TDNT*, I, 398–447.

Beelzebul, how much more will they malign those of his household.'
Here it is expressed in the couplet of verse 20(c)(d). As this and the
following couplet (20(e)(f)), which refers explicitly to preaching, have
the same rhythm as verse 19, it seems best to regard them as another
Johannine maxim, used in the community in connection with the risks
attaching to evangelistic work. Hence once more we have a maxim,
expounded with the aid of the teaching already given in 13: 16–20 in
the light of the pool of tradition that has come down to us in the Mission
Charge of Matthew 10.

The principle of agency to which John has referred in verse 20 is
important to him not only in connection with the position of the disciples, but also as one of the foundations of his christology. Jesus is the
ἀπόστολος of the Father. By introducing this theme John can now show
that the world's refusal of the teaching given by the disciples is nothing
less than rejection of God himself.

This theme is worked out in verses 21–4, comprising the third and
fourth stanzas of the composition. The opening words of verse 21 are
resumptive, summarising the two preceding stanzas. The principle of
agency is indicated by the phrase 'on my account' (διὰ τὸ ὄνομά μου).
It is significant that this phrase belongs to the Synoptic saying on the
hatred of the world, Matthew 10: 22 and parallels. Then in 21(b) this
principle is referred back to the Father. Once more the phrase used, τὸν
πέμψαντά με, is significant. It occurs in 13: 16(b), in the continuation of
the quotation that we had in verse 20, and also in 13: 20, which again has
a parallel in the Mission Charge at Matthew 10: 40. Verse 21 implies the
opposite of 13: 20(b) ('he who receives me receives him who sent me'),
and this could equally well be put in the form 'he who hates me hates
him who sent me'. This is in fact what is said in verse 23, resuming
21(b), except that 'my Father' is substituted for 'him who sent me'.
This change adds greater emotional force, but does not alter the point.
It is artistically necessary to prepare for the climax in verse 24.

The failure of the world to respond to the disciples arises ultimately
from their rejection of the Father. This rejection is due to lack of knowledge (21(b)). Knowledge in John's thought is inseparable from keeping
the word (20(e)(f)). The preaching of the word brings the knowledge of
God, and to keep the word is the practical expression of this knowledge
(cf. 8: 55).

We can now turn to the two conditional sentences in verses 22 and 24.
These are aimed at showing that the world's lack of knowledge of the
Father is a culpable failure, because it has been given the revelation of
the Father and has refused it. This point is first put in a straightforward

way in verse 22. Then verse 24 makes the same point in a different way, by means of carefully chosen variations within the same formal structure. All are important for John's purpose, as he builds this short discourse to its climax. Hence it is a mistake to bracket 24(b) as a rather pointless addition (Bultmann), in the hope of recovering a saying from the underlying revelation-discourse, parallel to verse 22. This verse is not a parallel to verse 22, but an adaptation of it. First, the *works* of Jesus replace his *speech*. This is not just a stylistic variation, but a step forward in the argument. The works of Jesus reveal not only his identity as the Father's agent, but also his unity with the Father. This point is put very strongly in 10: 22–39, which is the climax of the debates on the identity of Jesus (note especially 10: 25, 32, 37f). It is precisely because of the importance of Jesus' works from this point of view that John adds 24(b), 'which no one else did'. Jesus' works are unique in this respect, even though the disciples will perform works of a similar kind (14: 12).[25] For the works of Jesus comprise not only the miracles (signs) but also the Cross, in which his unity with the Father is supremely revealed. In fact, however, as John points out in his new version of the νῦν δέ clause (24(d)(e)), although the world has seen the works that lead inevitably to this conclusion, it has responded with hatred (the refusal of belief being the sin that, thus exposed, produces hatred), and this is directed against the Father as well as Jesus, because it is the truth of the unity between them that is rejected.[26] The pairs of phrases ('seen and hated', 'both me and my Father') heighten the emotional effect in making this crucial point.

Finally verse 25 places the coping-stone on the argument. The phrase 'written in their law', with its distancing of Jesus to emphasise that the Law is an authority that the Jews themselves accept quite apart from the teaching of Jesus, occurs also with a psalm quotation in 10: 34, and performs the same function in the argument. In 10: 30 Jesus has made the fundamental christological statement, 'I and the Father are one.' When challenged by the Jewish authorities, he appeals first to scripture ('your law') and secondly to the evidence of his works. Thus the two corroborate one another, and the truth so confirmed cannot be denied by the Jews without rejecting the Law that they themselves accept as divine revelation (cf. 5: 36–47). Similarly in verse 24 John has explained

---

[25] In this verse μείζονα means, not more impressive works, but works whereby the mission of Jesus is extended through the disciples, cf. Schnackenburg *Das Johannesevangelium, ad loc.* In 5: 20 the same expression is used to denote the eschatological acts to which Jesus' works point forward.

[26] In verse 24(d) the implied object of ἑωράκασιν is probably intended to be 'the works', and the following καί must be translated 'and yet' (BDF §444 (3)), as recommended by Barrett and Schnackenburg (cf. 6: 36).

the world's hatred from its reaction to Jesus' works, and here he affirms that this hatred also has the evidence of scripture. As the words quoted come from the Passion Psalms,[27] it is probable that John is building on previous work.

If we look back over the composition, it is striking how much of it alludes to earlier working. In verses 18–20 a triangular relationship was observed between the maxims of verses 18–19, 20(c)–(f), the sayings in John 13: 16–20, and the traditions used in Matthew 10.[28] These connections are also found in verses 21–4, but it does not seem safe to postulate a source for verse 22, which is the only verse that might claim to be taken from a revelation-discourse. The most impressive feature of this composition, however, is the debt that it owes to the central themes of the Johannine christology. It has been suggested earlier that one of John's objects in composing this piece was to restore the morale of the Church in the face of stronger hostility. We can now see that he has achieved this aim by taking up the persecution maxims, and by building around them a composition rooted in the christology of the Gospel and its scriptural evidence. The overall effect is to reassure the Christians that the increased pressure is only to be expected in the light of the Gospel tradition.

Next John inserts a fragment of his Paraclete material in verses 26f. If I was correct in claiming that he composed verses 18–25 for their present position in the discourse, we must also assume that his use of these verses here belongs to the same stage of redactional activity. We shall see that they make an excellent transition to the verses on persecution in 16: 1–4*a*.

15: 26 (a) But when the Counsellor comes,
      (b) whom I shall send to you from the Father,
      (c) even the Spirit of truth,
      (d) who proceeds from the Father,
      (e)   he will bear witness to me;
  27 (a) And you also are witnesses,
      (b)   because you have been with me from the beginning.

The problems of the Paraclete material fall outside the scope of this

---

[27] The most likely source is Psalm 69: 5, as this psalm is much used in the Passion apologetic (cf. B. Lindars, *New Testament Apologetic* (London, 1961), pp. 99–108), but the identical phrase is found in Psalm 35: 19. Other possible sources are Psalm 109: 3; 119: 161; Ps. Sol. 7. 1, cf. E. D. Freed, *Old Testament Quotations in the Gospel of John*, Supplements to Novum Testamentum 11 (Leiden, 1965), pp. 94f.

[28] Both Brown and Schnackenburg stress that this relationship does not necessarily imply that John had these traditions in precisely the form in which we now have them in Matthew.

paper.[29] Suffice it to say that I think that John introduced the verses on the Paraclete in 14: 16f, 26 at the same time as he inserted the new discourse of chapters 15 and 16. A notable feature of these verses is the piling up of appositional phrases in order to explain who or what the Paraclete is. Hence John is aware that the title is not self-explanatory. Indeed, he feels the need to add explanatory phrases each time he uses Paraclete material. So the same is true of 15: 26(b)(c)(d). These phrases may be regarded as resumptive, reminding the reader of the descriptions already given in 14: 17 and 26. They are not, however, foreign to the intention of the underlying homily, but are derived from it. They correctly represent the character and origin of the Paraclete (cf. 16: 7, 13–15). Moreover these phrases serve a definite purpose in the present context. The Paraclete's assistance to the disciples when faced with persecution derives its validity from the fact that he is the Spirit of truth and originates from the Father himself. He is sent by Jesus as his agent (26(b)), but he comes from the Father (26(d)).[30] So he is an authentic agent of God, comparable to Jesus himself and available as his substitute.

Thus 26(b)(c)(d), though formally an addition to the saying that John is using here (so Bultmann, Becker), have been added deliberately for the sake of the present context. Omitting these phrases, we have in 26(a)(e) and 27 a pair of couplets in the form of a chiasmus ('Counsellor comes – witness – witnesses – from the beginning'). By this means John expresses the joint witness of the Paraclete and the disciples. The use of the word 'witness' suggests a forensic setting, in which the disciples give the message (cf. 20(e)(f)) when on trial. The knowledge that they have the assistance of the Paraclete at such a moment is calculated to reassure them. Thus this fragment of the Paraclete homily adds to the assurance already given in verses 18–25, and indicates the form that the coming persecution may be expected to take.

It is universally recognised that these verses are based on the promise of the Spirit's aid to the disciples (Matthew 10: 19f; Luke 12: 11f and all three Synoptic versions of the Little Apocalypse; on these see Prof. Lampe, pp. 129–31 below). In fact it is very likely that this tradition is the starting-point of John's Paraclete homily, and that he has broadened the idea in the process (so Brown). But the fact that he has brought this

---

[29] See the excursuses in the commentaries of Brown and Schnackenburg; also G. Johnston, *The Spirit-Paraclete in the Fourth Gospel*, Society of New Testament Studies Monograph Series 12 (Cambridge University Press, 1970).

[30] For the synonymous parallelism of these two lines, cf. Schnackenburg, *Das Johannesevangelium, ad loc.* It is evident on this showing that ἐκπορεύεται is equivalent to the sending by Jesus, and is not really concerned with trinitarian relationships.

particular feature into the present context of persecution shows yet again that he has not forgotten the starting-point in the traditions of Matthew 10 and parallels.

It has now been shown that John has organised his material in such a way as to bring assurance to his readers during their time of testing and to restore their morale. This accounts, at least in part, for the unexpected feature of the use of a Paraclete fragment apparently out of context. After giving these assurances, John is ready to speak openly concerning the persecution. This is the subject of 16: 1–4*a*.

16: 1   (a)   I have said all this to you
       (b)   to keep you from falling away.
   2   (a)   They will put you out of the synagogues;
       (b)   indeed the hour is coming
       (c)   when whoever kills you
       (d)   will think he is offering service to God.
   3   (a)   And they will do this
       (b)   because they have not known the Father, nor me.
  4*a*   (a)   But I have said these things to you,
       (b)   that when their hour comes
       (c)   you may remember
       (d)   that I told you of them.

These verses make a suitable climax and conclusion to John's composition concerning the coming persecution. They cannot be analysed along the lines of source and redaction, and lack the rhythmical character that would suggest a debt to previous material. On the other hand the structure is not unlike that of 15: 18–25. These verses are thus best regarded as belonging to the same literary process.

The most obvious structural feature is the inclusion provided by ταῦτα λελάληκα ὑμῖν in verses 1 and 4*a*. This feature not only agrees well with the style of 15: 18–25, but also provides further proof that the composition of these verses has been undertaken in the course of the redactional work of chapters 15–16 as a whole. For the phrase ταῦτα λελάληκα ὑμῖν, with slight variations, is a special characteristic of John's editorial style in these chapters. In chapter 14 it occurs only at 14: 25, introducing the Paraclete verse 26. As we have seen, this is likely to be an insertion, made at the same time as the addition of chapters 15–16. Within these chapters it occurs at 15: 11; 16: 1, 4, 25, 33. Generally it marks a transition of thought, bringing the subject back to the present situation in order to point up by contrast the future conditions following the Passion. But 16: 4*a* is exceptional, as it does not open a fresh topic, and it is distinguished from the rest by the particle ἀλλά. This makes the phrase resumptive of verse 1.

The contents also of verses 1 and 4a are virtually equivalent, and betray John's great anxiety concerning the steadfastness of the Christians in his own day. In verse 1 he shows contact with the Gospel traditions by his use of σκανδαλισθῆτε, which is a feature of Jesus' warning about the flight of the disciples (Matthew 26: 31//Mark 14: 27). He will allude again to this tradition later at 16: 32. He had previously quarried from it in his Last Supper account, where the forecast of Peter's denials in 13: 38 is extremely close to Mark 14: 30, but the previous verses have been replaced by characteristic Johannine themes. In verse 4a the motif of forewarning also has precedents in the earlier tradition, being a feature of the Little Apocalypse (Matthew 24: 25//Mark 13: 23).

Within the inclusion of verses 1 and 4a there is another inclusion in verses 2 and 3, achieving a formal balance by the repetition of ποιήσουσιν (2(a), 3(a)). Thus the whole paragraph forms a chiasmus: λελάληκα – ποιήσουσιν – ποιήσουσιν – λελάληκα. The nodal point in the structure is thus 2(c)(d), which thereby receives particular emphasis. The ground is prepared in 2(b), which points to the future, using a phrase that denotes a climactic moment.[31] Hence this marks a stage beyond what is described in 2(a), and therefore still future at the time of writing. In 3(a) the future verb, which is repeated from 2(a), is now laden with the extra meaning provided by 2(b)–(d). But in 3(b) the tension is reduced, as John briefly recalls the theological explanation already furnished in 15: 21–4.

It thus appears that verse 2(c)(d) comprises John's most serious warning to his readers. It is a real fear that a violent persecution is about to begin. We cannot tell how far John's fears were realised. But violent attacks on Christians, causing death, are known to have taken place in the time of Bar Cochba's rebellion, and are referred to in a number of passages in Justin's *Dialogue with Trypho*.[32] John correctly points out that this action will be carried out with a genuinely religious motive.[33] The expression is compressed, and should be understood to mean 'will

---

[31] The phrase ἔρχεται ὥρα is used in various connections, but always with this sense, cf. 2: 6; 4: 21, 23; 5: 25, 28; 7: 30; 8: 20; 12: 23, 27; 13: 1; 16: 21, 32; 17: 1.

[32] Justin, *Dial.* 16; 95; 110; 122; 133. *Dial.* 16 also attests the application of the *Birkat-ha-Minim* in the Synagogue; cf. Davies, *Sermon on the Mount*, p. 278. For other references in Justin, cf. p. 49, n. 6.

[33] For the 'holy zeal' that fired Jewish movements from Maccabaean times onwards, cf. M. Hengel, *Die Zeloten* (Leiden, 1961), pp. 151–234.

think that he makes an act of worship equivalent to the offering of a sacrifice'.[34] John does not intend to justify the action by these words. It is much more likely that there is an ironical intention behind them. For of course the martyrdom of Christians is indeed an acceptable sacrifice (cf. 17: 19). Thus, in the very act of placing before his readers this alarming possibility, he provides the means of seeing it positively within the framework of Jesus' own sacrifice.

IV

In the preceding pages I have attempted to show that John 15: 18 – 16: 4a was penned as part of the process of the composition of chapters 15–16. These chapters, along with chapter 17, were added to the Gospel at a later stage. The passage that we have studied owes a small debt to previously written work on the part of the Evangelist, consisting of the 'maxims' in 15: 18–20 and the Paraclete material. But in the main it is a new composition, and the contributions from previous work are subordinated to the argument of the piece as a whole. It therefore follows that this passage is concerned with conditions at the actual time of writing, comparatively late in the redactional history of the Fourth Gospel. In composing this piece, the Evangelist has made use of his own previous work within the Gospel, and has also drawn afresh on the traditions, known to us from Matthew 10 and other Synoptic references, which were fundamental to his theological presentation of the Gospel. He is at pains to show the vital relevance of this theology to the urgent situation with which he now has to deal. His object is not to provide information on the persecution. Nor is it an attempt to give authoritative guidance by the literary device of an address by the Master.[35] It is rather an attempt to interpret the present situation in the light of the truth of the Gospel. He wishes to show how it is to be understood within the divine ordering of events, which has been revealed for all time in the person of Jesus, and supremely in his Passion. It is thus significant that John does not make any exemplary use of the sufferings of Jesus, as is done, for instance, by 1 Peter. Jesus is not held up as the model of patience, but as the declaration of the Father. The disciples are fore-

[34] The verb προσφέρειν should properly specify the thing offered, either gifts or sacrifices, whereas λατρεία denotes an act of worship, which may include such offerings. The use of τῷ θεῷ in this verse, rather than τῷ πατρί, indicates that John is employing conventional religious language. The idea expressed in this verse is echoed in Num. R. 21.4 (cf. Barrett, *NT Background, ad loc.*).

[35] This kind of motive is probably the best explanation of the pseudepigraphic books of the New Testament, especially the Pastorals.

warned of sufferings, so that, aided by the Paraclete, they may stand firm in their confession of faith and not fall away.

The situation that has evoked these reflections is a time of sharp conflict between the Church and Synagogue in John's circle. The Gospel in its earlier state included hints that there were secret Christians among the Jews who were hesitating to declare themselves for fear of reprisals. Some sort of ban from the Synagogue is implied, and this must be taken seriously, however difficult it is to correlate with information derived from Jewish sources.[36] When John writes 15: 18 – 16: 4a the situation, though not fundamentally altered, is becoming critical. There is a real risk of violent, even fanatical, conflict.

We know from various sources[37] that Jewish persecution of Christians continued in the early part of the second century. But the success of the policy represented by the *Birkat-ha-Minim* must have changed the situation radically. The Johannine Church ceased to be in an uneasy relationship with the Synagogue, but became totally separate from it. It thus comes about that the Epistles of John contain no certain allusion to persecution by the Jews. Instead, the Church has become a closed society, jealously guarding its traditions and keeping a close watch on its members.

In this situation the use that is made of the Johannine teaching on persecution is not without interest. The opponents are dissident members of the Church itself, whose identity has never been satisfactorily decided.[38] They can be referred to as 'the world', because their beliefs and behaviour put them on the side of the godless world over against the true members of the Church. Thus in 1 John 3: 1 'the world' fails to recognise the true members as the children of God because it does not know God. We are at once reminded of John 15: 21. The difference between 'the world' and the true members is fundamental, for 'the world' are children of the devil and the true members are children of God (1 John 3: 10). But they are not easily distinguished. The only ways

[36] See the discussion in Hare, *Persecution*, pp. 54ff.
[37] Cf. p. 49, n. 6 above, and Hare, *ibid.* pp. 76f; J. W. Parkes, *The Conflict of the Church and the Synagogue* (London, 1934), p. 132. There are even indications of a Jewish counter-mission to Christians in later strands of the New Testament and the Apostolic Fathers, cf. G. W. H. Lampe, '"Grievous Wolves" (Acts 20: 29)', in *Christ and Spirit in the New Testament: Studies in Honour of C. F. D. Moule*, ed. B. Lindars and S. S. Smalley (Cambridge University Press, 1973), pp. 253–68.
[38] R. E. Brown (cf. p. 48, n. 2 above) asserts that, in spite of showing similar tendencies, they cannot be certainly identified with any of the known heretical groups of the second century. Schnackenburg compares them with the opponents of Ignatius.

in which the children of the devil can be detected are by their failure to do right and by their lack of love for the brethren.

At this point the argument of 1 John 3 has two items that link up with our study. First, the author gives the example of Cain, a brother who proved himself a son of the evil one because he murdered his brother instead of loving him. 'And why did he murder him? Because his own deeds were evil and his brother's righteous' (verse 12). Here we have the same explanation of persecution as we found in connection with John 15: 19. It is the exposure of the world's sin that arouses the world's hostility.[39] This provides the explanation for our second item, which follows immediately in verse 13: 'Do not wonder, brethren, that the world hates you.' This appears to be a direct quotation either of John 15: 18 or of the underlying 'maxim'. Moreover there is a clear allusion to John 15: 13 in verse 16 ('he laid down his life for us'). Whether these passages depend directly on the Gospel as we have it, or on earlier forms of its materials, they are certainly secondary from the point of view of its thought. For here the author has taken up the themes of love and hatred, which are not directly correlated by John in chapter 15, and worked out a comprehensive scheme, whereby sonship of the devil and all forms of wrongdoing, especially hatred, are opposed to sonship of God, righteousness, and the love of the brethren. The result of this scheme is that 'the world' can be used to denote anyone who belongs to the former class, including an individual who fails to respond to the claims of charity (verse 17).[40] There is thus a single category, which applies equally to the 'antichrists' (2: 18–22) and 'false prophets' (4: 1–3) who have separated themselves from the congregation, and also to Diotrephes and his kind, who refuse hospitality to 'the brethren' (3 John 9f). This category cuts across the formal distinction between members of the Church and those outside, for there are those within the Church who do not truly belong to it (1 John 2: 19;[41] 4: 5f). Evidently

---

[39] M. Wilcox, 'On investigating the use of the Old Testament in the New Testament', in *Text and Interpretation* (cf. p. 48, n. 2), p. 240, has drawn attention to the parallel between this verse and Pal. Tg. Gen. 4.8, suggesting that the writer is dependent upon a Jewish exegetical tradition. The parallel is illuminating, but omits the essential point at issue here, i.e. the reason *why* Cain should have murdered his brother.

[40] 'The love of God' in this verse probably denotes the love that comes from God (genitive of origin), cf. R. Bultmann, *The Johannine Epistles*, Hermeneia (Philadelphia, 1973), *ad loc*. Schnackenburg, however, treats it as genitive of quality, i.e. 'divine love'.

[41] The Greek (ἀλλ' ἵνα φανερωθῶσιν ὅτι οὐκ εἰσὶν πάντες ἐξ ἡμῶν) is ambiguous. Bultmann takes the ὅτι clause to mean, 'not all (who so claim) belong to us'. Schnackenburg translates, 'they do not belong to us – all of them', citing BDF §275(5). The former seems best (so NEB, RV margin).

John's anxiety for the unity of the Church in John 17: 20–3 has been sadly justified.

Finally, the real test of the false brethren is the confession of faith (1 John 2: 22f; 4: 2f, 15; 5: 10; 2 John 9). This again could well owe a debt to John 15: 21–4. But once more the terms of reference are really quite different. In the Gospel it is a matter of faith in Jesus as such. In the Epistles it is a perverted form of this faith, held by those who claim to be true Christians (Brown would say, true followers of the Gospel of John), but are not. Failure to show love to the brethren is proof that they are false (1 John 4: 20). It is obvious that, in these circumstances of internal strife, the categories of love and righteousness have become constricted in their application, and so to some extent debased. Consequently the great Johannine themes of the Gospel can be seen to be losing their freshness. They are degenerating into stereotypes. The life of the Johannine Church does not match the greatness of John's vision, and his call to courageous discipleship. For that we have to return to the Gospel itself.

Interchange and suffering

MORNA D. HOOKER

In a book published more than twenty years ago, which he characteristically described as a 'slight essay', Professor Moule[1] discussed what he
termed the 'strange paradox' at the heart of Christian faith, arising from
'the finality and yet constantly repetitive nature of salvation – the
finished work of God in Christ, over against his continued work in the
Body of Christ which is the Church'. It is one aspect of this tension,
namely the relationship between the sufferings of Christ and those of
Christians, that I wish to explore in this essay.

In previous essays on the theme of 'Interchange',[2] I have argued for
the importance of the theme of participation for understanding the
Pauline view of redemption. In various key texts,[3] Paul expresses the
belief that – to adapt the words of Irenaeus – Christ became what we
are, in order that, *in him*, we might become what he is. Christ identified
himself with the human condition, bore the likeness of Adam, in order
that men and women might bear his likeness and become children of
God. Commentators have at times interpreted some of these passages
in substitutionary terms, but a careful analysis shows that this is a mis-
interpretation. It is not a case of Christ becoming what we are in order
that we might become what he once was. If we experience glory and life
as a result of Christ's self-humiliation and death, then this is because he
himself has been raised in glory; if righteousness comes to us as a result
of Christ being made sin, then this is because he himself has been
acknowledged as righteous at the resurrection. What happens to us, as a
result of what happens to him, happens only because we share in his
experience of vindication and reversal. In other words, Christ is so
identified with humanity, that he is able to act as our representative.

---

[1] *The Sacrifice of Christ* (London, 1956).
[2] 'Interchange in Christ', *JTS* n.s. 22 (1971), 349–61; 'Interchange and Atonement', *BJRL* 60 (1978), 462–81.
[3] 2 Corinthians 5: 21; 8: 9; Galatians 3: 13; 4: 4; Romans 8: 3, 14; Philippians
2: 6–10 and 3: 20f.

'Christ died for us so that we might live' (1 Thessalonians 5: 10) may sound like a simple exchange – but in fact our life depends upon the fact that we live 'with him'. Christ died for us, in order that we might share his resurrection. This is no simple exchange, but a sharing of experience, and the phrase '*with him*' emphasises the dependence of the believer upon Christ. The basis of Paul's understanding of the believer's participation in Christ is set out more clearly in Romans 5: 12–19, in his contrast between the representative figures of Adam and Christ. The argument that everything that happened in Adam has been reversed in Christ depends upon the belief that what happens to one man can affect all men. In the case of Adam, he is regarded as a representative and inclusive figure: what he did affects all men because they are all his descendants. In the case of Christ, he too can be understood as a representative figure because he is the Christ/Messiah: what he did affects all who share his experiences because they are 'in Christ'. In the former case, Adam's sin led to condemnation and death for all; in the latter, Christ's right-eousness led to acquittal 'for all'. Man's condition in Adam is reversed in Christ because Christ was willing to share in man's condition – i.e. to come under condemnation and sentence of death; the result is that men and women are able, in turn, to share in his vindication and resurrection.

In spite of the problematic πάντες in Romans 5: 18, it is clear that Paul does not think of this 'interchange' taking place automatically. It is necessary, not only for Christ to identify himself with us, but for us to identify ourselves with him. Our union with Adam is involuntary and automatic, but our union with Christ is the result of a deliberate act on our part, and therefore not completely analogous. Christ shares our situation of condemnation and death – but we in turn need to share in his death. It is true that 2 Corinthians 5: 14 states the representational view of Christ's death in such a way as to suggest that it necessarily involves the whole of humanity; nevertheless, the context makes clear that it is only those who identify themselves with Christ's death, and no longer live to themselves, who share his resurrection life. One obvious way in which this happens is in baptism. 'Do you not know', asks Paul in Romans 6: 3, 'that all of us who have been baptised into Christ Jesus were baptised into his death?' The following verses spell this out: 'we were buried with him in baptism into death *in order that*, as Christ was raised from the dead through the glory of the Father, we too might walk in newness of life' (verse 4). This pattern of death–resurrection is re-peated in verses 5 and 8, in parallel conditional sentences: 'if we have been joined to the likeness of his death, we shall also share his resurrec-tion'; 'if we died with Christ, we believe that we shall also live with him'. It is noticeable that in both statements the resurrection is understood as a future event: we have *already* shared Christ's death, and therefore we *expect* to share his resurrection. Verses 6–7 explain the significance of dying with Christ: because we have been crucified with him, we are no longer enslaved to sin, since dying sets us free. Verse 9 explains the significance of Christ's resurrection: he will never die again, for he is no longer subject to death. It should be clear from this why Paul finds it easier to speak of dying with Christ as a past event than to describe rising with Christ in the same way. For while he believes that sin should no longer rule the Christian (verse 14), the 'last enemy', death, is not yet destroyed, and though Christians have died with Christ, it cannot be said of them, as it is of Christ, that they 'will never die again'.[4] Nevertheless the death and resurrection of Christ have set a pattern for the Christian. Christ died to sin once and for all, and lives now to God (verse 10); Christians must therefore reckon themselves to be dead to sin and alive to God in Christ (verse 11). In other words, while the resurrection with Christ lies in the future, there is a sense in which we already share his resurrection life, because we are in him.[5] This is why we can 'walk in newness of life' here and now (verse 4). And this is why Paul can urge the Romans to present themselves to God 'as if' they were dead men brought to life (verse 13).

This particular passage explores the meaning of dying and rising with Christ in two ways: the first is baptism, the dramatic proclamation of Christ's death and resurrection in which the believer identifies himself with the historical event of Christ's crucifixion; the second is the ethical consequence, that one is therefore dead to sin. The two are woven together here because it is the second that Paul is concerned to stress, and he argues it on the basis of the first. Both of them, however, demonstrate that it is not enough for Christ to identify himself with humanity: the believer must also identify himself with Christ. The paradox of Christian salvation is that though Christ shares *our* death in order that we may share his life, the believer can only share that life if he, in turn, is willing to share *Christ's* death. In identifying himself with Christ, the believer makes an act of self-abnegation similar to Christ's own, and

---

[4] Cf. a similar distinction in 1 Corinthians 15. In verse 17, Christ's resurrection means that we *have* been released from sin; in verse 22, it means that we *shall* all be made alive.

[5] Cf. G. M. Styler, 'Obligation in Paul's christology and ethics', in *Christ and Spirit in the New Testament: Studies in Honour of C. F. D. Moule*, ed. B. Lindars and S. S. Smalley (Cambridge University Press, 1973), pp. 181–3, where he argues that Paul understands the Christian's union with Christ's resurrection as past and present as well as future.

trusts himself totally to the God who is able to raise the dead to life. This attitude of total reliance upon God is parallel to that which is expressed elsewhere in the familiar terms of faith that leads to justification: it is because he is content to abandon his own pretensions to righteousness that the Christian is able to share the verdict of acquittal pronounced on those who are in Christ (Romans 8: 1). This happens at baptism, but it happens again and again throughout the Christian life, which is a continual process of reckoning oneself dead to sin and alive to God.

These are not the only ways, however, in which the Christian identifies himself with the death of Christ. In Romans 8: 17 we have another form of this idea, expressed in terms that remind us of the statements about death and resurrection with Christ in Romans 6. This verse forms the climax of a section in which Paul argues that God has set men free from sin and death by sending his Son in the likeness of sinful flesh. Christians, however, are no longer 'in the flesh' (because Christ has died to the flesh) but 'in the Spirit', and this Spirit makes them children of God, and so joint heirs with Christ, who is the Son of God. Paul uses here another form of the idea that Christ participates in the condition of men (coming in the likeness of sinful flesh), in order that they might share in his condition – i.e. be sons of God. Verse 17*b* gives us another hint as to how this change of status takes place. We become God's children and joint heirs with Christ, only if we are prepared to share his sufferings: it is necessary to suffer with him in order to be glorified with him. The verse echoes the structure of the earlier verses in Romans 6, where dying with Christ was interpreted in terms of baptism and dying to sin:

6:4 συνετάφημεν οὖν αὐτῷ . . . εἰς τὸν θάνατον, ἵνα ὥσπερ ἠγέρθη Χριστὸς ἐκ νεκρῶν . . . οὕτως καὶ ἡμεῖς. ἐν καινότητι ζωῆς περιπατήσωμεν.

6:5 εἰ γὰρ σύμφυτοι γεγόναμεν τῷ ὁμοιώματι τοῦ θανάτου αὐτοῦ, ἀλλὰ καὶ τῆς ἀναστάσεως ἐσόμεθα.

6:8 εἰ δὲ ἀπεθάνομεν σὺν Χριστῷ, πιστεύομεν ὅτι καὶ συνζήσομεν αὐτῷ.

8:17 . . . εἴπερ συνπάσχομεν ἵνα καὶ συνδοξασθῶμεν.

It is significant that the theme of 'identification with Christ' is worked out in Romans 8 in terms of 'suffering with Christ'. Clearly it is not enough for the believer to identify himself with Christ in a once-for-all act, namely baptism. We have seen already that dying with Christ is a continuing process in relation to sin: as long as the believer continues to live 'in the flesh', he must not live 'according to the flesh', but must identify himself with Christ's once-for-all act in dying to sin (Romans 6: 10). Here in Romans 8 we meet another way in which dying with Christ needs to be worked out in the believer's life. It is only if we suffer with him that we shall be glorified with him. We may become children of God and heirs of glory through Christ's act of self-identification with us, but if we are indeed to share his glory, we must identify ourselves with his suffering. Once again, we find the paradox that though in identifying himself with us Christ made an act of self-abnegation, those who are 'in Christ' must in turn identify themselves with *his* humiliation if they are to share his glory: the pattern of death–resurrection, suffering–glory must be worked out in them.

The theme of suffering leading to glory is found in an earlier section of Romans, in 5: 1–5. It is interesting to note that this follows immediately after the summary statement in 5: 1, which is similar to 8: 1. Both these verses sum up Paul's belief that through Christ's death Christians are free from condemnation in God's sight, and introduce a statement about what it means to live in Christ. In chapter 5, Paul says that we rejoice in hope of sharing the glory of God, and goes on to say that we even rejoice in our sufferings. Why? Because suffering produces endurance, endurance produces tried character, and tried character produces hope. As for this hope – the hope of sharing God's glory – we know that this will not be disappointed, since we have already received a pledge of the future through the work of the Holy Spirit. Support for this confidence is provided by a typically Pauline argument: 'if while we were enemies we were reconciled to God by the death of his Son, much more, now that we are reconciled, shall we be saved [from wrath] by his life' (verse 10; similarly verse 9). Christ's death 'for us' is seen as a supreme demonstration of God's love. It is interesting that in a context that describes how we are justified through the death of *Christ* and will be saved by him from wrath, we find also the theme that *our* sufferings work towards our glorification.

A similar theme is found in Philippians 3. Once again, the idea occurs in the context of a passage that contains the theme of 'interchange'. The form in which this latter theme is expressed is unusual, in that the thought of Christ's participation in our condition is spelt out in chapter 2 (in the famous so-called 'Christ-hymn'), whereas that of our participation in Christ's status does not occur until the very end of chapter 3. Nevertheless, the echoes of chapter 2 are clear: the one who was found in the *form* of a slave and the *fashion* of a man, who *humiliated* himself to a shameful death, is going to re*fashion* our body of *humiliation*, con*forming* it to his own body of glory.[6] Paul does not say in Philippians, as he says elsewhere, that Christ became what we are *in order that* we might become what he is. Nevertheless, he works out in 3: 21 the meaning of Christ's exaltation for the believer: because Christ took the form of a slave and was found in the likeness and fashion of a man, those who are in Christ share in what he is by virtue of his exaltation. It is certainly clearer in Philippians than anywhere else that this is no simple exchange: the reversal of status belongs to Christ, and believers hope to share in this reversal.

Yet it is also clearer in Philippians than elsewhere that this idea of our participation is far from being automatic. Christ shares our humiliation – but if we are to share his glory, then we must share his humiliation. Once again this is not confined to the idea that we are baptised into Christ's death, but is worked out in terms of the Christian's attitude to life, and indeed the attitude of the whole Christian community. The introduction to the 'hymn' makes this clear. Paradoxical as it may seem, Christians are urged to become *like Christ* in his self-emptying – which meant, for him, becoming *like us*.[7] This is spelt out even more forcefully in chapter 3, where Paul describes how he has abandoned every source of confidence 'in the flesh' – including even righteousness under the Law. Everything that he formerly prized he now considers as worthless and no better than rubbish for the sake of gaining Christ. He has identified himself with Christ's act of 'self-emptying', in order that he might be found in Christ (3: 9); in doing so, he has forsaken the righteousness of the Law, which is based on claims about what one has, for the righteousness that comes from God through faith – a faith that has nothing else on which to rely except God himself. The meaning of the phrase πίστις χριστοῦ in this verse has been the subject of much debate, and the context supports the arguments of those who wish to understand it as a reference to the faithfulness or faith of Christ himself;[8] this

---

[6] The details are given in 'Interchange in Christ', pp. 356f.

[7] Some commentators argue that the passage is to be understood as an appeal to act in the manner appropriate to those who are in Christ, and not as an appeal to act in a manner similar to that of Christ himself. This distinction is an unnecessary one, however, resulting from a dogmatic dismissal of the notion of imitating Christ. See M. D. Hooker, 'Philippians 2: 6–11' in *Jesus und Paulus, Festschrift für W. G. Kümmel*, ed. E. Earle Ellis and E. Grässer (Göttingen, 1975), pp. 151–64. Cf. also C. F. D. Moule, 'Further Reflexions on Philippians 2: 5–11' in *Apostolic History and the Gospel, essays presented to F. F. Bruce*, ed. W. Ward Gasque and Ralph P. Martin (Exeter, 1970), pp. 264–76; and H. D. Betz, *Nachfolge und Nachahmung Jesu Christi im Neuen Testament* (Tübingen, 1967), pp. 163–9.

[8] See e.g. G. Hebert, '"Faithfulness" and "Faith"', *Theology* 58 (1955), 373–9; T. F. Torrance, 'One Aspect of the Biblical Conception of Faith', *ExpT* 68

interpretation avoids the tautology that results from taking both occurrences of the word 'faith' in this verse as references to the faith of the
believer. Moreover, it fits well into the theme of participation with
which Paul is here concerned. If it is correct, then Paul is saying that he
abandoned the righteousness of the Law for the righteousness that came
about through the faith of Christ himself, a righteousness that comes
from God and is received by faith. 'Faith' sums up exactly Paul's description of Christ's self-emptying in Philippians 2, since in exchanging
the form of God for the form of a slave, Christ was relying totally on
God. This faith was vindicated at his exaltation, which proclaimed him
righteous in God's sight. It is with this faith – this willingness to empty
oneself of all pretensions and accept God's gift – that Paul now identifies
himself, believing that by being found in Christ he will share Christ's
righteousness. This interpretation is supported by the threefold use in
this section of the verb ἡγέομαι, which was used in 2: 6 in the first line
of the passage about Christ. Paul counted, and continues to count,
everything he once prized as loss and as rubbish, in order to gain
Christ and be found in him. In him he is given the righteousness that
comes through Christ's own faith – a righteousness from God, based on
faith.

But this status of righteousness before God is not the end of the
matter. Paul's purpose is to know Christ, to experience both the power
of his resurrection and the fellowship of his sufferings; it is to be conformed to Christ's death, if only by doing so he may attain the resurrection from the dead. It is noticeable that the idea of knowing Christ
and the power of his resurrection is here immediately qualified by the
reference to sharing his sufferings. Possibly Paul is here opposing teaching that emphasised the experience of the risen Lord in such a way as to
deny both future hope and present suffering: for Paul, life in Christ
means experiencing the power of Christ's resurrection – but only as one
experiences also his suffering. It was because Christ emptied himself
that God exalted him (Philippians 2: 9), and it is those who share his
sufferings who share his resurrection. In order to attain the resurrection
of the dead, one must become like him in death (3: 10f). Those who do
not recognise this are 'enemies of the cross' (3: 18). Although the image
of being conformed to Christ's death reminds us of baptism, we notice
that Paul uses a present participle, συμμορφιζόμενος, to denote a continuing process, with resurrection as a future goal. It is clear that Paul

(1957), 111–14, and comments by C. F. D. Moule, pp. 177, 222; R. N. Longenecker in *Reconciliation and Hope*, ed. R. J. Banks (Exeter, 1974), pp. 146–8.
The debate goes back to a suggestion made by Haussleiter in an article published in 1891. See also P. Vallotton, *Le Christ et la foi* (Geneva, 1960).

does not understand dying with Christ simply in symbolic terms. Those who hope to share in his resurrection must be conformed to his death – and that means sharing in his sufferings. It is through Christ's death and resurrection that the Christian is pronounced righteous: but this does not mean that Christ's sufferings are a substitute for ours. To say 'Christ died for us in order that we might live' is only half the story: we need to die *with him* in order to live *with him*. Dying with Christ is a continuing process, and this means that resurrection can never be totally realised in this life. In Philippians 3: 12–16, Paul stresses that it is still a future goal for which he must strive. He does not claim to have reached perfection: possibly he is alluding here to Christians who did make such claims. Paul himself is still aiming for the prize that awaits him at the end of the course. The image is similar to that which Paul uses in 1 Corinthians 9: 24–7, a passage that is of particular interest since Paul clearly envisages that there is a situation in which he might *not* win the prize.

It is clear from these passages that, however much Paul may stress the Cross as the decisive event in man's salvation, there is a sense in which, to use his own words, the Christian community must work out its own salvation (Philippians 2: 12). Christ dies as man's representative, not his substitute – and this means not only that Christ's death embodies the death of others, but that they must share his dying.

It is of course in 2 Corinthians that we meet the most extended treatment of this theme of sharing in the sufferings of Christ. In the opening thanksgiving, Paul describes the way in which, though the sufferings of Christ overflow in his direction, the consolation that comes through Christ overflows in equal measure (1: 5–7). In this case, however, the sufferings are not interpreted simply in terms of Paul's own experience, but in relation to that of the community in Corinth. Paul's affliction leads to the Corinthians' comfort and salvation, his comfort to theirs – when they patiently endure the same sufferings. Paul is confident that when they share his sufferings, they share also his comfort. It is interesting to notice that we have here a remarkable parallel to the pattern that we have found elsewhere. Just as Christ's death leads to life for Christians, so Paul's affliction leads to comfort and salvation for the Corinthians. Just as Christ's resurrection brings resurrection and glory (to those who are prepared to suffer with him), so Paul's experience of comfort brings comfort to the Corinthians (provided they share his sufferings).

Going on to describe the nature of the affliction that he has experienced, Paul says that although it was so severe that he despaired of his own life, this taught him to rely on God, who raises the dead to life. It was in sharing Christ's situation of helplessness that he learned to share his hope in God (2 Corinthians 1: 8–10). Under apparent sentence of death, Paul was delivered from danger, and so, in a sense, brought back to life. The difference between the two experiences of 'interchange' referred to in 2 Corinthians, the one linked with Christ's death and the other with Paul's sufferings, is that the second experience derives from, and is dependent on, the first. It is because Paul shares in Christ's sufferings that his own are of benefit to others: it is those who are in Christ who experience the life that comes through death.

Paul takes this theme up again in chapter 4 of 2 Corinthians, a passage that follows on from the defence of his ministry in chapter 3 and may well reflect accusations from his opponents about his weakness and lack of dignity. Immediately after declaring that Christians are changed into Christ's likeness and glory, Paul describes how this 'treasure' is continued in 'earthen vessels' – once again, in order that we may learn to rely upon the power of God (verse 7). This passage provides us with Paul's fullest exploration of the theme of life-through-death. In a series of striking phrases, he describes various ways in which he is 'always carrying in the body the death of Jesus, in order that the life of Jesus may also be manifested' in his body (verses 8–10). It is by sharing the dying of Jesus that he is able to experience the life of Jesus – a theme so important that Paul restates it in verse 11. Then once again he moves onto the idea that his own sufferings can benefit the Corinthians: 'So death is at work in us, but life in you' (verse 12).

He now introduces a quotation from the Psalms. 'Having the same spirit of faith, according to that which is written – "I believed, therefore I spoke" – we also believe, and therefore speak' (verse 13). In discussing the word 'same' here, commentators are divided between those who think that it refers to the Psalmist[3] and those who suggest that it refers to the Corinthians.[10] The former suggestion seems awkward, since the Psalmist's words are introduced into the argument as an ordinary proof-text,[11] while the latter suggestion does not really fit the context. It is

[9] E.g. C. K. Barrett, *The Second Epistle to the Corinthians* (London, 1973), *in loc.*

[10] E.g. R. H. Strachan, *The Second Epistle of Paul to the Corinthians* (London, 1935); W. Schmithals, *Gnosticism in Corinth*, trans. John E. Steely (Nashville and New York, 1971), p. 162.

[11] If the Old Testament quotation is intended to refer us to its original context, then it would certainly be appropriate here, for verses 1–9 of the psalm describe the sufferings of the psalmist. However, the wording of the citation in 2 Corinthians reproduces exactly the LXX version, where what is verse 10 in the Hebrew text begins a new psalm – a psalm of deliverance. If Paul is quoting from the LXX, as the wording suggests, then it would seem that he is

important to note that Paul clearly understands faith here as faith in God, who raised Christ from the dead and brings life out of death. This is the faith that Paul claims to share. If he intends any answer to the commentators' question 'the same faith as whom?' perhaps it is 'Jesus'. It is the death of Jesus that has just been mentioned in verses 10f and is referred to again in verse 14, where Paul expresses confidence that the one who raised Jesus will raise 'us' with Jesus. If the interpretation of Philippians 3:9 given above is correct, then possibly we have here a parallel to the idea that in his death Christ demonstrated faith in the one who could raise him from the dead, and that those who are prepared to share his dying share his faith. It is significant that in 2 Corinthians 4, as in 1:9, the theme of suffering with Christ is interwoven with that of faith in God who raises the dead.

In verse 15 Paul reiterates the thought expressed in verse 12 that his sufferings benefit the Corinthians. But not only the Corinthians. His temporary affliction is insignificant when compared with the eternal glory towards which it is working. As in Romans 8:17 and Philippians 3:10f, we find Paul emphasising that the sufferings of believers play a role in bringing about future glory. The process of glorification is not yet complete (cf. 3:18).

The opening verses of 2 Corinthians 5 continue the theme of faith in God to bring life out of death (verses 1–5), and lead on to the thought that the end of the process will mean not only glory but judgement (verse 10). This is a theme that is hinted at in Philippians 3:12–16 (cf. also 1 Corinthians 9:24–7). Paul's doctrine of justification through faith does not exclude the idea of future judgement, and the reward and punishment of good and evil.

This chapter contains also a verse that sums up neatly some of the ideas that we have been examining. The statement that Christ has died for all in verse 14 might be understood – and has sometimes been understood – as substitutionary.[12] But Paul immediately adds the words 'therefore all have died', showing clearly that he understands Christ to have died as man's representative. Yet this death is something that men need to appropriate for themselves. Christ died for all, says Paul, so that 'those who live might live no longer for themselves but for him who for their sake died and was raised'. By living *for* him, they share his self-giving and are controlled by his love. This is why, if anyone is in Christ,

---

using the quotation atomistically. The Hebrew wording of the verse is difficult, and is variously interpreted, but its meaning seems to be significantly different from the LXX.

[12] E.g. Leon Morris, *The Cross in the New Testament* (Exeter, 1967), p. 220.

Morna D. Hooker

there is a new creation (verse 17): just as death leads to life, so the old gives way to the new. The idea that dying with Christ means living under the control of Christ is spelt out also in Galatians 2: 20f.

But Paul is concerned primarily in 2 Corinthians 5 with his own apostolic calling. He has been entrusted with the ministry of reconciliation – reconciliation that resulted from Christ being 'made sin for our sake' (verse 21). Inevitably, Paul's own ministry means sharing in the humiliation and suffering of Christ (6: 4–10). Once again, however, we find Paul claiming to experience 'life' through 'death'; he comes to know joy through sorrow, and finds himself possessing everything through having nothing. Familiar, too, is the idea that this 'interchange' of experience benefits others: although he is poor, Paul makes others rich. We have only to turn on to 8: 9 to discover that this is not an experience that Paul claims for apostles alone. The Corinthians are exhorted there to give generously, and so to follow the example of Christ himself, who 'being rich, became poor for your sake, in order to make you rich by his poverty'.

The idea of imitating Christ is linked in 1 Thessalonians with the theme of suffering. In the opening thanksgiving, Paul describes the Thessalonians as having become 'imitators of us and of the Lord' in that they 'received the word in much affliction, with joy inspired by the Holy Spirit'. In the following chapter, he says that they 'became imitators of the churches of God in Christ Jesus which are in Judaea; for you suffered the same things from your own countrymen as they did from the Jews, who killed both the Lord Jesus and the prophets' (2: 14f). Suffering is assumed, here, to be the lot of all who believe the Gospel. If they are persecuted, the Thessalonians are following in the footsteps of the Lord himself, as well as of their apostle and of the churches in Judaea.

The suffering endured by the Thessalonians was caused by persecution, and was therefore the direct result of their Christian faith. Much of Paul's own suffering was clearly due to his apostolic call, and we are not surprised to find him describing it as a sharing in the sufferings of Christ. What *is* perhaps surprising is that he appears to make no distinction between this and what we might perhaps describe as 'ordinary' suffering – the pain that results from the simple fact of being human. It is as though *all* suffering, whether it is persecution or the thorn in the flesh of 2 Corinthians 12: 7–10, has been baptised into Christ, and can be transformed through the experience of interchange. In other words, the power of Christ's resurrection can be experienced in suffering that results from being 'in Adam', as well as in suffering that comes through being 'in Christ'.[13] Perhaps it is because he thinks of all suffering as due, ultimately, to Satanic powers opposed to God, that Paul makes no distinction between persecution and 'natural' events.

The most famous of all the passages in the Pauline epistles that refer to sharing the sufferings of Christ is Colossians 1: 24. Paul's own sufferings are described here as being ὑπὲρ ὑμῶν, and as 'filling up what is lacking of the afflictions of Christ'. Most commentators are concerned to stress what Paul does *not* mean here: in the words of J. B. Lightfoot, 'St. Paul would have been the last to say that [Christians] bear their part in the atoning sacrifice of Christ.'[14] Lightfoot went on to point out that 'the idea of expiation or satisfaction is wholly absent from this passage'. It is indeed only because commentators have approached Colossians 1: 24 with preconceived notions about the Pauline understanding of Christ's death that it has caused them difficulties. One can go further than Lightfoot and suggest that the ideas of expiation or substitution (which are not necessarily the same thing) are in fact far from central in Pauline thought, so that their absence here is by no means surprising. The interpretation of Christ's death as a once-for-all event is *one* model used by New Testament writers, but is not the only one. When Paul speaks of Christ's death in relation to sin, *then* he describes it in once-for-all terms. But the theme of dying-to-live is an ongoing process, in which Christians share. In describing his own sufferings as 'for you', Paul says no more than he says throughout 2 Corinthians. The belief that his sufferings can benefit others does not involve the idea that they also atone for the sins of others. Indeed, there are two occasions when Paul speaks about suffering ὑπὲρ Χριστοῦ. It might perhaps be possible to explain both away as meaning little more than 'as Christians'. But in 2 Corinthians 12: 10, Paul is acting as Christ's apostle and representative in accepting weakness, insults and hardships. And in Philippians 1: 29, Paul uses the phrase twice, and writes that it has been granted to the Philippians τὸ ὑπὲρ Χριστοῦ πάσχειν. Paul speaks often of Christ suffering ὑπὲρ ἡμῶν: but here we find him using a parallel phrase in describing the sufferings of Christ's followers. It is not so surprising, then, in Colossians 1: 24, to find him writing of his own sufferings as 'filling up what is lacking in the sufferings of Christ', or describing this as of benefit to Christ's body, the Church.[15] A somewhat similar idea –

13 See also 'Interchange in Christ', p. 359.
14 *Saint Paul's Epistles to the Colossians and to Philemon*, 2nd. ed. (London, 1876), *in loc.*
15 It seems strange that τὰ ὑστερήματα τῶν θλίψεων is normally understood as a reference to the Church's quota of sufferings. Since Paul elsewhere regards it as part of his vocation to share Christ's sufferings on behalf of the Church, it

albeit in this case a hypothetical one – is found in Romans 9: 3, where Paul expresses his willingness to be ἀνάθεμα...ἀπὸ τοῦ Χριστοῦ ὑπὲρ τῶν ἀδελφῶν μου.[16]

Colossians 1: 24 provides an interesting example of the way in which commentators have allowed their theological convictions to influence their interpretation of the text. The belief that Christ's death is decisive and once-for-all has led some of them to shy away from the straightforward meaning of the words. Another example of this can be seen in the refusal to allow that Paul ever speaks of imitating Christ.[17] Colossians 1: 24 reflects the conviction that we have found elsewhere in Paul's writings, that it is necessary for the Christian to share in the sufferings of Christ and that this participation in suffering can be of benefit to other members of the Christian community. This necessity is not based on the idea that there is a set quota of messianic sufferings that need to be completed. Rather it arises from the representative character of Christ's death. If Christ died for all, this means not only that all have died, but that they must continue to work out the meaning of dying with Christ. The acceptance of Jesus as Messiah means a willingness to share his experiences. In this sense, at least, the sufferings of Christ are no substitute for ours, but a pattern to which we need to be conformed.

The tendency to stress the belief that Christ's death was a substitute for ours to the exclusion of the Pauline conviction that Christians must participate in the suffering of Christ is perhaps a very early one. The Corinthians, e.g., seem to have been unable to grasp the idea that there was any place for suffering and humiliation in their calling: for them, resurrection with Christ was a *past* event, and this meant that they shared already in his glory, fullness and riches (cf. 1 Corinthians 4: 8). Christ had suffered – and they experienced the resulting glory. He had become for them the substitute for humiliation and death. They failed to see the necessity to share his sufferings.

The failure of the antinomians to see the need to die with Christ to sin provides an interesting parallel. For them, too, the death of Christ was a once-for-all act bringing them release. Neither group understood Paul's insistence that the Christian life was a continuous process of self-identification with Christ. The Corinthians wanted instant glory, the

seems more likely that it is Paul's own quota of sufferings, which he sees as still needing to be completed. See also the contribution of W. F. Flemington to this volume, pp. 84–90.

[16] The idea that Paul's sufferings can lead to salvation for others reappears in 2 Timothy 2: 10. But the saying has lost the passion of Paul's own sayings and reads like an assessment of his apostolic achievements.

[17] Cf. p. 75, n. 7, above, on the interpretation of Philippians 2.

antinomians instant salvation. For Paul, these are the goal of Christian living, achieved through sharing Christ's sufferings.

In contrast to the Corinthian stance, Paul emphasised the Gospel of Christ crucified (1 Corinthians 1: 23). This Gospel is not a mere objective fact to be believed, however, but a way of life to be accepted. Christian discipleship means identification with the crucified Lord. Faith in God means faith in the one who raises the dead – a faith shown by Christ himself. In insisting that faith is the only way to find righteousness Paul was not being arbitrary, but spelling out the very nature of his Gospel. For the way of the Cross, as it is set out in Philippians 2: 6–8, is the supreme example of what Paul means by faith: those who accept this way make no claims upon God, and rely totally on his grace. Those who follow this path of faith must be prepared to share the humiliation and suffering that it brings, if they wish to experience also the glory that God gives.

On the interpretation of Colossians *1 : 24*

W. F. FLEMINGTON

'It is now my happiness to suffer for you. This is my way of helping to complete, in my poor human flesh, the full tale of Christ's afflictions still to be endured, for the sake of his body which is the church' (Colossians 1: 24, NEB).

In an earlier letter St Paul had indignantly repudiated the idea that it was he who had been crucified for the sake of others.[1] In this passage he asserts the value for others of the sufferings which he is enduring, and speaks of them as 'the afflictions of Christ'. How are these two points of view to be related to each other?

It is clear that Colossians 1: 24 must have considerable importance for any consideration of the place of suffering and martyrdom in the New Testament. In his commentary on the epistle Professor C. F. D. Moule devotes more than five pages to the study of this verse, and it will be helpful for us at the outset if we avail ourselves of the convenient distinction that he draws between two main lines of interpretation:[2]

(1) That which links the verse with Pauline teaching about Christians as those who are 'in Christ'. 'Christ's sufferings (on the cross and throughout his ministry) are necessarily shared by Christians...their union with him involves their participation in his sufferings.'

(2) That which links the verse with the conception of the 'messianic woes'. 'There is a "quota" of sufferings which "the corporate Christ", the Messianic community, the Church, is destined to undergo before the purposes of God are complete.' Professor Moule is inclined to think that the two interpretations should be combined, but of the two he regards 'the second as the more uniformly probable and...the dominant idea'. John Austin Baker in *The Foolishness of God* makes considerable use of this conception of the messianic woes, and in a footnote commends Professor Moule for applying it to the interpretation of Colossians 1: 24.[3]

---

[1] 1 Corinthians 1: 13.
[2] C. F. D. Moule, *The Epistles of Paul the Apostle to the Colossians and to Philemon*, Cambridge Greek Testament Commentary (Cambridge University Press, 1957), p. 76.
[3] J. A. Baker, *The Foolishness of God* (London, 1970), p. 239 n. 2.

In what follows, while fully recognising the relevance and importance of the idea of the messianic sufferings, I want to put in a plea for a little further consideration of the first line of interpretation, namely, that which links the verse with Pauline teaching about Christians as those who are 'in Christ', and in so doing I want to recall another exegesis of this verse, which in my judgement accords more closely with Paul's thinking.

I may have missed something vital, but I am often puzzled by the way in which the central words of this verse are apt to be cited in a truncated form, with a full stop inserted where there appears to be no justification for such a pause in the original. Thus the passage is read, 'I fill up that which is lacking of the afflictions of Christ', and the words that follow, 'in my flesh', are omitted. A representative example occurs in T. W. Manson's work, *The Teaching of Jesus*. He wrote, 'The Apostle does not hesitate to speak of his own sufferings as supplying what is lacking in the sufferings of Christ.'[4] Again, we may note the words of W. L. Knox, 'Christ...through His servants must continue to suffer until the whole quantity of suffering needed for the redemption of the world was completed.'[5] In the hands of less scholarly exponents this view can find a looser and more popular expression – Calvary provides the example, but the world's salvation is to be fully effected only by a continuing atonement in which the followers of Christ can share and to which they can successively contribute. Such a position often seeks support from words of Jesus himself, who called men to take up their cross and follow after him,[6] and it agrees with much modern thinking, which sees the Cross of Christ not as something unique but rather as the supreme example of sacrificial service.[7] In a century during which so many have given their lives in two world wars such teaching can bring comfort and reassurance to those who have been bereaved.

Yet as an adequate exegesis of Colossians 1: 24 such an interpretation

---

[4] T. W. Manson, *The Teaching of Jesus* (Cambridge University Press, 1931), p. 232.
[5] W. L. Knox, *St Paul and the Church of the Gentiles* (Cambridge University Press, 1939), p. 166.
[6] E.g. Mark 8:34 and parallels; but contrast Dr O'Neill, above, pp. 11–16, and note words of the scholar whom we honour in this volume: 'Although indications can be found that his disciples stand beside him and take a share in his work, even being invited to share his cup, yet there is no hint of a crudely "pluralist" view, that is, Jesus is not just one among many equals. His disciples are with him, but he is not one of them' (G. M. Styler, 'Stages in Christology in the Synoptic Gospels', *NTS* 10 (1963–4), 403).
[7] Cf. the hymn that has been frequently sung at Remembrance Day services, 'O valiant hearts', with its reference to 'lesser Calvaries'.

must be disputed for two reasons: first, it contradicts what St Paul taught elsewhere about the Cross of Christ, and, secondly, it is singularly inappropriate in an epistle addressed at this particular time to the church at Colossae.

(1) If there is one thing central and determinative in Pauline theology it is the finished and decisive character of what God through Christ effected by means of the Cross. 'What the law could never do...God has done: by sending his own Son...as a sacrifice for sin' (Romans 8: 3). 'God was in Christ reconciling the world to himself' (2 Corinthians 5: 19). The scholars whom I have cited for the earlier interpretation of Colossians 1: 24 would not for a moment have denied such a decisive act of God in Christ. Thus Wilfred Knox, on the page containing the passage that I have quoted, could also write, 'Jesus had reconciled man to God...through death.' But if this reconciliation had taken place, it is not easy to see why Knox should continue, 'but this work of reconciliation had to be completed by the sufferings of his ministers'.[8] J. B. Lightfoot in his classic treatment of the subject tried to avoid the difficulty by drawing a distinction between the sufferings of Christ that were (to use his Latin term) *satisfactoriae* (having sacrificial efficacy) and those that were *aedificatoriae* (having ministerial utility) – a distinction that has not won much support among more recent commentators.[9] These quotations all seem to illustrate how great scholars, when they interpret Colossians 1: 24 in this way, are continually having to qualify what they say for fear of being misunderstood.

(2) The second reason why it is unsatisfactory to say of this verse that St Paul 'speaks of his own sufferings as supplying what is lacking in the sufferings of Christ' is that such a position is quite inconsistent with the reply St Paul makes to his opponents at Colossae. The precise nature of the Colossian 'heresy' is hard to determine, but it is clear that the teachers whom St Paul is opposing accorded to Christ a place in the work of redemption that fell far short of what in St Paul's judgement was right and fitting. As Professor Moule puts it in the introduction to his commentary, Paul's opponents at Colossae regarded 'Jesus...as only one among the many who controlled the approaches to salvation'.[10] Over against such an estimate of Christ Paul warns his readers:

'Be on your guard; do not let your minds be captured by hollow and delusive speculations, based on traditions of man-made teaching and

[8] Knox, *Paul and Gentiles*, p. 166.
[9] J. B. Lightfoot, *Saint Paul's Epistles to the Colossians and to Philemon*, 3rd ed. (repr. London, 1892), p. 164.
[10] Moule, *Colossians and Philemon*, p. 33.

centred on the elemental spirits of the universe and not on Christ. For it is in Christ that the complete being of the Godhead dwells embodied, and in him you have been brought to completion.'[11]

In such a situation surely for St Paul to have suggested in 1: 24 that the work of Christ was not yet complete, that his sufferings needed supplementation, would have served only to provide his opponents with fresh ammunition. So absurd a conclusion suggests that we might do well to seek another exegesis.

Let us look again at the verse, excising the full stop that is so often gratuitously placed at the end of the truncated quotation, 'I fill up that which is lacking of the afflictions of Christ.' In the Authorised and Revised Versions this clause is followed (as in the Greek) by the words 'in my flesh', but some of the modern translations seem to go out of their way to separate the clause, 'that which is lacking of the afflictions of Christ' (τὰ ὑστερήματα τῶν θλίψεων τοῦ χριστοῦ), from the words, 'in my flesh' (ἐν τῇ σαρκί μου). Thus the NEB, altering the order of the original, renders the latter phrase, 'in my poor human flesh', and places it in front of the clause, 'the full tale of Christ's afflictions still to be endured', separating the phrase off with double commas. The RSV, very similarly (though without the use of commas), puts the words 'in my flesh' first, rendering, 'in my flesh I complete what is lacking in Christ's afflictions'. I want, instead of this, to argue for following the order of the Greek, and taking the phrase, 'in my flesh', after, but closely in conjunction with, the words that in the original precede it. We should then translate, 'I fill up that which is lacking of the afflictions of Christ in my flesh' – so construing everything from τὰ ὑστερήματα down to ἐν τῇ σαρκί μου as a single composite phrase. In classical idiom, no doubt, a repeated article before ἐν τῇ σαρκί μου would have been desirable; but this can scarcely be demanded in Hellenistic Greek. According to this way of taking the passage, the defect that St Paul is contemplating lies not in the afflictions of Christ as such,[12] but rather in the afflictions of Christ as they are reflected and reproduced in the life and behaviour of Paul his apostle. St Paul strives continually to live ἐν χριστῷ, but he knows that in his life there is, as it were, an unpaid balance that needs to be made up before the reproduction of Christ's sufferings in Paul's person is complete. St Paul rejoices because in all that he is suffering on behalf of the Colossians he is reducing his un-

---

[11] Colossians 2: 8f.

[12] Cf. Moule, *Colossians and Philemon*, p. 77, who points out that θλῖψις 'is nowhere in the NT demonstrably used of the actual sufferings of Jesus on the cross or in his ministry'.

paid balance, he is making the reproduction a little more like the perfect original. Let me make clear that to take the clause thus closely with the words 'in my flesh' is in no sense my own interpretation. A. S. Peake in The Expositor's Greek Testament took it this way.[13] So did E. F. Scott in The Moffatt Commentary.[14] An admirably lucid statement of this exegesis is to be found in the work by Hoskyns and Davey, *The Riddle of the New Testament*.[15] They write of this verse that it 'does not mean that there was something lacking in Christ's suffering, but that there was something lacking in St Paul's. He desires that his body may be, as it were, the arena where the obedience to God may be as wholly displayed as it had been in the Passion of Jesus Christ.'[16]

To take the words 'in my flesh' with those immediately preceding them as a single composite phrase just carries to its logical conclusion the Pauline teaching about those who are 'in Christ'. The Christian, by his incorporation in Christ called and empowered to re-enact what Christ did, is continually striving to make that reproduction in his own person more complete. The centrality of this conception in Pauline thinking is indicated also by the use of verbs compounded with the preposition σύν ('with').[17] According to St Paul, the man who is 'in Christ' is enabled to share with him in crucifixion, death, burial,

---

[13] A. S. Peake, *The Epistle to the Colossians*, The Expositor's Greek Testament, ed. W. Robertson Nicoll, III, 515.

[14] E. F. Scott, *The Epistles of Paul to the Colossians, to Philemon and to the Ephesians*, Moffatt New Testament Commentary (London, 1930), pp. 30f: 'Paul rejoices in all new hardships because they bring him nearer to his ideal of a life completely conformed to Christ.'

[15] E. Hoskyns and N. Davey, *The Riddle of the New Testament* (London, 1931), pp. 226f.

[16] Hoskyns and Davey use the word 'body', whereas the word used by St Paul is σάρξ ('flesh'). He could not well use σῶμα because in the latter part of the verse he needed that word for the Body of Christ, the Church. But σάρξ is here used in a morally neutral sense, as an equivalent for σῶμα. For another example we may compare 1 Corinthians 5: 3, 'absent in body' (ἀπὼν τῷ σώματι) with Colossians 2: 5, 'even...though I am absent in flesh', (εἰ... καὶ τῇ σαρκὶ ἄπειμι). In these two passages σῶμα and σάρξ are virtual equivalents. We may note also the rhythmic parallelism in 2 Corinthians 4: 10 and 11, where ἐν τῷ σώματι ἡμῶν (verse 10) is balanced by ἐν τῇ θνητῇ σαρκὶ ἡμῶν (verse 11). For further examples of σάρξ = σῶμα see the excursus at Romans 8: 11 by H. Lietzmann in his Handbuch zum Neuen Testament (*An die Römer*, 3rd ed. (Tübingen, 1928)).

[17] The references are: συνσταυρόω (Romans 6: 6; Galatians 2: 20); (cf. also Romans 6: 8, where the verb ἀποθνήσκω is followed by the preposition σύν); συνθάπτω (Romans 6: 4; Colossians 2: 12); συνεγείρω (Ephesians 2: 6; Colossians 2: 12; 3: 1); συνζάω (Romans 6: 8; cf. 2 Corinthians 4: 10f); συνκαθίζω (Ephesians 2: 6). Compare Prof. Hooker, above, pp. 70–83.

resurrection and a new quality of life. Some of these verbs are used in passages that refer to the rite of baptism. For St Paul part of the meaning of baptism is that the rite foreshadows and anticipates that continual dying to sin and rising again to new life in which the whole subsequent behaviour of the man 'in Christ' is meant to consist. We recall what St Paul wrote in 2 Corinthians 4: 10: 'Wherever we go, we carry death with us in our body, the death that Jesus died, that in this body also life may reveal itself, the life that Jesus lives.' The advantage of this way of interpreting Colossians 1:24 is that, on the one hand, the Pauline conviction about the decisive and finished character of what God through Christ did upon the Cross is fully maintained. This conviction goes back to the moment of St Paul's conversion, when for him a crucified Messiah ceased to be a stumbling-block and came instead to dominate his theology. On the other hand, this way of taking the passage gives full scope for the scarcely less important Pauline insight that the benefits of Christ's work can be fully appropriated by the Christian only as, by incorporation ἐν χριστῷ, in the Body of Christ, he is enabled to exhibit the same readiness to suffer as marked the life and death of his Master.

So we come back to the question with which we began. What is the relation between 1 Corinthians 1: 13, which repudiates the idea that St Paul had been crucified for others, and Colossians 1: 24, which asserts the value for others of St Paul's sufferings, and describes them as 'the afflictions of Christ'? Our answer must be that in one sense the Cross of Christ is unique and unrepeatable in so far as it is the 'sacrifice for sin', (Romans 8:3 and cf. 3:25), the divine way of bringing about the world's salvation. It was in reference to this supreme divine Act that St Paul could indignantly ask: 'Was it Paul who was crucified for you?' (1 Corinthians 1: 13). But in another sense the Cross is representative and capable of being reflected and mirrored in the life of Christians. The love of God in Christ that there embraced sacrificial suffering is the pattern for the Christian. By incorporation 'in Christ' he must continually seek more and more completely to reproduce it in his own life, and St Paul believes that this can bring benefit to the Body of Christ, which is the Church. It was in reference to this other aspect of the Cross that St Paul could write the words of Colossians 1: 24. Among modern translators James Moffatt seems best to have rendered the verse: 'I am suffering now on your behalf, but I rejoice in that; I would make up the full sum of all that Christ has to suffer in my person on behalf of the church, his Body.'

In an age when for many people Christian faith is hard to come by,

W. F. Flemington

Pauline theology may seem utterly remote and unreal. But in our own time there are some whose life and conduct force us to ask whether St Paul's conviction about the Cross of Christ may not give us the clue to the secret of this strange and baffling universe. In July 1941 during the Nazi occupation of Poland, because of the supposed escape of a prisoner from the camp at Auschwitz, it was decided that ten men should die. They were to be locked up in an underground room with no food or water. One of them, Franciszek Gajowniczek, was a married man with a family. A Franciscan priest came forward and took his place. Father Maximilian Kolbe not only died in his stead, but during more than two weeks of agony he supported the others, as they died, with his prayers and his example, until he and three others were the last to die. Thirty years later, at a Synod in Rome on 17 October 1971, Maximilian Kolbe was beatified in the presence of the man for whom he had given his life. Cardinal Wojtyla (later to become Pope John Paul II) recalled his action and its effect, especially on the Nazi guards: 'The SS themselves were astounded: "*So was haben wir nie gesehen*" (we never saw anything like it before), they said.' Father Kolbe has been described as 'a man who embodied in his own person the love that Christ showed towards all men'. The future Pope summed it up in the words, 'this man of flesh and blood...carried out his commitment to the end'.[18]

In Charles Wesley's hymn, 'O Thou who camest from above', as it is often sung, the last verse reads:[19]

> 'Ready for all Thy perfect will,
> My acts of faith and love repeat,
> Till death Thy endless mercies seal,
> And make the sacrifice complete.'

But in the last line Charles Wesley originally wrote 'my sacrifice'.[20] (It was probably his brother, John, who altered the possessive pronoun to the definite article.[21]) Was Charles Wesley combining the wording of Romans 12: 1 with the thought lying behind Colossians 1: 24?

[18] The quotations are taken from Mary Craig, *Man from a Far Country* (London, 1979), pp. 134ff. In chapter 11 of this life of Pope John Paul II the author has told the full story of the life and death of Father Kolbe. I am grateful to the Reverend Richard Harries, Vicar of All Saints' Church, Fulham, for kindly giving me this reference.

[19] E.g. *The Methodist Hymn-Book*, no. 386; cf. *Hymns Ancient and Modern*, no. 698.

[20] *The Poetical Works of John and Charles Wesley*, ed. G. Osborn (London, 1870), IX, p. 59. *The English Hymnal*, no. 343, has kept the original reading.

[21] *A Collection of Hymns for the Use of the People Called Methodists*, 3rd ed. corrected (1782), no. 318. Cf. also J. Telford, *The New Methodist Hymn-Book Illustrated*, 4th ed. (London, 1944), p. 203.

Preparation for the perils of the last days: *1 Thessalonians 3: 3*

E. BAMMEL

The Christian's hope in the trials and afflictions of the day is expressed in the lines of the prayer:

> 'Herr lass mich nur nicht wanken,
> Gib mir Beständigkeit
> Dafür will ich Dir danken
> In alle Ewigkeit.'

N. Selnecker, the author of this hymn echoes 1 Thessalonians 3:3 or rather the interpretation this passage has received from Luther to E. v. Dobschütz and M. Dibelius.

Intellectual doubts – 'Unsicherheit in der Glaubensüberzeugung', as it is put by v. Dobschütz[1] – and lack of fortitude are temptations and experiences which, separately and in combination, manifested themselves once and again in nascent church history. In the context of 1 Thessalonians, however, such considerations are rather surprising. Was this really the problem the community and their spiritual adviser had to grapple with? Paul had characterised the Thessalonians not only as πιστεύοντες but as those in whom the word of God is active (2: 13), nay, in whom the εὐαγγέλιον manifested itself πληροφορίᾳ πολλῇ (1: 5). He had expressed his joy at the state of the Thessalonian Christians in formulations of which the unqualified praise is absent from the other Pauline letters. He had even described them (2: 19) as the στέφανος, as the very achievement[2] he hopes to present to Christ at his coming. How is it possible that he could have proceeded in the next verse already to an expression of uneasiness about the state of their belief?

---

[1] *Die Thessalonicher-Briefe* (Göttingen, 1909), p. 264.

[2] The reference to ἀγαλλίασις (= eschatological rejoicing; cp. Luke 1: 14; Acts 2: 46; John 5: 35; 8: 56), which is documented by A and Tertullian, is in keeping with the flow of the sentence. Awkward, however, is the hybrid στέφανος ἀγαλλιάσεως. Might it be that the variant is based on an earlier alternative text, which ran: στέφανος καὶ ἀγαλλίασις?

True, Paul speaks of ὑστερήματα of their πίστις in the following paragraph (3: 10), of shortcomings he wishes to fill up during the visit he longs to undertake, which he sets out to cope with already on the next pages, in four sections that contain teaching material on different questions. What he expounds to them is a quantitative addition to their belief, that means to the body of Christian teaching they had been acquainted with before.[3] Correspondingly ὑστερήματα points to gaps of information[4] rather than material shortcomings and basic weaknesses.

On the other hand, the interference of Satan, referred to in 2: 18, might be taken to allude to experiences on the spiritual level and therefore be regarded as an indication of temptations, either imminent or already affecting the Thessalonians. This is, however, not necessarily the case. Paul had found Satan active in events that prohibited him from visiting the Thessalonian community. Surely, he thinks of external events in this case. It is likely that the happenings that might affect the community consisted of similar events or, indeed, of the very same event.[5] The allusion to the missionary work of the apostle at the end of the sentence (καὶ...ὁ κόπος ἡμῶν), which leads back to the 'temptation' of 2: 18, may give additional weight to this impression. If it was the awareness of Paul's hindrance, this could be taken as a kind of spiritual temptation. Could such an assumed temptation, however, be styled as θλῦψις and even as an event that is a *must* in the eschatological period? The parallelism in the wording between the two parts of verses 1–5, striking as it is,[6] is made yet more pointed by the fact that verses 3*b*, 4 stand alone. These, however, are the very verses that interpret verse 3*a*, as becomes obvious from the repetition of θλίψεις in verbal form in the middle of verse 4, a fact that demands a meaning for σαίνεσθαι that is different from the hypothetical temptation that might have been caused by Paul's impediment. Verse 5 describes, or alludes to, a feeling of uneasiness on the part of Paul, which proved to be unjustified,[7] while verses 2*b*, 3*a* refer to guidance that is still valid (see verses 3*b*, 4).

[3] It is the *fides quae creditur*, as in 3: 5 (and Philippians 1: 27), which is invoked.

[4] Cp. Colossians 1: 24.

[5] V. Dobschütz puts it like this: 'Irrewerden der Thessalonicher auf Grund seines Fernbleibens: damit versucht sie der Versucher' (*Die Thessalonicher-Briefe*, p. 138); cp. p. 129: 'er befürchtet, sie müssten einen ungünstigen Eindruck hervorrufen'.

[6] The parallel features are μηκέτι στέγοντες – ἐπέμψαμεν – ὑπὲρ τῆς πίστεως – μηδένα σαίνεσθαι in 3: 1f and μηκέτι στέγων – ἔπεμψα – τὴν πίστιν – μή πως ἐπείρασεν in 3: 5. This is rather unusually repetitive.

[7] Paul carries on describing his relief when he received the news from Timothy: στήκετε ἐν κυρίῳ. It is therefore likely that verse 5 gives expression to the inquiry that was made with the mission of Timothy. The parallelism between

Nor is the little[8] we know about the meaning of σαίνεσθαι from parallel texts of such a nature that it substantiates such an interpretation. Dibelius had suggested the meaning: 'erschüttert' (meaning 'emotionally shaken'), although he had rightly stated in the second edition of his commentary that attestation is lacking: 'freilich fehlen die Belege'.[9] In the second and third edition he listed Diogenes Laertius, VIII.1.41: οἱ δὲ σαινόμενοι τοῖς λεγομένοις ἐδάκρυόν τε καὶ ᾤμωζον καὶ ἐπίστευον εἶναι τὸν Πυθαγόραν θεῖόν τινα. From this reference, which he seems to have taken over from E. v. Dobschütz,[10] he concludes that the passage exhibits the meaning of the word in our verse, 'die für unsere Stelle passende Bedeutung'. In fact, however, the passage is the story of the return of Pythagoras from Hades, the state of excitement caused by the narration of his experience, the weeping and swearing of those present and the resulting exclamation Πυθαγόρας θεῖός τις. Σαινόμενοι expresses even more than ἐδάκρυον καὶ ᾤμωζον the shock and perturbation caused by the unexpected reappearance of Pythagoras. Three stages are indicated: the first shock, the more-or-less inarticulate expressions of consternation, and finally articulate confession and homage. The parallel points to a physical alteration and by no means to *Wankelmut*, infidelity or apostasy.

The other relevant parallel comes from Origen's *Dialogue with Heraclides*, a papyrus that was not published until 1949. Origen sums up one discourse by saying: all the questions that vexed us (ἔσηνεν)[11] have been examined.[12] Admittedly the context requires a wider meaning than in the other parallel but not that of a commotion or an aberration.

Pythagoras had been in the nether world, whereas the Thessalonians

verses 1f and 5 might be explained by the assumption that Paul cites the letter of recommendation he had handed to Timothy. Verse 5 would represent this letter more closely than verses 2f, whereas from verse 2*b* onwards Paul slips to problems that had not yet, or not sufficiently, been dealt with by Timothy. The extraordinarily full description of the office (*Amt*) of his assistant would equally be explained by such an assumption.

[8] H. Grotius (*Annotationes in Novum Testamentum* (3 vols., Amsterdam, 1641–50), vol. II, p. 659) removed the difficulty by postulating a special Cilician usage ('puto sic usos Cilicas' etc.). The material is listed by v. Dobschütz, *Die Thessalonicher-Briefe*, pp. 133f.

[9] *An die Thessalonicher* I/II (Tübingen, 1925), p. 15.

[10] *Die Thessalonicher-Briefe*, p. 134.

[11] 'disturb' (D. E. H. Whiteley, *Thessalonians* (Oxford, 1969), p. 52) is a psychologising translation.

[12] Cp. H. Chadwick, 'I Thessalonians 3³: σαίνεσθαι', *JTS* n.s. 1 (1950), 156–8. For the word in a sense like that in the *Dialogue*, see Origen, *In Joh.* I. 35; II. 13 (7) (GCS (1903), pp. 44, 69); VI. 9 (6) (*ibid.*, p. 118) exhibits the sense of excitement.

are to encounter the turmoil of the last days. The facing of the *extrema* is the feature common to both, the *tertium comparationis*. Σαίνεσθαι seems to indicate the reaction in such a situation. Would this assumption throw any light on the meaning of σαίνεσθαι?

Descriptions of how men will be affected when they encounter the ultimate reality are not infrequent in Jewish literature. They occur particularly in accounts of visions vouchsafed to men enlightened from above. Enoch is filled with fear and trembling (φόβος...καὶ τρόμος), when he enters the heavenly hall.[13] Already, when he sees an angel, Sophonias trembles and cannot remain standing.[14] Enoch – so it is maintained in the Slavonic version of his visions – on seeing the Ophanim, is fearful and trembles with great terror.[15] Ishmael, when he encounters the princes of the Merkaba and the Seraphim at the entrance to the seventh hall is seized with trembling and shuddering (*nirtaᶜti we-nizdaᶜzaᶜti*), falls down and is benumbed by the radiant image of their eyes.[16] Even the place, where the visionary stands, trembles.[17] The experience is even more shattering when the seer proceeds to encounter the divine sphere proper. Abraham falls to the ground when he hears the divine voice; he cannot stand any longer; his mind is terrified and he trembles.[18] Having arrived before God Enoch becomes afraid and falls down on his face,[19] the visionary lies like one dead,[20] he is near to death,[21] his mind is confused[22] and is filled by terror and great fear.[23] The seer experiences what is expressed in the sentence, typical of rabbinic logic: how fearful and awful it is to come before the face of the ruler of the earth, how much more terrible and awful it is to

---

[13] He is shaken and trembling (σειόμενος καὶ τρέμων) and falls down. The Lord orders him to go forward and one of his angels raises him and sets him on his feet (Enoch 14.13f, 24f).

[14] Apoc. Soph. 8.3 (G. Steindorff, *Die Apokalypse des Elias, eine unbekannte Apokalypse und Bruchstücke der Sophoniasapokalypse* (Leipzig, 1899), p. 151).

[15] Slav. Enoch 20.1.

[16] Hebr. Enoch 1.7 (H. Odeberg, *3 Enoch or The Hebrew Book of Enoch* (Cambridge 1928), Hebrew part, p. 2).

[17] 4 (2) Esdras 6: 29; cp. 10: 26 (B. Violet, *Die Apokalypsen des Esra und des Baruch in deutscher Gestalt*, GCS 32 (Leipzig, 1924), p. 54).

[18] Apoc. Abr. 10.2–4.

[19] Slav. Enoch 21.2. The experience of a mystic who touches the Name is similar: 'Strong trembling seized me and I could summon no strength, my hair stood on end and it was as if I were not in this world. At once I fell down, for I no longer felt the least strength in any of my limbs' (cited by G. Scholem, *Major Trends in Jewish Mysticism* (London, 1955), p. 151).

[20] 4 (2) Esdras 10: 30.

[21] *Ibid.* 10: 34.

[22] *Ibid.* 10: 30 (probably = ἀπηλλοιώθη: cp. Violet *ad. loc.*).

[23] Syr. Bar. 54.1.

come before the face of the ruler of heaven.[24] His impression coincides
with the experiences the angels themselves are exposed to: they tremble
and fear before Metatron[25] and before Chayyliel.[26] Before their
creator they exist in fear, awe and trembling, with commotion, anguish,
terror and trepidation.[27] It is in the elaborate description of the Ethiopic
Enoch that it is mentioned that the seer whose heart is excited at the
beginning of the vision is commanded by God's angel to stand up ('to
stand like a man') at the end of it, is strengthened and advised to take
courage.[28] In another version of the vision he himself asks for strengthening[29] and for explanation of what happened to him.[30] Even more
detailed is the account in the Sophonias apocalypse, where at different
stages of the story, each indicating a station in the heavenly journey, it
is mentioned that the visionary is filled with fear[31] and that in consequence he is advised by angels to be strong and to have no fear.[32]
The repetition of the key words makes it abundantly clear what is
considered typical in the eyes of the composer of the apocalypse.
Extreme weakness,[33] mental incapacity during the experience and the
need of strengthening after it[34] are the characteristic phenomena.

All these features are present in the narration of Ḥag. 15, where it is
narrated that four persons entered Paradise, one who dies, one whose
mind becomes confused, a third who becomes a heretic and finally one
returns unharmed. The names of those who have the experience are
supplied in the account and it is probably due to this fact that turning to
heresy is introduced as a possible outcome. Apart from this, typical
stages of the experience are separated. The account is an artificial
schematisation. In Hebr. Enoch 16.2 it is said of Acher that he feared
and trembled before Metatron and that his soul departed from him;
thus, at least two of the features that characterise different persons in
Ḥag. 15 are used to describe one person here, the very person who is
stigmatised as a heretic in the other account.

The same can happen on the earth. Methusalem's spirit is confused

---

[24] Slav. Enoch 39.8.   [25] Hebr. Enoch 14.1.
[26] *Ibid.* 20.1.   [27] *Ibid.* 35.6; cp. 48 (B).
[28] Eth. Enoch 10.30.   [29] *Ibid.* 12.7.
[30] *Ibid.* 10.37; 12.8.
[31] Apoc. Soph. 1.2; 5.2; 8.3.
[32] *Ibid.* 1.3; 5.6; 12.5; 13.5.
[33] An exception may be Isaias, of whom it is said that he is absorbed in the
vision of God (Asc. Is. 5.7).
[34] The sequence is different in Hebr. Enoch: the spirit of the seer is restored
at God's command by Metatron at the beginning (*heḥezir nishmathi*, 1.9);
his weakness is removed after an interval (1.10f.), and so he is able to encounter the heavenly revelations.

when he has spoken with the Lord before the altar.[35] Nir is confused
when the angel of God talks to him.[36] When the high priest stays on in
the Holy of Holies, while having a vision, those who wait outside fear
that he has died.[37]

What is experienced by the chosen individual in an exalted moment
is only a foretaste and symbol of what is to come in reality at the end of
the days. It will be the general fate, when the eschatological events dawn.
The earth quakes, trembles and sways, knowing that it will undergo a
transformation.[38] This will be a sign for men of the coming events.[39]
The inhabitants of the earth will be seized by great horror[40] – *excursus
mentis*, as it is put in the parallel text of 4 Esdras 13: 30. Again: the
quaking of places and the confusion of peoples as well as the machina-
tions of the masses and the bewilderment of the leaders are viewed as
signs of the end.[41] They are viewed as signs that God rises to pronounce
judgement.[42] The Syriac Baruch presents a sequence of twelve periods of
tremors (*Erschütterungen*), the sixth of which – the central item – is
explicitly called 'tremor'. The words are the same as in the descriptions
of visionary experiences. Vision of God and vision of the *Endzeit*
merge in one another. It is for this reason that the seer asks at the end of
a vision for 'strengthening until the end'.[43] The situation the faithful
will meet in the time of Antichrist is therefore alluded to by the phrase
φεύγουσιν, μετὰ τρόμου.[44]

---

[35] *Vom Priestertum Methusalems, Nirs und Melchisedeks*, II. 16, in N. Bonwetsch,
Die Bücher der Geheimnisse Henochs, TU 44.2 (Leipzig, 1922).

[36] *Ibid.* 4.4.

[37] Yoma 53*b*.

[38] 4 (2) Esdras 6: 14f; Apoc. Soph. 18.3ff.

[39] 4 (2) Esdras 6: 13.

[40] *Ibid.* 5: 1: ἐν ἐκστάσει ἐκστήσονται or ληµφθήσονται; Syr. Bar. 25.3. Syr. Bar.
70.2ff names confusion of mind and tremor of the heart. Cp. the topos of
the *gerim gerurim* in rabbinic literature (see 'Gerim gerurim', *Annual of
the Swedish Theological Institute* 7 (1970), 127–31). Maybe the enigmatic
remark in Mark 10: 32a: ἀναβαίνοντες...ἐθαµβοῦντο is illuminated by this.
The fear that is said to have seized those who accompanied Jesus is due
to a premonition of the coming events (cp. Luke 19: 11); it illustrates the
eschatological tension. The juxtaposition with the prediction of the Passion
of the Son of Man (verses 32b–34) gives verse 32a an accent different from
the one it would have had as an entity on its own.

[41] 4 Esdras 9: 3.   [42] Apoc. Soph. 18.3ff.

[43] 4 Esdras 12: 6. The end is not the end of the vision (as Violet assumes),
which is over already, but the end of days. It is in keeping with this, that,
after having returned to the waiting people, the seer assures them that God
remembers them εἰς τέλος (12: 47 – for a discussion of the translations of the
verse see Violet, p. 172).

[44] Ephraem, Λόγος εἰς τὸν Ἀντίχριστον, II. 223, quoted by W. Bousset, *Der Antichrist* (Göttingen, 1895), p. 144.

If it is God himself (or his angels), who, one hopes, will take away the tremor[45] by the direct action from those who encounter him in a vision, it is different with the terror that is caused by the unfolding of the eschatological events and, connected with it, by the activities of anti-divine forces. It is the knowledge, the hope and assurance that God is the leader, that will enable men not to have fear and not to tremble.[46]

The words used in 1 Thessalonians 3: 2 are strikingly similar to those employed in the Jewish apocalyptic texts: στηρίξαι – σαίνεσθαι – θλίψεις[47] represent a cluster of ideas that receive their full meaning when set against the eschatological features of the whole epistle. The eschatological function of Jesus – not the Cross – forms the climax of the first chapter – a chapter that seems to represent faithfully the main points of Paul's missionary preaching, as it was carried out at that time.[48] Chapter 2 concludes by interpreting the meaning of the Jewish persecution against the Christians in the unfolding of the eschatological events. The fourth chapter contains detailed teaching about the fate of the faithful at the time of salvation. The fifth chapter starts with an eschatological warning and concludes with the exhortation or petition that the Thessalonians may be kept undamaged in the Παρουσία. This is the wider context. Chapter 3 ends with a proleptic presentation of the community to the returning Christ and starts with a reference to the eschatological woes (θλίψεις, verses 3f[49]), which receive their meaning in God's salvific design (κείμεθα, verse 3[50]). This makes it likely that an interpretation that makes use of the parallels to the terms in verse 2 is tenable. On the other hand, it is significant that Paul places στηρίξαι at the beginning and speaks of σαίνεσθαι in a manner at variance with the majority of the apocalypses: it is applied already to the eschatological sufferings and, in consequence of the positioning of στηρίξαι, preceded by μηδένα: that is to say, because the action of στηρίξαι comes first, it appears in the context of an exhortation about what is to be avoided.

What is striking in Paul's eschatological exposition is the equal

[45] Characteristic is Slav. Enoch 21.3, where the Lord informs the seer through Gabriel not to fear and to stand up (cp. 22.1ff, where the removal of fear is achieved by God through the anointing and clothing of Enoch).
[46] 6 Esdras 16: 76. Correspondingly Ezra prays that he may not be overpowered by fear when he sees the punishments and he is allowed to see men who pass through the flames unwaveringly. The vision is an anticipatory experience of what will happen in the progression of the eschatological events.
[47] θλίψεις means sufferings in Colossians 1: 24 and persecutions in Matthew 24: 10 v. l (א): it points to *Fährlichkeiten* rather than *Anfechtungen*.
[48] Cp. A. Oepke, *Die Missionspredigt des Apostels Paulus* (Leipzig, 1920).
[49] Cp. especially Colossians 1: 24.
[50] For the interpretation cp. E. Stauffer, *Die Theologie des Neuen Testaments* (Stuttgart, 1941), p. 166 (ET, p. 187).

emphasis in two directions. Diagnosis of the events in time: the Jewish persecution,[51] the self-assured cry: peace and security,[52] even the martyrdom and death of the faithful have their meaning in the progression of the final events. On the other hand: warning against the Thessalonians' drawing conclusions or rushing to infer consequences: neither the abandoning of work (4: 11) nor carelessness (5: 6) can be allowed. 3: 2 seems to fit into this approach. 2: 14ff had explained that the persecution by those who are θεῷ ἐνάντιοι and the divine revenge against them indicate necessary stations in the final events. It would have been tempting for the Thessalonians to deduce from this the nearness of the παρουσία and to enter into a state of ἔκστασις. Paul remonstrates vigorously against this. Is it the apostle's privilege to interpret the signs of the time, to communicate what he deems appropriate and to withhold what is beyond the understanding of the community? Or is he not even sure about the actual sequence of events? In any case, he considers it necessary to commission Timothy to deal with the matter. His message is not only a παράκλησις – the same word is used in 4: 10 to introduce the warning against excitement and idleness– but even more so a στηριγμός – the eschatological meaning of the word is highlighted by 3: 13. That means, the σαίνεσθαι that appears as unquestionable fact in the apocalyptic material is no longer an inevitable fate (*Schicksal*).

Paul may have been trained in encountering mystical experiences already in his former Jewish past, he may have had the experience of divine intervention in the different trials he had passed through[53] and he may have received the assurance that it would be granted to him not to be submerged in the θλίψεις ahead. He could not, however, feel the same assurance about this with respect to the newly established community. He may have had the confidence not to σαίνεσθαι, while the neophytes might be exposed to this shattering physical experience without the necessary training. They needed the counselling of both Paul and his fellow-missionary to cope with the danger of physical exhaustion. Paul is all the more able to be confident about the success of Timothy's intervention as he is, in Paul's opinion, the collaborator of the one ὅς[54] καὶ ποιήσει (5: 24).

[51] Cp. E. Bammel, 'Judenverfolgung und Naherwartung: Zur Eschatologie des ersten Thessalonicherbriefes', *ZTK* 56 (1959), 294–315.

[52] Cp. *idem*, 'Ein Beitrag zur paulinischen Staatsanschauung', *TLZ* 85 (1960), cols. 837–40.

[53] Cp. Romans 8: 15, 26. The whole passage is dotted with martyrological terms.

[54] Referring to God, as 2: 12 shows.

Σαίνεσθαι is considered as a danger. Quite a number of remarks are made in the letter on the disposition in which the Christians have to face the coming events. The warning against drunkenness (5: 17) and the reference to disorderliness (5: 14) may allude to side effects of σαίνεσθαι. His challenge to gird yourself with the armour of faith, love and hope of salvation, described so vividly in 5: 8, his concern for ἀμεμφία ἐν ἁγιωσύνῃ (3: 13) and his prayer that πνεῦμα, ψυχή and σῶμα may be intact at the moment of the παρουσία may spell out the message Timothy had been entrusted with and give a positive version of the remark in 3: 2. Surprisingly frequent in these passages is the reference to the integrity of the person, which has to be preserved to the end. It is at this point that the ethical emphasis, so typical for the whole Christian approach to eschatology, comes in as well.

Σαίνεσθαι is not the expression of ethical shortcomings, but it may result in deviations; especially while the time before the end is prolonged. Paul does not encourage his followers to reserve σαίνεσθαι for the ultimate stage of the eschatological events, he discourages it completely. Instead, στήκειν is the watchword, which indicates the Christian's disposition *vis-à-vis* the coming events.[55] Jewish presupposition and Christian departure from it become recognisable at this point.

Commentators have noticed the parallel in 2 Thessalonians 2: 2 but thought that the words ἀπὸ τοῦ νοός give a different emphasis. If the interpretation suggested here is tenable, this is not right. On the contrary, σαλεύεσθαι ἀπὸ τοῦ νοός is an exact parallel to σαίνεσθαι, and to this there is appended the word θροεῖσθαι, which seems to express the joyful and eager expectation of the παρουσία of the Lord.

It was A. von Harnack who had suggested that the second letter was written shortly after the first, that it was written to the same place but to a different house community, which was Jewish in character and had to be instructed in a different way.[56] This verse, which starts with a parallel to the first letter such as could not have been invented by a later imitator, and goes on to tackle special dangers, gives some support to the great scholar's theory.

1 Thessalonians is Paul's chief tractate on the *ars patiendi in nomine Christi*. His readers had received the Gospel in θλίψεις (1: 6; 3: 7),

---

[55] 1 Thessalonians 3: 8. Cp. 1 Corinthians 16: 13. The eschatological meaning of στήκετε is confirmed by the preceding γρηγορεῖτε: even the following κρατειοῦσθε may receive its colour by reference to the weakening that, according to the Jewish apocalypses, happens *in extremis*.

[56] 'Das Problem des zweiten Thessalonicherbriefes', *Sitzungsberichte der königlich preussischen Akademie der Wissenschaften* (1910), 560–78.

that means in this case real persecutions (2: 14f; 3: 4*b*), nay some of them had already laid down their lives (4: 14[57]), he himself has suffered in an ἀγών[58] that was caused by human adversaries, while, at the same time, the ἀγών was the focal point of a battle between God and Satan (2: 18; 3: 5), of a battle that (Paul is sure about this at this time)[59] was due to reach its climax before long.

There is no hint that the Thessalonians had wavered in these trying circumstances. On the contrary, Paul notices their χαρά in these vicissitudes (1: 6) and found God active (2: 13) in their response to the challenge. Even death in persecution was sustained willingly – but questions as to the fate of those who lost their lives had arisen. Martyrdom as such does not seem to have constituted a temptation. Still, there is one point that made the apostle feel concerned; the σαίνεσθαι of the Thessalonians in face of the coming events, a reaction that was imminent or had already been initiated in an anticipatory way. Confronting this danger Paul uses words borrowed from martyrological language, here στήκειν and, in a partly related passage in his last letter, συναθλοῦντες.[60]

[57] For the interpretation cp. v. Dobschütz, *Die Thessalonicher-Briefe*, p. 191, who takes a different line.

[58] 2.2. Cp. the verb ἄγω = to bring someone to trial, an accused person to court; cp. F. Preisigke, *Wörterbuch der griechischen Papyrusurkunden*, vol. 1 (Berlin, 1925), s.v. The situation is illustrated in the same verse from the viewpoint of the martyr by προπαθόντες, whereas the action of the persecutor is indicated by ὑβρισθέντες.

[59] 'Judenverfolgung und Naherwartung', pp. 305ff.

[60] Philippians 1: 27f. The parallelism to 1 Thessalonians 3: 2 is striking: στήκετε... συναθλοῦντες τῇ πίστει...μὴ πτυρόμενοι...ὑπὸ τῶν ἀντικειμένων. Πῇ πτυρόμενοι is used instead of μηκέτι σαίνεσθαι. It is an open question whether the term means 'shying' or refers to the trembling that is the beginning of being scared off. The reference to the problem of martyrdom, although not exclusive (cp. ἔνδειξις...σωτηρίας), is here, however, much more marked than in 1 Thessalonians 3.

Maintaining the testimony of Jesus: the suffering of Christians in the Revelation of John[1]

J. P. M. SWEET

'They overcame him by the blood of the Lamb and by the word of their testimony' (Revelation 12: 11). Every reference in the New Testament to Christ's death can be brought under the heading of either victory or sacrifice, as John Knox has shown.[2] In Revelation the two 'stories' are intertwined, two elements in a single narration; I wish to explore their relationship, and in particular the aspect of testimony in the sufferings and the victory of both Christ and Christians.

(1) (a) Christian suffering is the result of witness, which is not just their testimony *to* Jesus, but the testimony *of* Jesus, which they maintain.

(b) Faithfully maintained, this witness brings suffering to them, as it did to him, from the world it provokes and torments.

(c) It does not consist in the suffering, but in speaking up for the true God in word and behaviour against the world's idolatry and immorality.

(d) It is ultimately victorious not by the moral effect of the suffering it incurs, but by God's vindication, which shatters the opposition.

(2) In Revelation seen as a whole the victory of witness brings about conversion and healing, as opposed to the hardening effect of the retributive plagues. This reading is supported by appeal to its structure and its use of scripture, particularly Zechariah 12–14 and Genesis 49, which involves a 'rebirth of images'. It appears that the ground of the victory is sacrificial death.

(3) The relationship between the two 'stories' may be stated thus: (a) 'Victory' offers a metaphorical explanation of how the atonement works. The world, turned away from God, is in the grip of illusion ($\tau\grave{o}$ $\psi\epsilon\hat{v}\delta os$), evidenced by idolatry issuing in immorality, and is penetrated

---

[1] In preparing this paper in honour of Geoffrey Styler, my only regret is that it cannot be read before the Seminar and reduced to clarity, perhaps even cogency, by his masterly minutes.

[2] *The Death of Christ* (New York, 1958; London, 1959), chapters 7 and 8.

by reality (ἡ ἀλήθεια), the word of God, the presence of which – in Christ, in Christians, and finally at the parousia – defeats the lie.

(*b*) But the *final* victory of truth over illusion is grounded from the beginning in 'sacrifice' – his, and their, apparent defeat in suffering fidelity. Here there is no explanation, only mystery.

Before developing these points I must outline the view of Revelation on which they are based.[3]

(1) The book is an integrated whole, whatever the pre-history of its materials. In particular the letters to the churches belong with the apocalyptic part, bound in by little touches, as at 13: 9f; 16: 15; 21: 7; in fact for us they shed light on the apocalyptic part, which is largely enigmatic, though at the time it must have been clear enough, and was intended to shed light on a situation in which discernment was desperately needed.

(2) That situation was for the most part one of *prosperity*; persecution was local and selective, the result of 'faithful witness': that is the picture given by the letters – only one death is mentioned (Antipas, 'my faithful witness', 2: 13), and that is by implication some time ago; only two churches, at Smyrna and Philadelphia, are fully faithful and suffering for it – and if we accept Irenaeus' dating towards the end of Domitian's reign,[4] we have no external evidence for general persecution; at best, hints of local and selective punishment, which could be avoided by recantation and token worship of the state gods, as in Pliny's letter to Trajan, or presumably by eschewing obtrusive non-conformity in the first place.[5]

(3) In this situation of creeping conformity to the world around, the purpose of Revelation was to recall the churches to the primitive witness to God and obedience to his Law, over against the idolatry and immorality of the 'world' – to set out the true nature, role and destiny both of the world, into conformity with which many Christians were sliding, led by influential prophets, and of the Church to which by baptism they belonged. In other words the apocalyptic part is not so much an attack on the world to encourage the Church, as an attack on the Church, which is embracing the world – to its own deadly danger,

---

[3] It is set out more fully in my SCM Pelican Commentary (London, 1979).

[4] There is no good reason not to, *pace* J. A. T. Robinson, *Redating the New Testament* (London, 1976) – see my commentary, pp. 21ff.

[5] Revelation 13 may seem to reflect general persecution but is in fact genuinely predictive; John's stance is the time of the 'sixth head' (17: 10), when the beast is to outward appearances *crushed* (cf. 13: 3, 12, 14 and p. 116, n. 44). Its return, bringing the great θλῖψις (7: 14; cf. Mark 13: 19) or πειρασμός (3: 10), is imminent, and John's task is to prepare the churches for it.

and in betrayal of its true role of convicting the world by its witness, for the world's salvation.

(4) For the structure of the book I follow Farrer's commentary:[6] it is provided by the four 'sevens' – letters, seals, trumpets, bowls – linked with the themes of the Lord's apocalypse (Matthew 24 and parallels). This leads one to focus on the following concerns: (*a*) deception in the Church (2, 3 – Matthew 24: 4, 10–12); (*b*) assurance for the faithful in a world breaking up (4–7 – Matthew 24: 6ff); (*c*) witness, over against idolatry and its apparent triumph[7] (8–14 – Mark 13: 9–23); (*d*) the triumph of witness (19: 11ff), flanked by the demolition of 'Babylon' and the building of 'Jerusalem' (15: 1 – 22: 5 – Matthew 24: 29–31).[8]

I. 'MAINTAINING THE TESTIMONY OF JESUS'

Christian suffering in Revelation is the result of witness, 'maintaining the testimony of Jesus'. This witness, suppressed by the world but vindicated by God, finally overcomes the world.

(*a*) In their afflictions Christians are at one with their Lord, and distinct from 'all who dwell on earth' – a moral rather than demographical category, which does not, or should not, include Christians. John writes to them as their brother who 'shares with them in the suffering and the sovereignty and the endurance which are in Jesus' (1: 9). The hundred and forty-four thousand who have the slaughtered Lamb's name on their foreheads follow him wherever he goes; as with Isaiah's lamb led to slaughter, 'no lie was found on their lips' (14: 1–5; Isaiah 53: 7–9). The redeemed have defeated the accuser 'by the blood of the Lamb and by the word of their testimony, for they did not hold their lives too dear to lay them down' (12: 11).

This μαρτυρία is naturally taken as their witness *to* Jesus, but other verses speak of the testimony *of* Jesus, which they 'had' or 'held' (ἔχειν) – see 1: 2, 9; 12: 17; 19: 10; 20: 4 – and though the genitive could be objective, most scholars take it to be subjective because of the

---

[6] (Oxford, 1964); note his demonstration of the links between the themes of the first four letters, and the themes of the four 'sevens' (pp. 83–6).

[7] With Farrer I take the 'third woe' (11: 14) to be the kingdom of the beast, set up by Satan on his expulsion from heaven (12: 12), i.e. the Roman Empire (13); what the world takes to be its greatest blessing is in fact its worst disaster (14: 9–11).

[8] The cosmic demolitions, as in the OT, symbolise the pulling down of corrupt social and political structures, and the 'gathering of the elect' is presented by John as the adorning of a bride or building of a city – terms used by Isaiah of the gathering of the exiles from Babylon (49: 17f; 54: 11f).

parallel phrases 'word of God', 'commandments of God', together with
the word 'held', which implies something received.[9] They maintain
Jesus' testimony, which, like the word of God, has been committed to
them. Just as Mr Styler has shown that Jesus is for Paul not only the
model and the motive but also the actual basis of ethical obligation,[10]
so Christian witness in Revelation seems to be not specifically testimony
to Jesus (though it may include that – see (c), pp. 106f) but the witness of
Jesus in them, inspiring them to bear witness, ἡ γὰρ μαρτυρία Ἰησοῦ
ἐστιν τὸ πνεῦμα τῆς προφητείας (19: 10): he is the faithful and true
witness, and the servants of God 'hold' his testimony, which is the
inspiration of true prophecy (in the sense of being God's spokesman).

In what then does this 'testimony of Jesus' consist? In the light of
1: 5: 'Jesus Christ the faithful witness, the firstborn of the dead', and
1 Timothy 6: 13; 'Jesus Christ τοῦ μαρτυρήσαντος ἐπὶ Ποντίου Πειλάτου
τὴν καλὴν ὁμολογίαν, it is tempting to say 'his death on the Cross',
but this is only true if it is taken as shorthand for his whole attestation
of God in word and deed, which was consummated on the Cross.[11]
His words to Pilate at John 18: 37 are to the point: 'For this I was born
and came into the world, to bear witness to the truth'; and in 1 Timothy
6 his ὁμολογία is appealed to as motive for 'keeping the commandment',
which probably means 'the rule of faith and life enjoined by the gospel,
to which Timothy had pledged himself at baptism'.[12] Jesus' ὁμολογία
or μαρτυρία is both his verbal witness to his Father, summed up at his
trial, and his obedience to his Father, summed up in Gethsemane and
on the Cross.[13]

So Christians in their suffering are at one with their Lord, and set
over against the earth-dwellers: though not physically exempted from
'the ordeal which is coming upon the whole world' (3: 10), they will be
kept safe spiritually by 'the seal of the living God', which they receive
on their foreheads (7: 2, 3, with probable reference to baptism). This

[9] E.g. N. Brox, *Zeuge und Märtyrer* (Munich, 1961), pp. 94f; A. A. Trites,
The New Testament Concept of Witness (Cambridge, 1977), pp. 156–8; for
the objective genitive, H. von Campenhausen, *Die Idee des Martyriums in der
alten Kirche* (Göttingen, 1936), p. 42, and G. W. H. Lampe, below, p. 135.

[10] 'The basis of obligation in Paul's Christology and Ethics' in *Christ and
Spirit in the New Testament: Studies in Honour of C. F. D. Moule*, ed.
B. Lindars and S. S. Smalley (Cambridge University Press, 1973), pp. 183–7.

[11] Cf. Trites, *NT Concept of Witness*, pp. 158f. A. E. Harvey, *Jesus on Trial*
(London, 1976), shows that the whole of the Fourth Gospel can be seen as the
account of an extended 'trial' of Jesus, which becomes in fact the trial of the
world (pp. 110ff).

[12] J. N. D. Kelly, *The Pastoral Epistles* (London, 1963), p. 144.

[13] On 1 Timothy 6: 13 and Revelation 19: 10 contrast Professor Lampe's
remarks below, pp. 133–5.

seal sets them apart as the twelve tribes (the hundred and forty-four thousand) of the Israel of God, who were chosen to be his witnesses[14] against the idolatrous nations (Isaiah 43: 9–12; 44: 8, 9): just so Christians are to maintain the testimony of Jesus, himself the faithful witness and servant of God (cf. Isaiah 43: 10), and to keep God's commandments (12: 17), over against the idolatry and immorality of the earth-dwellers – which are now infecting the Church itself (2: 14, 20). Structurally there is a correspondence between the sealing in chapter 7, set between the opening of the sixth and seventh seals, and the 'prophesying' of John and the two witnesses in 10: 1 – 11: 13, set between the sixth and seventh trumpet blasts. The seal is given for a purpose – for witness, which includes purity of life in obedience to God's Law (which can also be called $\mu\alpha\rho\tau\acute{\nu}\rho\iota\upsilon\nu$; cf. 15: 5; Exodus 31: 18) – and it can be exchanged for a different mark by those who forget this purpose, and prefer the more tangible security and rewards that go with following the beast.

(*b*) For this witness, faithfully maintained, though it gives invulnerability and success for a time to the 'two witnesses' (11: 5, 6) as to Jesus in his ministry, must bring suffering and death. When their time has come, when they have 'completed their testimony' (11: 7; $\acute{o}\tau\alpha\nu$ $\tau\epsilon\lambda\acute{\epsilon}\sigma\omega$-$\sigma\iota\nu$; cf. John 19: 30, $\tau\epsilon\tau\acute{\epsilon}\lambda\epsilon\sigma\tau\alpha\iota$), the agent of this world's ruler kills them in the 'great city', where also their Lord was crucified, and the earth-dwellers declare a public holiday because these two prophets had tormented them (11: 7–10). Truth is always painful to those in the grip of illusion ($\tau\acute{o}$ $\psi\epsilon\hat{\upsilon}\delta\upsilon\varsigma$), and the true prophet has always earned persecution (cf. Luke 13: 33) – so much so that suffering had come to be one of the marks of a true prophet, when tests were needed, and the prophet had become a martyr-figure.[15] John himself had already suffered for his testimony on the usual understanding of 1: 9: 'I was in the island called Patmos because of the word of God and the testimony of Jesus'. In his vision he was called to 'prophesy' after eating the 'little scroll', which though sweet in his mouth was bitter in his belly (10: 9–11).

John was a 'prophet', and though prophets were a distinct class within the Church in practice, potentially all the Lord's people were prophets[16] – if they were true to their baptismal vocation – and all were called to the same witness as their Lord, and the same result. The 'two

---

[14] Not only witnesses to his deeds and demands, but also, in accordance with Jewish legal practice, his advocates (Trites, *NT Concept of Witness*, p. 115).

[15] Cf. H. Kraft, *Die Offenbarung des Johannes* (Tübingen, 1974), pp. 23f.

[16] See D. Hill, 'Prophecy and Prophets in the Revelation of St. John', *NTS* 18 (1972), 401–18.

witnesses', though clearly modelled on Elijah and Moses (and perhaps contemporary figures), represent not a special element within the Church, but the whole Church in so far as it is faithful to its prophetic vocation:[17] Revelation 11: 1–13 follows the vision of the little scroll, and has significant links with the accounts of Jesus' sending out the twelve and the seventy two by two, the minimum number for valid witness (Matthew 10; Luke 10[18]). It is perhaps not a coincidence that only two of the seven lamps of Asia, at Smyrna and Philadelphia, are fully faithful in their witness. They suffered for it at the hands of the Jews, who thereby showed themselves servants of Satan (2: 9; 3: 9). Christians who kept a low profile and did not provoke the Jews (where they were strong) by open witness, could keep out of trouble. At Sardis (where the remains of the huge synagogue can still be seen) the Church had the reputation of being alive but was in fact dead (3: 1). By implication the majority had failed to confess Christ (3: 5). Their (false) security could hardly have been achieved without a *modus vivendi* with the Jews.[19]

It is not only verbal witness to the true God and his will that attracts persecution, but also the obedience to his commands that goes with it : purity of life, over against the immorality that stems from idolatry, is equally painful to the godless. This is eloquently set out in the Wisdom of Solomon: 'Let us lay a trap for the just man...he is a living condemnation of all our ideas. The very sight of him is an affliction, because his life is not like other people's, and his ways are different... Outrage and torment are the means to try him with...let us condemn him to a shameful death' (2: 12–20) – cf. 1 Peter 4: 4, and Revelation 12: 17:' the dragon went off to make war[20] on the rest of the woman's seed, those who keep the commandments of God and maintain the testimony of Jesus'.

(*c*) Witness in Revelation leads to suffering; suffering is not in itself the content of the witness, as it became in the later usage of the word. The form of the testimony that John expected Christians to maintain

---

[17] Zechariah had seen a lampstand of gold, with seven lamps on it (the model used for the church in Revelation 1–3), and two olive trees on either side (Revelation 11: 4), representing Zerubbabel, the scion of David, and Joshua (Jesus) the high priest – prototypes both of Jesus and of his Church, which he has made 'a kingdom and priests' (Revelation 1: 6; 5: 10).

[18] See P. S. Minear, *I Saw a New Earth* (Washington, 1969), pp. 290–2.

[19] C. J. Hemer, 'A Study of the Letters to the Seven Churches of Asia', Manchester Ph.D. dissertation 1969, pp. 315f, 339–41.

[20] His agents are the two beasts (13), signifying the Roman Empire and its religion, which are to bring suffering and death to all who are faithful to the seal of their baptismal vocation and do not exchange it for the mark of the beast.

seems to be very much that of the primitive kerygma,[21] as delivered to Gentiles: attack on idolatry, announcement of Jesus' death and resurrection as the defeat of the powers behind idolatry and the harbinger of universal judgement, and summons to repentance – turn from idols to the true and living God (1 Thessalonians 1: 9, 10; Acts 14: 15–17; 17: 29–31; 24: 25; Revelation 14: 6, 7), and turn to a holy life from the immorality that stems from idolatry (1 Thessalonians 4: 3–8). John, like Paul, worked with the conventional Jewish analysis set out in Wisdom 13 and 14: 'the invention of idols is the root of immorality; they are a contrivance which has blighted human life' (14: 12) – cf. Romans 1: 18–end; Revelation 9: 20, 21.

Such would have been the content of the little scroll, which fed John's 'prophesying' (10: 10, 11), followed by that of the two witnesses (11: 3ff), for it is a scaled-down version of the great scroll of chapter 5, which no doubt contained God's gracious purpose for the world (else why weep that it cannot be opened?), but also evokes the Law-tables of Sinai (Exodus 32: 15) and Ezekiel's scroll full of lamentations, mourning and woe (Ezekiel 2: 10); its unsealing unleashed the horseman plagues of 6: 1–8, and the first horseman, who rides out victoriously to conquer, most probably represents the proclamation of the Gospel.[22] It may seem crazy to put evangelism on a par with war, famine and pestilence, but (i) proclamation of the Gospel, as a testimony to (or against?) the nations, is mentioned along with these plagues in the Lord's Apocalypse, which is the model for Revelation 6: 1–8 (Mark 13: 9, 10 and parallels); (ii) the two witnesses are to smite the earth with every plague (11: 5, 6) – symbolic language for the sword of the Spirit, which is the word of God (cf. Isaiah 11: 4; Mark 13: 11; Luke 21: 15; John 16: 8ff); (iii) the Gospel, as John understands it, is no cosy announcement of God's love, but proclamation of his victory and summons to submit: fear God, the true God who made heaven and earth, and give him glory, for the hour of his judgement has come (14: 6, 7); the coming destruction of 'Babylon' (the cause of the earth-dwellers' infatuation) and punishment of those who worship the beast (14: 8–11) is part of the proclamation; (iv) the scene at 6: 2 is picked up at 19: 11–16: a white horse, and one seated on it called the Word of God, who is followed by the armies of heaven

---

[21] E.G. Selwyn asked 'whether the term κήρυγμα has not been worked too hard, and whether the word μαρτυρία and its cognates would not describe better the primitive and indispensable core of the Christian message', in 'Eschatology in 1 Peter', *The Background of the New Testament and its Eschatology*, ed. W. D. Davies and D. Daube (Cambridge University Press, 1956), p. 395 – quoted by Trites, *NT Concept of Witness*, p. 1.

[22] So Cullmann in *Background of NT*, pp. 415f; see my commentary, pp. 136–8.

(the faithful witnesses) on white horses, and out of his mouth goes a sharp sword to smite the nations. The apostolic κήρυγμα or μαρτυρία is in itself an anticipation of the parousia.

(*d*) But if we follow the story of the two witnesses through, it is not just their witness, nor their death, that finally shatters their opponents, but their vindication – their resurrection and ascension, which (like their witness and death) echo Christ's: here again we are close to the primitive kerygma, which centred not on his ministry and death but on his resurrection and parousia. Their going up in a *cloud*, in the *sight* of their *enemies*, and the *penitence* of the survivors of the earthquake – all this is a deliberate echo of the programmatic words at 1: 7: 'Behold, he is coming with the clouds, and every eye shall see him, all those who pierced him, and all the tribes of the earth shall mourn for him' – a coming which, as we have seen in the discussion of 6: 2 and 19: 11–16, is in some sense anticipated in Christian witness, which is by no means without present effect (cf. p. 116).

But the effect lies in the testimony, not in the moral effect of the suffering that the testimony incurs. It is no doubt true that undeserved suffering and death, lovingly borne, work on men's consciences and turn their hearts, but in Revelation, and in the rest of the New Testament, just as the suffering of the μάρτυρες is not the content of the μαρτυρία, so it is nowhere said that awareness of their *suffering* brings men to repentance. Even in 1 Peter, where there are more references to suffering for righteousness' sake than anywhere else, this is nowhere inculcated for its saving effects on the persecutors – it is simply what Christians are called to, in imitation of Christ; the prelude of judgement on the persecutors and of glory for the Christians.[23]

Even in the Gospels it is hard to find any suggestion that the sight of innocent *suffering* turns men's hearts. The centurion's confession in Mark follows his seeing 'how Jesus died', but that refers to the 'great cry' (15: 37–9), and Matthew and Luke both make the confession dependent on the external phenomena, which in Matthew are linked with the resurrection (27: 51–3; 28: 2). Matthew 27: 54 is particularly

---

[23] Certainly 1 Peter 3: 1–4 does envisage the converting power of women's silent obedience and purity (cf. 2: 12), and in Revelation the effect of faithful witness is crucial (p. 116). So too is that of purity: just as the Church's witness is set over against the world's idolatry in the trumpets section, so in the bowls section the harlot's immorality is set in contrast with the purity of the Bride, which is 'the righteous deeds of the saints' (19: 8). With Isaiah in mind we may see the Bride–City, so adorned, as the beacon that draws in the nations. But again the *final* effect lies not in human purity alone but in its vindication by God – the City coming down out of heaven from God (21: 10).

close to Revelation 11: 13: 'the centurion and his men who were keeping watch over Jesus, when they saw the earthquake and all that was happening, were terrified, and said, Truly, this man was the son of God'; cf. 'The rest in terror gave glory to the God of heaven.'

But was this terror perhaps the fear of the Lord that is the beginning of wisdom?

2. VICTORY – MACCABAEAN OR CHRISTIAN?

Is the victory over the godless world and its inhabitants, which is depicted in Revelation 6–20 with such violence, simply punitive and destructive? Is there no more than the 'Maccabaean' understanding of martyrdom as bringing mercy for God's people, glory for the martyrs and punishment for the persecutors?[24] Or is it a victory over the root cause of men's godlessness, which leads to their conversion? Does Revelation 11: 13 depict unavailing terror and remorse, or saving awe and repentance? The language can bear either construction. ἔμφοβος is used of the effect of Jesus' resurrection on women and disciples (Luke 24: 5, 37), but also of Felix's barren reaction to Paul's testimony (Acts 24: 25). 'Give glory to God' is a regular biblical phrase for humble submission (cf. 1 Samuel 6: 5–8), and is used in Revelation with the sense of turning from idols to acknowledge God at 14: 7; 15: 4, in marked contrast with 16: 9, 11: 'they did not repent to give him glory...they cursed the God of heaven for their pains, and did not repent of their works' (cf. 9: 20, 21). But the result of homage can only be seen from the context. In the case of Abraham, for example, it was positive (cf. Romans 4: 20 in contrast with 1: 21), but it cut no ice in 1 Enoch: the kings of the earth ask for 'respite to glorify and give thanks and confess their faith before his glory', but 'their faces shall be filled with darkness and shame before that Son of Man, and they shall be driven from his presence'; they will be handed over to angels for punishment because they have oppressed his elect, and will be a spectacle for the elect to enjoy (62.5, 10; 63.11, 12).

The same question is raised by Revelation 1: 7, which we have seen is picked up at 11: 7–13: is the mourning '*for* him' (the natural meaning of ἐπ' αὐτόν) or '*because of* him' – penitent compunction or self-pitying realisation and remorse? Can one see constructive penitence here and at 11: 13 in the light of the eternal torment of those who worship the beast (14: 9–11, rather Enochian), the wine-press of the wrath of God (14: 20), and the related picture of total destruction at 19: 11–21?

[24] Cf. 2 Maccabees 7: 9–13, 31–8; 4 Macc. 6.27–9; 17.20–2.

But if not, what are we to make of the Song of Moses and of the Lamb, which celebrates the coming of 'all the nations' to worship before God, 'the king of the nations' (15: 4, citing Psalm 86: 9)? What of the final vision of the nations and their kings bringing their glory into the new Jerusalem (not at all Enochian), and the tree of life, the leaves of which are for the healing of the nations (21: 24 – 22: 5)?

Three factors may support the positive interpretation:

(a) The structure of Revelation

(i) In the trumpets section the plagues of chapters 8 and 9 are the fruit of idolatry and immorality,[25] and their effect is to harden men: 'the rest who were not killed by these plagues did not repent' of their idolatry or of their crimes (9: 20, 21). But at 11: 13 the rest who were not killed by the earthquake, which followed the witnesses' ascension, gave glory to God. The whole interlude 10: 1 – 11: 13, which represents Christian witness, is explicitly bound in with the trumpet plagues by the announcements of the three 'woes' (8: 13; 9: 12; 11: 14). There is thus a deliberate contrast of effect between the plagues caused by idolatry and those caused by witness, which at first sight seem to be out of the same stable[26] – 'they have power over the waters to turn them to blood [cf. 8: 8], and to smite the earth with every kind of plague' (11: 5, 6). Retribution hardens men, but witness, consummated in death and vindicated by God, shatters the Babel of human arrogance and complacency; men come, like Nebuchadnezzar, to their senses and give glory to the God of heaven (cf. Daniel 4: 28–end). We may distinguish, like Paul, between a godly wound that brings saving repentance and a worldly wound that brings death (2 Corinthians 7: 10), and we may admit that John, unlike Paul (except in 2 Thessalonians 1, if it is his), gets carried away in his pictures of retribution.

(ii) But the destructions and tortures of 6–20 are encapsulated within the visions of God as Creator and Redeemer (4, 5) and of the new creation, in which there is healing for the nations and the curse of Genesis 3 is removed (21: 1 – 22: 5). The ingathering of the nations and their kings (21: 24ff) seems impossible to western minds after their total destruction in 19: 11ff, and is sometimes explained away as referring to

[25] This is the implication of Wormwood (8:11) in the light of the OT references (Amos 5: 6f; 6: 12; Jeremiah 9: 15; 23: 15); it is 'the star of the new Babylon which has poisoned by its idolatry the springs of its own life' (G. B. Caird, *The Revelation of St. John the Divine* (London, 1966), p. 115, to whom I am deeply indebted in all that follows).

[26] But these 'plagues' are in fact caused by the truth, the word of God (cf. pp. 105 and 107).

Gentile as opposed to Jewish Christians, but this is not a distinction John recognises, and there is no hint that these are not genuine ἔθνη.[27] Or it is said to be mere scriptural colour, drawn from Isaiah, but this is not how John uses scripture elsewhere. His use of Ezekiel, Daniel and Zechariah shows a creative grasp of each book as a whole: the same goes for Isaiah.[28]

Destruction *and* ingathering: it is a double picture, as in the book of Isaiah taken as a whole, and as in the book of Psalms, which early Christians also took as a whole and cited as 'David'; the destruction of men, in so far as they are idolatrous and wicked, as in Psalm 2 (quoted in Revelation *passim*) or 9 and 10; the ingathering of men, as God's creatures, as in Psalm 86: 9 (quoted in Revelation 15: 4) or 87. But in Revelation the two are not simply put side by side: the former is subsumed under the latter, as if the good kine had swallowed up the bad. The whole earth has been drawn into the sanctity of the Holy City, which is one great Holy of Holies, totally informed by God's presence and man's adoration. Only what is unclean is left outside (21: 8, 27; 22: 15).[29]

This may be supported by another structural observation: it is one of the angels of the seven last plagues who shows John both the judgement of the harlot Babylon and the descent of the Bride, New Jerusalem (17: 1; 21: 9), whose adornments are described in deliberate contrast: destruction and recreation are the work of the one God, two sides of the one coin. It is not simply that the one is replaced by the other, but that all in the old creation that had been corrupted and spoiled is taken up, cleansed and purified, into the new.

(b) *The use of Zechariah*

The mourning of Revelation 1: 7 comes from a passage deeply significant to early Christians, Zechariah 12–14. God says

> 'In that day I will seek to destroy all the nations that come against Jerusalem [12: 9]. And I will pour upon the house of David and the inhabitants of Jerusalem a spirit of grace and mercy, and they shall look upon me [or 'him'] whom they have pierced, and they shall

---

[27] The view follows from taking the hundred and forty-four thousand and the uncountable multitude of chapter 7 as two different groups rather than (with most commentators) as two aspects of the one reality – see my commentary, pp. 150f.

[28] Without the chauvinism of, e.g., 49: 23; 60: 10–16; contrast Revelation 21: 24 – 22: 2.

[29] This reservation does not destroy the point, which is the paradoxical appearance in the Holy City of the ἔθνη who had apparently been destroyed (but by the word of God). John was not a dogmatic universalist.

mourn for him...as for a first-born [10]. In that day there shall be great mourning...as in the valley of Megiddo [11]. The land shall mourn, every family (or tribe) apart [12]... In that day a fountain shall be opened for the house of David and the inhabitants of Jerusalem for sin and uncleanness [13: 1]... I will cut off the names of the idols from the land...and remove the prophets and the unclean spirit from the land [2]'.

There is not space to discuss this passage in detail.[30] It was clearly crucial in the primitive Passion apologetic, and before A.D. 70 was presumably taken as a prophecy of Jewish repentance for the crucifixion. But after A.D. 70 this would hardly do. Matthew 24: 30 and Revelation 1: 7[31] show that 'land' in Zechariah 12: 10 (and therefore also in 13: 2) was taken as 'earth', as MT *'ereṣ* and LXX *γῆ* allow. If now it is the Gentiles (who after all carried out the crucifixion, and pierced Jesus' side, John 19: 34–7[32]) who mourn for their victim, the first-born (cf. Revelation 1: 5), then it would be possible to take the spirit of grace and mercy as given to the house of David for the benefit of the attackers of Jerusalem (12: 9, 10), to make them see and repent; equally the fountain would be for the nations, to cleanse sin and its causes from the earth (13: 1, 2).

There can be no proof that this is how John read Zechariah, but we can note that the gathering of the nations against Jerusalem and the destruction of devil, beast and false prophet (20: 8–10) echoes the gathering of the kings to Armageddon ('mountain of *Megiddo*') by the unclean spirits like frogs that proceed from the Satanic trinity, and it is followed by the vision of the fountain of life (22: 1). Zechariah 14 takes up the same motifs, which are all echoed in Revelation 20–2: the nations gathered against Jerusalem (14: 2); the fountain (14: 8); removal of the curse (14: 11); the survivors come up to keep the feast of Tabernacles, or ingathering (14: 16); Jerusalem is all holy (14: 20).

It may be all part of a creative reinterpretation of scripture in the light of the Cross, a rebirth of images.

[30] See B. Lindars, *New Testament Apologetic* (London, 1961), pp. 122–7: F. F. Bruce, *This is That* (Exeter, 1968), pp. 110–13.

[31] The conflation of Zechariah 12: 10 with Daniel 7: 13 shows that we are dealing with a *testimonium*, which may have been used without respect to context. But John, at least, read Zechariah as a whole.

[32] J. R. Michaels made the attractive suggestion that ὁ ἑωρακὼς μεμαρτύρηκεν is part of the fulfilment of ὄψονται εἰς ὃν ἐξεκέντησαν, referring to the spearman, whom mediaeval legend identified with the confessing centurion of Mark 15: 39 – correctly! ('The Centurion's Confession and the Spear Thrust', *CBQ* 29 (1967) 102–9.)

(c) Rebirth of images

The slaughtered lamb at 5: 5, 6 raises similar problems. Is it a sacrificial victim, evoking the lamb of Passover and of Isaiah 53? Or is it the militant young ram of the Jewish apocalypses, its seven horns and eyes symbols of power and omniscience, which has been fused with the lamb of sacrifice?[33] If so, is the understanding of sacrifice 'Maccabaean', or does its redemptive power extend to God's enemies? What is the relation of the lamb to the lion of the tribe of Judah? For D. H. Lawrence it was but 'a lion in sheep's clothing': 'we never see it slain, we only see it slaying mankind by the million'.[34]

Again there is no space for a full discussion, but following Caird I believe that the key lies in the distinction between hearing (the lion) and seeing (the lamb).[35] 'Hearing' points to the inward and theological, 'seeing' to the outward and empirical. Thus on the one hand 5: 5, 6 is a symbolic expression of 1 Corinthians 1: 23f: 'Christ crucified, a stumbling block to Jews and folly to Gentiles, but to us...the power of God and the wisdom of God', and on the other it represents the astonishing empirical fulfilment of the traditional belief symbolised by the lion of Judah (Genesis 49: 8–12), militant violence transmuted into sacrificial suffering, a rebirth of images that can then be seen throughout the book. Take the wine-press. In the Targum version, probably familiar to John and many of his hearers,[36] the lion prophecy is glossed from Isaiah 63: 1–6: 'How noble is the king, Messiah, who is going to arise from the house of Judah...setting in order the order of battle... reddening the mountains with the blood of their slain. With his garments dipped in blood, he is like one who treads grapes in the press.'[37] If Genesis 49 has been transmuted, so, we may suppose, has Isaiah 63, as used at Revelation 14: 20 and 19: 12–15 – as indeed is indicated by the words 'outside the city',[38] and by the robe 'dyed with blood' *before* the

33 Cf. C. H. Dodd, *The Interpretation of the Fourth Gospel* (Cambridge University Press, 1953), pp. 231f, referring to 1 Enoch 89 and Test. Jos. 19.8; for the Testaments see J. C. O'Neill, *Journal for the Study of the New Testament* 2 (1979) 2–30, who argues for a pre-Christian expectation of a Messiah ben Joseph in the guise of the lamb of God, both militant and suffering, saving both Jews and Gentiles.

34 *Apocalypse*, Penguin ed. (London, 1974), pp. 58f.

35 *Revelation of St. John*, pp. 73–5; cf. my commentary, pp. 175f.

36 See M. McNamara, *The New Testament and the Palestinian Targum to the Pentateuch* (Rome, 1966), pp. 97–125, 189–237.

37 Ps.-Jon. on Genesis 49: 11, quoted from J. W. Bowker, *The Targums and Rabbinic Literature* (Cambridge University Press, 1969), p. 278.

38 Cf. Hebrews 13: 11–14; Acts 7: 58 (Stephen); Mark 12: 8 and parallels; Luke 4: 29: on this view the wine-press contains the blood not of God's enemies but of Christ and those who maintain his testimony.

slaughter of the enemy.[39] God's victory over his enemies is bound up
with his defeat at their hands, his piercing them with their piercing
him – not tit for tat, but one long-drawn-out struggle.

Everything the New Testament says about Christ's death can be
brought under the headings of sacrifice and victory, and both 'stories'
are necessary for a full statement of the truth. In fact in Revelation they
are intertwined: 'they overcame him by the blood of the Lamb, and by
the word of their testimony'. The victory over the accuser in heaven
(12: 7–9) – a symbolic picture of Pauline 'justification' – is won not by
Michael but by Christ; Michael's is merely a mopping-up operation,
or in Caird's analogy, he 'is not the field officer who does the actual
fighting, but the staff officer who is able to remove Satan's flag from the
heavenly map because the real victory has been won on Calvary'
(*Revelation of St. John*, p. 154). Christ's death, the result of his good
confession before Pontius Pilate, is a sacrifice, 'freeing us from our
sins' (1: 5), and as such is the ground of his 'conquest', which entitled
him to break the seals and set the final drama going – its momentum
maintained by Christian maintenance of his μαρτυρία ἄχρι θανάτου.

Sacrifice is the ground of victory, but we still have to ask how sacrifice
is understood.

(i) Is it human action or passion, which somehow covers the gap
between God and man, or God's action or Passion into which men are
caught up? In Revelation surely the latter: the Lamb is 'at the heart of
the throne' (7: 17), and was slain 'from the foundation of the world'
(13: 8);[40] Christians are associated with him in his sacrifice as in his
testimony (7: 14; 12: 11; 14: 4, 5).

(ii) Is it for God's enemies or simply for the elect? The case for a positive
interpretation of 1: 7 and 11: 13 is cumulative, but so also is the negative
view, which to anyone who reads 6–20 on its own must seem irresistible.
There can be no clinching argument, but it may help acceptance of the
positive view to insist that it does not involve John Knox's third 'story',
the moral theory of the atonement (which he rightly says is not found
in the New Testament), to the effect that God overcomes his enemies
by the demonstration of sacrificial love, in the death of Christ and his
witnesses, instead of by the violence through which the beast conquers

[39] 'The Rider bears on his garment the indelible traces of the death of his
followers, just as he bears on his body the indelible marks of his own passion
(1: 7; cf. John 20: 20–7)' (Caird, *Revelation of St. John* pp. 243f). Cf. also
A. T. Hanson, *The Wrath of the Lamb* (London, 1957), pp. 159ff.
[40] This is the natural sense of the Greek, though rejected by RSV, NEB, JB
and many commentators in the light of 17:8. For the meaning, cf. 1 Peter
1:19f.

(11: 7; 13: 7). God's victory is just as violent, but it is violence of a different kind, the impact of truth on illusion: destructive, agonising (to victor as well as victim), but finally liberating and healing, indeed the only way to true liberation and healing. The cure is not love or gentleness but truth, a sharp two-edged sword to smite – and heal.

> 'The wounded surgeon plies the steel
> That questions the distempered part.'

> 'Who then devised the torment? Love.'[41]

3. VICTORY AND SACRIFICE

If sacrifice is the ground of victory, how is it related to the testimony of Christ and his witnesses, which, when vindicated by God, shatters the earth-dwellers? The two 'stories' work on different levels.

(a) The story of the overcoming of idolatry by witness offers a more intelligible and in one sense a deeper understanding of the atonement than that of the overcoming of sin's defilement by sacrifice. If we look to the disease rather than the treatment, then it seems that defilement is not itself the disease but its result or symptom – though of course symptoms are 'illness' and need treating. Defilement in Revelation is bound up with idolatry, and idolatry is a function of man's turning away from his creator, so that his 'senseless mind is darkened' and he defiles the creation, starting with himself (Romans 1: 18ff); he becomes a victim of 'false consciousness' and 'alienation'. Or using the Satan myth, which is another way of talking about human declension from God in its cosmic social effects, man is in bondage to the 'father of lies' (τὸ ψεῦδος), the ruler of this world (John 8: 31ff);[42] or in another version, non-worship of God becomes the worship of not-God, or demons (Deuteronomy 32: 7, quoted 1 Corinthians 10: 20; cf. Revelation 9: 20), which lie behind idolatry and draw men into it; there can be no

---

[41] T. S. Eliot, *Four Quartets*, East Coker IV; Little Gidding IV. Cf. Revelation 1: 5, 'to him who loves us and freed us from our sins by his own blood' – words addressed to the elect, certainly, but his death is part of God's eternal purpose for the world (13: 8), and the elect are ἀπαρχή (14: 4), the first of the total harvest, chosen for the sake of the rest. John's message is addressed to (or against) them, not the world. God's love for the world is not mentioned (it could perhaps be taken for granted: cf. 1 John 2: 2 etc.), but is evidenced in the cost of redemption.

[42] I think it is justifiable to fill in the theology underlying Revelation's pictures from Paul and the Fourth Gospel. In Ephesus John could well have been exposed to both streams, as well as to the prophetic–apocalyptic stream that also influenced Paul; cf. E. S. Fiorenza, 'The Quest for the Johannine School: the Apocalypse and the Fourth Gospel', *NTS* 23 (1977), 402–27.

spiritual vacuum, and turning away from God sets up a rival 'kingdom' or κόσμος, based on unreality (ψεῦδος) but terribly powerful in its effects.

This kingdom can be destroyed by tearing down the false and deceiving structures (or rather letting them poison and destroy themselves – cf. the plagues of trumpets and bowls, Revelation 8, 9, 16). But the root cause can only be dealt with by supplying the basic deficiency, which is God, ἀλήθεια; that is, by witness to the truth (John 18: 37), which is not just verbal but the coming of God himself; and this *coming* must be not momentary but an abiding *presence* (παρουσία can mean both) carried through to the end, like a course of penicillin, if the cure is to be complete. This presence we have in the historical testimony of Jesus, the Word made flesh, carried on in those who maintain his testimony, and consummated in what we call the parousia, which gives place to the Holy City, one of whose names is 'The Lord is there.'[43] Thus faithful testimony to the truth *is* the defeating of Satan who deceives the whole earth; obedience to God's commandments *is* the crushing of the ancient serpent's head.[44]

(*b*) But nowhere is it suggested that witness or the suffering that goes with it completes the conversion of the world in itself – only in its final vindication by God (1(*d*) above). Its immediate outward effect is overall to intensify opposition (12: 12 – 13: 18). Not that Christian witness had *no* outward effect – far from it (11: 5f; cf. p. 108, n. 23); Gospels and Acts are full of it – but that these victories, though real enough, are only partial and proleptic. Revelation is concerned not with individual conversions but with the defeat of the Satanic trinity – the powers behind human resistance – which can only be carried out finally by God. In this final sense the victory-over-Satan story is incomplete. Witness to the truth could go on for ever, attracting some and repelling others. What dynamic lies behind the final moment of truth?

Here we are driven back to the sacrifice story at a deeper level. The dynamic behind the final victory is the same as that which lies behind Christ's first-fruits victory in his resurrection (1: 5), behind Satan's expulsion from heaven (12: 7–9). It is given in the word ἐσφαγμένον,

---

[43] Ezekiel 48: 35, which lies behind Revelation 21: 3ff.

[44] Cf. Genesis 3: 15 in the Targum version, which lies behind Revelation 12: 9–12, 17; 13: 3: 'when the offspring of the woman keep the commandments of the Law, ... they will smite you on the head; but when they abandon the commandments of the Law, ...you will wound them in the heel' (Bowker, *Targums*, p. 122). The healing of the beast's smitten head, and its painful consequences for Christians, is perhaps to be connected with disobedience, like that at Pergamum and Thyatira; cf. 1 p. 102, n. 5.

which sums up his whole faithful obedient μαρτυρία ἄχρι θανάτου and that of his μάρτυρες. The serpent's head is crushed not by divine *fiat*, but by divine presence, and this presence conquers not by superhuman power and wisdom but by fidelity to itself, at the cost of itself. It is this incalculable cost to God, and to those who take his part, that the sacrifice story conveys.

If cleansing of defilement seems to us a more superficial and impersonal metaphor than liberation from the source of defilement (as is perhaps implied by the remark that the author of Hebrews conceives sin as stain rather than chain), this may be because we are used to mechanical quasi-magical means of cleansing – like the 'miracle' detergents, gentle, soft and kind to the hands. It is different if we think in medical terms – sharp, drastic, dangerous and costly to both doctor and patient:

> 'The wounded surgeon plies the steel
> That questions the distempered part;
> Beneath the bleeding hands we feel
> The sharp compassion of the healer's art...'[45]

We can in some sense say how the victory of ἀλήθεια over ψεῦδος 'works', but if we ask how it is *finally* to be achieved, we can only point to a mystery, the hidden wisdom of God, which is beyond this age and its rulers – a lamb standing ὡς ἐσφαγμένον, and the souls of τῶν ἐσφαγμένων because of the word of God and the testimony they maintained, who were told to rest until the number of their fellow-servants who were to be slain like them was complete (6: 9–11). The two 'stories' are ultimately one (12: 11). Sacrifice is not simply a mechanical act of expiation or propitiation but belongs to the being of God himself, and therein lies the victory.

[45] T. S. Eliot, *Four Quartets*, East Coker IV.

Martyrdom and inspiration

†G. W. H. LAMPE

The Christian Church owes its survival of almost three centuries of intermittent persecution during the critical period of its formation and growth, and its emergence at the end of that time as a movement powerful enough to establish a position of total dominance in the Roman Empire, to its clear and uncompromising idea of martyrdom. This was a tradition that it had inherited to a large extent from Judaism, like itself a martyr-religion in the sense of a religion that actively and systematically trained its adherents collectively (as distinct from the individual heroes produced by Greco-Roman philosophies, such as Socrates, or the Stoic dissidents in the early Empire) for a vocation to witness to their faith not only at the cost of, but actually by means of, suffering and death. For Christians, however, the conviction that the martyr was the ideal disciple held an even more central place in belief and practice, for it was rooted in the event that stood at the heart of the Gospel, the death of Jesus. Their doctrine of martyrdom was, indeed, largely derived and developed out of the response of the orthodox Jewish resistance movement to the persecution under Antiochus Epiphanes, but there are significant differences of attitude between such writings as Daniel, 2 Maccabees and 4 Maccabees, on the one hand, and the New Testament and second-century Christian literature on the other. The former tend to be primarily defensive. The stories told in Daniel and the accounts of the words and the heroic endurance of the Maccabaean martyrs are designed to encourage their readers to resist the attempts of brutal heathen rulers to force them to abandon their religion – to worship idols, to eat unclean food, and so to apostatise from the Law. The Christian martyr, too, has to resist, through torture and death, the efforts of the authorities to make him renounce his faith; but it is he who really takes the initiative. The martyr is, as the word 'martyr' denotes, a witness, and as a witness he is, as it were, on the offensive against the persecuting power. Unlike the Jewish martyr, his

† Prof. Lampe read the proofs of this essay before his death on 5 August 1980.

aim is not merely passive resistance to attempts to compel him to abjure his ancestral way of life (as by forcing him to eat pork), but active testifying to a Gospel. For the central point of conflict between the Church and both the Synagogue and the Roman authorities lay in the realm of belief. Their controversy turned on the cardinal Christian belief that 'Jesus is Lord.' This was the essential theme of the Church's witness, provoking the Roman State in the second century to confront Christian believers with the demand that they should curse Christ and acknowledge that 'Caesar is Lord.'[1] The Christian was essentially a missionary, and martyrdom was for him the supreme and most effective mode of evangelism. A trial of Christians before a Roman governor was therefore always for them a show trial. It was their great opportunity for propaganda, when they could confess Christ before the rulers of the world. Death by a public execution set the seal on their testimony in the presence of the crowds, and by writing and circulating their *acta* the Church secured for it still wider and more lasting publicity.

This immensely significant idea could be expressed in a variety of theological terms and imagery. There was what might be called a 'pneumatology' of martyrdom, in so far as the martyr's testimony was believed to be inspired by the Holy Spirit and the Christian who confessed his faith in circumstances of persecution was regarded as closely akin to the prophet as a recipient of revelation and a proclaimer of God's word. It is this aspect of the idea of martyrdom that it is the purpose of this essay to explore. There was also a 'christology' of martyrdom, a 'soteriology', an 'anthropology' and a 'demonology'.

All these facets of the idea of martyrdom have their roots in the New Testament or in pre-Christian Judaism, and they find parallel expression in such classical expositions of the early Church's thought on this subject as the *Martyrdom of Polycarp* and the *Letter of the Churches of Lyons and Vienne* to the churches of Asia, describing the great outbreak of persecution in the year 177. By a 'christology' of martyrdom I mean the interpretation of the faithful disciple's suffering and death as the imitation of Christ, a concrete and literal realisation of that death and burial with Christ which is figuratively enacted in every convert's baptism,[2] and as the consummation of so intimate a personal union with Christ that the Lord himself can be said to suffer in the person of his loyal follower. In the New Testament this understanding finds expression in such passages as Acts 9: 5 (to persecute the Christian community is to persecute Jesus himself), John 15: 20 (Christ's disciples

---

[1] *Mart. Polyc.* 8.2, 9.2–3; cf. Pliny, *Epp.* x.96.3f.
[2] Romans 6: 3; Colossians 2: 12.

must expect to suffer similar persecution to that which was directed against their Master), the hymn quoted at 2 Timothy 2: 11 ('If we have died with him, we shall also live with him; if we endure, we shall also reign with him'), and especially in 1 Peter where it is very prominent, particularly in 4: 13 ('Rejoice in so far as you share Christ's sufferings, that you may also rejoice and be glad when his glory is revealed'). It underlies the evident concern of Luke to draw a close parallel between the death of Jesus and that of Stephen, the first martyr. Ignatius, who does not use the actual 'martyr' terminology, dwells on this aspect of his approaching death: it is his entry upon true discipleship, it means the attainment of Christ, and by it he will become 'an imitator of my God'.[3] In the *Martyrdom of Polycarp* the theme of *imitatio Christi* is further developed in the correspondence between the details of his story and those of the Passion narratives in the Gospels, in the claim that the martyr becomes a participant in Christ, and in the writer's comment that, although the Church's enemies were foolish to suppose that the surviving Christians might apostatise from Christ to worship the martyrs, they do love and reverence them as disciples and imitators of the Lord.[4] Here, too, we find the belief that the Lord in person stands by the Christian sufferers and converses with them.[5]

When martyrdom is interpreted in this Christocentric fashion it is the actual suffering and death of the Christian disciple that is of primary significance rather than his verbal testimony; for, according to the *Epistle of Lyons and Vienne*, Christ himself suffers in the body of the martyr and defeats the devil there. In the same document the martyr Blandina is said to put on Christ, the invincible athlete, and, in the manner of her death, to be a representation of Christ on the Cross.[6] It is probably under the influence of this emphasis on Christian martyrdom as participation in the suffering and death of Jesus that the word μάρτυς and its cognates tend in the second century to lose the sense of 'witness', at least as their primary meaning, and a distinction comes to be drawn between the martyr who literally dies with Christ and the confessor who witnesses to him before persecutors but does not actually suffer the death penalty. Thus Tertullian, instead of using a Latin equivalent for μάρτυς in the sense of 'witness', has to take over the Greek word and employ it in Latin as a technical term for 'martyr', a person who has died for and with Christ.

The 'soteriology' of martyrdom takes up the idea that was so prom-

---

[3] Ignatius, *Eph.* 3.1; *Rom.* 4.2–3, 5.3, 6.3.
[4] *Mart. Polyc.* 1.2; 6.2; 7.1; 17.3.   [5] *Ibid.* 2.2.
[6] Eusebius, *H.E.* v.1.23, 42, 41.

inent in Judaism, that the death of the martyr effects atonement for
Israel by expiating the people's sins or propitiating the wrath of God.
The martyr's death, according to 4 Maccabees,[7] makes satisfaction on
behalf of the people, and his soul is a ransom for their souls. This is
an interpretation of martyrdom that, although it seems to have been of
cardinal importance for early Christian reflection on the significance
of the death of Christ himself,[8] received comparatively little emphasis
in respect of the sufferings of his disciples. Its influence, however,
can probably be seen in the application of sacrificial imagery to martyrdom. Thus Paul speaks of the possibility that he may 'be poured as a
libation upon the sacrificial offering' of the faith of the Christian community,[9] Ignatius of his life as an exchange for his readers' lives,[10] and
Polycarp is described as a 'whole burnt offering' and 'a rich and
acceptable sacrifice'.[11]

An 'anthropology' of martyrdom means, to use a rough and ready
and perhaps rather unfair designation, a somewhat anthropocentric
view, which treats the conflict waged by the martyr against his oppressors' efforts to make him recant as an external projection of the inward
struggle in the human soul between the flesh and the spirit (in the sense
of the lower nature or passions, on the one side, and the higher, rational,
self on the other). This is a central theme of 4 Maccabees, where the
martyrs' heroic resistance to every form of torture, and their steadfast
refusal to yield to any persuasion to abandon their loyalty to the Law,
are a supreme example of the conquest of the passions by reason
(λογισμός). The martyr, Eleazar, was 'king over the passions'.[12] It may
be a little unfair to characterise this interpretation as anthropocentric,
for it is of course assumed that the Maccabaean loyalists are divinely
inspired and fortified, and this presupposition underlies the author's
description of Eleazar raising his eyes to heaven (which signifies communion with God) while he 'keeps his reason inflexible'.[13] It is,
nevertheless, an interpretation in which divine inspiration and personal
communion with God are emphasised less strongly than the classical
cardinal virtues, especially fortitude and self-control under the hege-
mony of reason. It thus has close links with Stoic morality and furnishes
a bridge between Christian ideas of martyrdom and the philosophical
tradition of heroic virtue. Thus Clement of Alexandria refers to the

---

[7] 4 Macc. 6.28f; cf. 1.11; 17.22.
[8] Notably at Mark 10: 45; Matthew 20: 28.
[9] Philippians 2: 17; cf. 2 Timothy 4: 6.   [10] *Eph.* 21.1.
[11] *Mart. Polyc.* 14.1–2.
[12] 4 Macc. 7.10.
[13] *Ibid.* 6.5–6.

work of Timotheus of Pergamum on the fortitude of the philosophers,[14] and Tertullian commends the example of pagan 'martyrs' such as Mucius Scaevola, Heraclitus, Empedocles and Dido.[15] There may be a hint of a similar idea of transcendent heroism and of the conquest of the flesh by the spirit in the *Martyrdom of Polycarp* 2.3 (notwithstanding the writer's insistence on 'the grace of Christ') where we are told that the martyrs despised worldly tortures, and that for them the fire was cool, because they were no longer human beings but already angels. It is a way of looking at martyrdom that soon lent itself to spiritualisation: the martyr is one particular kind of ascetic, and his example can be followed, even when there is no external persecution, by those who steadfastly practise ἀπάθεια.[16]

The 'demonology' of martyrdom is the reverse side, as it were, of the belief that the faithful confessor is inspired by the Holy Spirit and dies as an imitator of Christ and a participant in his victory over the demonic powers. Just as the real object of the persecutors' attack is not primarily their individual victims but the faith that they profess and, ultimately, the God in whom they trust, so the opponent against whom the Christian 'athletes' contend is really the devil. Satan is the tempter of the faithful, seeking to cajole or frighten them into apostasy, possessing Judas the archetypal traitor,[17] trying to 'sift' the disciples of Jesus in the moment of the crisis of his arrest,[18] sitting enthroned at a centre of the imperial cult where Christians were faced with the choice between confession and denial, and always, until his final overthrow, the present and active enemy.[19] The struggle was symbolised for the martyr Perpetua by her fight in a dream against an Egyptian wrestler,[20] and it is Satan who 'eagerly strives' to make the martyrs of Lyons and Vienne utter some blasphemy, who supposes that he has 'devoured' (cf. 1 Peter 5: 8) Biblis who had 'denied' instead of confessing Christ, and who inspires the persecutors who are 'full of the devil' and are his ministers.[21]

It is, however, with the positive aspect that we are now concerned: the confessor of Christ as a Spirit-possessed and prophet-like person. According to this tradition, it is the faithful Christian's testimony that is of central significance. To deliver it may well mean to incur death, but whether the result is death, a lesser penalty such as imprisonment or exile, or, exceptionally, release is comparatively unimportant. Death is almost incidental; it is the witness before hostile authorities that is the

---

[14] *Strom.* IV. 56.2.   [15] *Apol.* 50; *Ad Nat.* 1.18.
[16] Clement of Alexandria, *Strom.*, IV.13ff.   [17] Luke 22: 3; John 13: 27.
[18] Luke 22: 31.   [19] Revelation 2: 13; 12: 9; 20: 2.
[20] *Mart. Perp.* 10.   [21] Eusebius, *H.E.* v.1.16, 25, 27, 35.

essence of 'martyrdom', and the role of the Spirit is not primarily to bring consolation and strength in physical suffering, but to inspire confessors to proclaim the Lordship of Christ with uninhibited freedom (*parrhesia*). This concept, in which the inspiration of the Spirit finds expression in evangelistic witness, has deep roots in the Old Testament. It is linked with the vocation of the whole people of God: '"You are my witnesses", says the Lord, "and my servant whom I have chosen, that you may know and believe me and understand that I am He"'; and to the 'servant...in whom my soul delights', who is either identical with, or symbolical of, God's faithful witnessing people, it is said: 'I have put my Spirit upon him.'[22] Within this general vocation to witness there is the special and more sharply focused testimony of faithful individuals, more particularly in the face of hostility and persecution. It is probably in these circumstances that the devotee of the Law prays in Psalm 119: 41–6 for inspiration to testify to it before rulers:

> 'Let thy steadfast love come to me, O Lord,
> ...then shall I have an answer for those who taunt me,
>   for I trust in thy word.
> And take not the word of truth utterly out of my mouth...
> I will also speak of thy testimonies before kings,
>   and shall not be put to shame.'

In the unprecedented situation of religious persecution in the Maccabaean era the 'wise', typified by the figure of Daniel himself and the 'Three Children', are confessors and sufferers for Judaism, and, as with the righteous man, the 'son of God' and 'servant of the Lord', of Wisdom 2: 12ff, faithful witness carries the assurance of resurrection or immortality.[23]

The prophets come to be regarded not only as men inspired by God's Spirit but also as martyrs. Collectively, the prophets were messengers of God to Israel whose message was constantly rejected: 'The Lord', says the Chronicler, 'sent persistently to them by his messengers...but they kept mocking the messengers of God, despising his words, and scoffing at his prophets.'[24] They were even put to death: 'I will send witnesses to them, that I may witness against them, but they will not hear, and will slay the witnesses also.'[25] Witness and prophecy are thus

---

[22] Isaiah 43: 10; 42: 1.
[23] Daniel 12: 2–3; Wisdom 3: 1–8.
[24] 2 Chronicles 36: 15–16.
[25] Jub. 1.12.

identified, and the prophet gives his testimony under the inspiration of the Spirit. Thus

> 'the Spirit of God took possession of Zechariah the son of Jehoiada the priest; and he stood above the people, and said to them, "Thus says God, 'Why do you transgress the commandments of the Lord, so that you cannot prosper? Because you have forsaken the Lord, he has forsaken you.'" But they conspired against him, and by command of the king they stoned him with stones in the court of the house of the Lord.'[26]

Later, Isaiah was reckoned as another Spirit-inspired prophet–martyr, who was absorbed in a vision of the Lord (like Stephen, according to Acts 7: 55–6) so that he did not hear the order to recant, and whose 'lips spoke with the Holy Spirit' until he was sawn in twain.[27]

Individually, each of the Hebrew prophets came to have martyrdom ascribed to him, and the stories of their trials and sufferings typified the ideal of the Jewish martyr. To such prophets as Zechariah and Jeremiah and Isaiah there were added Abel, Abraham, Isaac, Joseph, Phinehas and Daniel as examples of faithful servants of God who were ready to suffer for their loyalty, even though they did not necessarily have to undergo actual death.[28] This tradition passes over into Christianity. It is implied in the parable of the Wicked Tenants of the Vineyard, where the servants sent by the owner are ill-treated and killed,[29] and where the murder of his son comes as the climax of the succession of martyrdoms. It is more explicitly stated in Jesus' denunciation of the scribes and Pharisees as the sons of those who killed the prophets,[30] by Paul who, again, sees the death of Jesus as the climax of the long story of Jewish persecution of the prophets,[31] by Luke in the speech of Stephen, where the inspiration of the prophet–martyrs is related specifically to their role as foretellers of the coming of the 'Righteous One',[32] and by the writer to the Hebrews for whom the prophets are examples of endurance.[33] Ignatius similarly speaks of the persecution of the prophets, whose inspiration he ascribes, somewhat in the manner of 1 Peter 1: 11, to the grace of *Christ*.[34]

The further implication of the references in the New Testament to the persecution of the ancient prophets is that the disciples of Jesus stand in the same succession of inspired and suffering witnesses. Matthew's

[26] 2 Chronicles 24: 20–1.   [27] Mart. Isa. 5.7, 14.
[28] 4 Macc. 6: 17, 23; 13: 9; 14: 20; 16: 3, 20–1; 18: 1, 11f, 23.
[29] Mark 12: 1–5.   [30] Matthew 23: 29–33; Luke 11: 47–8.
[31] 1 Thessalonians 2: 15.   [32] Acts 7: 52.   [33] 11: 32ff.
[34] *Magn.* 8.2.

Great Sermon is addressed to the disciples of Jesus. It is they who
receive the blessing that belongs to those who are persecuted for
righteousness' sake; they are to rejoice and be glad 'for your reward is
great in heaven, for so men persecuted the prophets who were before
you'.[35] Jesus himself, whose death in Jerusalem will follow the pattern
of the persecution of the prophets,[36] will send a new succession of
prophets and wise men and scribes, or, as Luke has it, prophets and
apostles, and

> 'some you will kill and crucify, and some you will scourge in your
> synagogues and persecute from town to town, that upon you may
> come all the righteous blood shed on earth, from the blood of
> innocent Abel to the blood of Zechariah [Matthew adds 'the son
> of Barachiah'], whom you murdered between the sanctuary and
> the altar.'[37]

For Paul, similarly, the persecution of the prophets was part of a single
continuous story, which includes the death of Jesus and the expulsion
of the apostle himself, and also the obstruction of his Gentile mission.[38]
Luke's account of the death of Stephen also implies very clearly that
this martyrdom is to be understood against the background of the killing
of the prophets and the murder of the Christ whom they had foretold.[39]
This inclusion of the disciples and missionary witnesses of Jesus within
the succession of prophet–martyrs sets the keynote for the presentation
of the Christian confessor in the New Testament writings as a person
inspired and possessed by the Spirit in a special degree. Before we
leave the allusion to the persecution of the Old Testament saints in
Matthew 23: 35, however, it may be worth noticing the strange reference
to Zechariah as 'son of Barachiah'. It has some relevance to the history
of early Christian understandings of martyrdom because of the curious
appearance of the name Zechariah (Zacharias) in the story of the
martyrs of Lyons and Vienne. One Vettius Epagathus came forward
courageously and testified to the innocence of the Christians. He was
arrested himself, and was

> 'asked this one question, if he too were a Christian. And having
> confessed (ὁμολογήσαντος) in a very clear voice, he also was taken up
> into the inheritance (κλῆρος) of the martyrs, being called the advo-
> cate (παράκλητος) of Christians, but having within himself the

---

[35] Matthew 5: 10–12. [36] Luke 13: 33–4.
[37] Matthew 23: 34–5; Luke 11: 49–50. [38] 1 Thessalonians 2: 15.
[39] Acts 7: 52–7.

Paraclete, the Spirit of Zacharias [a variant reading has 'the Spirit more than that of Zacharias'], which he showed through the fullness of love, being well pleased to lay down even his own life for the defence (ἀπολογία) of the brethren.'[40]

This passage of the *Epistle of Lyons and Vienne* is highly instructive as an illustration of the 'pneumatology of martyrdom'. The allusion to the 'Spirit of Zacharias', however, if that is the correct reading as seems probable, appears to be unique. The Epistle offers a partial explanation: that Vettius was likened to the Lucan Zacharias because he 'walked in all the commandments and ordinances of the Lord, blameless'.[41] This, however, suggests no real reason why the Paraclete, the inspirer of the martyr's confession, 'I am a Christian', should be called, or even compared with, the 'Spirit of Zacharias'. It is of course true that Zacharias, like the other chief characters in Luke's infancy stories, was an inspired prophet; he was 'filled with the Holy Spirit and prophesied' in the words of the *Benedictus*.[42] This again, however, has no apparent connection with a martyr's inspired confession. There is the further complication that the name Zacharias stands second in the list of the martyrs of Lyons in the Hieronymian martyrology and the martyrology of Bede, after that of the bishop, Pothinus, and in Gregory of Tours and the Brussels MS 207–208 after that of Vettius Epagathus, which heads the list.[43] The suggestion is probably correct that this 'Zacharias' is not another martyr unmentioned in the *Epistle*, but a Christian surname given to Vettius on the lines of Ignatius' surname Theophorus.

The strong likelihood is that von Campenhausen is right in inferring that by 177 the Lucan Zacharias was already thought to have been an inspired martyr.[44] There was great confusion in antiquity between the various Zechariahs in the Bible. Zechariah the son of Jehoiada was, as we have seen, prominent in the tradition concerning martyr-prophets, and he continued to have an important place in rabbinic thought.[45] Sozomen's *Ecclesiastical History* concludes with the discovery of his remains at Caphar-Zechariah near Eleutheropolis in Palestine. A local landlord was told by the prophet in a dream to dig in a garden, where he would find a double casket, wooden within, leaden without, together with a crystal vessel of water and two snakes 'of moderate size, gentle

---

[40] Eusebius *H.E.* v.1.10.   [41] Luke 1: 6.   [42] Luke 1: 67.

[43] Gregory of Tours, *De gloria martyrum* 49. See D. H. Quentin in *Analecta Bollandiana* 39 (1921) 134–5.

[44] H. von Campenhausen, 'Das Martyrium des Zacharias' (*Historisches Jahrbuch* 77 (1958)) in *Aus der Frühzeit des Christentums* (Tübingen, 1963).

[45] See S. H. Blank, 'The Death of Zechariah', *HUCA* 12–13 (1937–8).

and harmless so as to appear quite tame'. The prophet was duly found, dressed in a white robe 'as being, I suppose', says Sozomen, showing some confusion with Zechariah's father, 'a priest'. Beneath his feet, outside the coffin, there lay a child who had been given a royal burial, with a golden crown, golden sandals, and rich vesture. The abbot of the monastery at Gerar, another Zacharias, came across an old and uncanonical Hebrew document, which showed that on the seventh day after Zechariah's martyrdom the son of King Joash died suddenly, and the king buried him at the prophet's feet by way of expiation. Sozomen adds that the prophet was intact, his hair shorn, a straight nose, a beard of moderate length, a rather short head, and eyes somewhat deeply set and overshadowed by the eyebrows.[46] The *Vitae Prophetarum* included among the *spuria* of Epiphanius tell us that the priests buried Zechariah beside his father, and that from then onwards there were no revelations in the Temple, by theophanies, visions of angels, oracles, ephod, or Urim and Thummim.[47]

Yet although Zechariah the son of Jehoiada was famous as the prototype of inspired prophet–martyrs and attracted to himself some interesting legends, he had early become confused with the prophet Zechariah the son of Barachiah, as our text in Matthew shows. This caused much trouble to ancient commentators. Chrysostom, for instance, asks who the Zechariah of Matthew 23: 35 can be: some say it is the father of John the Baptist, some the prophet Zechariah, some another person, a priest with two names whom scripture also calls Jehoiada.[48] Chrysostom does not attempt an answer to his own rather confused question (he has the excuse that in the LXX the son of Jehoiada appears as Azariah). Jerome does better. He explains that some say this is indeed the son of Barachiah, the eleventh of the Twelve Prophets, but that he is never said to have been killed between the Temple and the altar; indeed, in that Zechariah's time there were only ruins of the Temple. Some think Matthew is referring to the father of the Baptist, slain, according to apocryphal fancies, because he proclaimed the advent of Christ. Others think this is really the Zechariah who was killed by Joash; but he was the son of Jehoiada the priest, not of Barachiah. Jerome adds that in the Gospel of the Nazarenes the text reads 'son of Jehoiada' for 'son of Barachiah', and that Christians of the simpler sort point out certain red rocks between the ruins of the

---

[46] 9.17.
[47] C. C. Torrey, *The Lives of the Prophets*, Journal of Biblical Literature Monograph Series 1 (Philadelphia, 1946).
[48] *Hom. 74.2 in Matt.* (*PG* LVIII, 681).

Temple and the altar, or in the gateways leading to Siloam, which they believe to be stained with the blood of Zechariah.[49]

By the fourth century there was thus a well-established confusion between three Zechariahs. In fact the introduction of Luke's Zacharias into the conflation of the son of Barachiah with the son of Jehoiada was already known to Origen, and developed by him. According to Origen the reference in Matthew 23: 35 is to the father of the Baptist. Scripture does not tell us that he was the son of Barachiah, nor that he was slain by the scribes and Pharisees between the Temple and the altar; but there is a tradition that there was a place in the Temple reserved for virgins to stand and pray. Mary went there after the birth of her child, and those who knew of the birth objected. Zacharias then defended her right to stand there as a virgin, and for this apparent breach of the Law he was slain between the Temple and the altar. Origen makes the rather effective point that those who reject that story must explain why Jesus says that the scribes and Pharisees actually killed Zacharias themselves (ἐφονεύσατε), not that, as in the case of the prophets, they are the sons of those who so acted. He adds, however, that there may have been two men called Zacharias, and two fathers of men called Zacharias with the same name.[50] Elsewhere Origen adds another stone to this edifice of confusion: he claims that Josephus says that the Lucan Zacharias was the son of Barach, having identified the father of the Baptist with Josephus' Zechariah, son of Barach, murdered in the Temple during the Jewish War.[51]

Another story to account for the supposed martyrdom of Luke's Zacharias is told by Epiphanius, perhaps from an early Gnostic source: Zacharias was killed in the Temple because he had discovered that the object of Jewish worship was a man in the form of an ass.[52] A third tale, known to Peter of Alexandria,[53] and later appended to the *Protevangelium of James*, makes Zacharias the high priest. Herod's officers appear, hunting down the children, and ask the whereabouts of the child John, who has escaped with his mother into the country. Zacharias refuses to tell them, makes a martyr's confession in the curious form, 'I am a martyr of God', and is slain beside the altar.[54]

It would seem, then, that the process that led to the identification of the Paraclete that Vettius the martyr 'had within himself' with the

[49] *Comm. in Matt.* 23: 35–6.
[50] *Comm. ser. in Matt.* 25.
[51] *Fr. 457 in Matt.*; Josephus, *B.J.* IV.5.4.
[52] Epiphanius, *Haer.* 26.12; Josephus, cf. *C. Apion.* 2.7 and, for the similar slander directed against Christian worship, Tertullian, *Ad Nat.* 1.11.
[53] *Can.* 13.   [54] *Protev. Jac.* 8.3, 23–4.

'Spirit of Zacharias' was as follows: Zacharias was known from Luke
1: 67 to have been a Spirit-possessed prophet; he was identified with
the Zacharias of Matthew 23: 35 (who had already been confused with
the canonical prophet, the son of Barachiah) and was therefore believed
to have been a martyr; he may also have already been thought to have
been not only a priest, as in the Third Gospel, but high priest, and it is
therefore conceivable that he would be regarded as an inspired prophet
on the ground of John 11: 51, which ancient commentators generally
took to mean that the high priest was endowed with the gift of prophecy
ex officio.

All this, however, is of very minor importance in comparison with the
main point, which is the fact that the *Epistle of Lyons and Vienne*
provides such striking evidence of the early Church's belief in the
plenary inspiration of those who witnessed to Christ before persecutors.
Since Vettius was spokesman or advocate for Christ and his disciples, it
was really the Paraclete himself who spoke in him. His companions,
says the Letter, had the Holy Spirit as their counsellor (σύμβουλος).[55]
Similarly Tertullian urges confessors not to 'grieve the Spirit who has
entered prison with you,'[56] and Cyprian claims that it is the duty of a
Christian leader to speak, if he is arrested and brought before the
authorities, because the one who really speaks is 'God within us' ('Deus
in nobis positus').[57] Here lay the great strength of the Christian movement; it was realistically understood that Christ's followers could
expect only hatred and persecution, since that had been the lot of Christ
himself; but in the decisive choice between confession and denial, and
in witness before heathen rulers, it would be the invincible Spirit that
would control and inspire their actions and words.

This belief was already firmly established by the time of the formation of the Synoptic traditions. Certain passages in the Gospels constitute the foundation of the development of the Christian idea of
witness and martyrdom as a primary operation of the Holy Spirit. In the
Synoptic apocalypse (Mark 13: 9–11 and the parallel at Luke 21: 12–15)
Jesus warns his disciples of coming persecution (this warning being also
reproduced at Matthew 24: 9ff): 'They will deliver you up to councils
(συνέδρια) and you will be beaten in synagogues; and you will stand
before governors and kings for my sake, to bear testimony before them.
And the gospel must first be preached to all nations.' An unambiguous
promise of direct inspiration accompanies this warning: 'And when they
bring you to trial and deliver you up, do not be anxious beforehand

[55] Eusebius, *H.E.* v.3.3.   [56] *Mart.* 1.   [57] *Ep.* 81.

G. W. H. Lampe

what you are to say; but say whatever is given you in that hour, for it is not you who speak, but the Holy Spirit.' According to Luke, Jesus, having warned the disciples that they will be brought before kings and governors, tells them that 'This will be a time for you to bear testimony.' Persecution is thus the great opportunity to further the Christian mission by public witness, which, being divinely inspired, must ultimately prove irresistible. 'Settle it therefore in your minds, not to meditate beforehand how to answer; for I will give you a mouth and wisdom, which none of your adversaries will be able to withstand or contradict.' Here the phrase 'a mouth and wisdom' is equivalent to prophetic inspiration, Jesus himself being the giver of it, as, according to Luke and John, he is the giver or mediator of the Holy Spirit.

The promise that Mark sets in the context of the eschatological discourse appears in Matthew (10: 17–20) in the 'mission charge' at the sending out of the Twelve. Again, it reflects the conditions in which the post-resurrection witness of the Church was being carried out. Luke reproduces the promise again in a remarkable context at 12: 11–12: 'And when they bring you before the synagogues and the rulers and the authorities, do not be anxious how or what you are to answer or what you are to say; for the Holy Spirit will teach you in that very hour what you ought to say.' Luke's context is, first, as in the Matthaean 'mission charge', the eschatological promise: 'Every one who acknowledges me before men, the Son of man also will acknowledge before the angels of God; but he who denies me before men will be denied before the angels of God,'[58] the first part of which is closely paralleled in Mark 8: 38// Luke 9: 26. Here the scene in an earthly court where a faithful confessor 'acknowledges' (ὁμολογεῖν) the Lord is projected on to the heavenly court. Just as the Christian disciple confesses Christ, so before the angels of the heavenly court Christ will testify to the faithfulness of his servant. So, too, the apostate who has taken the opposite course and denied (ἀρνεῖσθαι) Christ will in turn be denied by him in the presence of the angels. In Luke the negative side of this combined promise and warning is developed by the insertion into this same context of the saying concerning blasphemy against the Holy Spirit.[59] The setting of this in Mark and Matthew is quite different, and Luke's introduction of it into the context of the promise that confessors can rely on plenary inspiration is very striking. 'Every one who speaks a word against the Son of man will be forgiven; but he who blasphemes against the Holy Spirit will not be forgiven.' Luke evidently understands the blasphemy that is un-

58 Luke 12: 8–9; Matthew 10: 32–3.
59 Luke 12: 10; Mark 3: 29; Matthew 12: 32.

forgivable to be the denial of Christ before men, to which he has just referred. Such denial amounts to a direct repudiation of the promised inspiration of the Spirit. It is the blasphemy against the Spirit, interpreted by Luke as the Spirit operating in the missionary witness of the Church, and transferred by him from the context of the Galilean mission of the earthly Jesus, in which Mark and Matthew place it, to that of the Christian confessor on trial before synagogues, rulers and authorities. This is the disastrous act of apostasy, which the missionary Church treated in a manner similar to that in which an army treats desertion in face of the enemy. Luke apparently believes that it was possible to 'speak a word against the Son of man' during the earthly life of Jesus without incurring this ultimate sin; the Spirit-inspired community with its commission to witness to the end of the earth[60] had not yet come into being, and the unforgivable sin belongs to the post-resurrection, or rather for Luke the post-Pentecostal, era of mission.[61]

The promise of inspiration and its fulfilment in early Christian experience is a frequent theme in the New Testament writings. Acts 4: 5ff describes the first appearance of apostles before a court. A most formal and solemn assembly of rulers and elders and scribes, with the high priest and all who were of the high-priestly family, inquire by what power or by what name Peter and John had healed the crippled man at the Temple gate and preached to the crowd. In reply Peter makes his *apologia* 'filled with the Holy Spirit', and the court has to recognise the characteristic mark of inspiration, boldness or freedom of speech (*parrhesia*). After their release the Christian community corporately prays that God may grant his servants to speak his word with all *parrhesia*, and in answer the place where they were praying was shaken, and 'they were all filled with the Holy Spirit and spoke the word of God with boldness'.[62] Thus on their next appearance before the authorities Peter and the apostles were able to claim: 'We are witnesses to these things, and so is the Holy Spirit whom God has given to those who obey him.'[63] The story of Stephen is so told as to leave no doubt that he is an inspired man. He is full of grace and power; his opponents cannot withstand the wisdom and the Spirit with which he speaks; when he begins his *apologia* before the sanhedrin the members of the court see

---

[60] Acts 1: 8.
[61] This raises the question of the relation between apostasy in the early Church and the tradition of Peter's denial of Jesus. I have discussed this elsewhere, e.g. in W. R. Farmer, C. F. D. Moule and R. R. Niebuhr (eds.), *Christian History and Interpretation* (Cambridge University Press, 1967), pp. 356–8.
[62] Acts 4: 29–31.
[63] Acts 5: 32.

that his face is like the face of an angel; and as his hearers turn on him in fury he, 'full of the Holy Spirit', sees the glory of God and Jesus standing at the right hand of God.[64] Stephen is, in fact, presented by Luke as a prophet and seer and martyr.

Of the Pauline writings Philippians is the most important from this standpoint. Paul's imprisonment is a means by which the progress of the Gospel is furthered; it brings him to the attention of the whole praetorium and to all others, and it encourages his Christian brethren to speak God's word fearlessly; through the gift of the Spirit of Jesus Christ he can confidently hope that he will not be put to shame (that is, fail to meet the challenge), but that Christ will be honoured in his person, whether he dies or survives, with all *parrhesia*; suffering for Christ's sake is a sign of perdition to the persecutors, but of salvation to the sufferers; he and his supporters are engaged in a contest together (like athletes) in the faith of the Gospel.[65] Many of the leading ideas in later Christian thought about martyrdom are adumbrated here, as well as the central belief that the person who suffers for the Gospel receives an outpouring of the Spirit of Jesus Christ. At the same time it is worth noticing that Paul has a remarkably down-to-earth view concerning martyrdom. What matters to him is the mission. It may be furthered either through his own death or through his continuing work for the churches. When he tells his readers that they are full partakers of the grace given to him, it is the grace of his own missionary calling that he has in mind rather than of vocation to a martyr's death. Paul is fully ready to accept death as the consequence of his mission of witness, but he is far from sharing the later ideas of a martyr's death in itself being the goal and crown of discipleship and the supreme mode of union with Christ.

Ephesians 6: 19–20, whether Pauline or not, reproduces Pauline thinking (as well as that expressed in Acts 4: 29–31) when the writer asks his readers to pray that he may receive the gift of speech to make known the mystery (that is, the revelation) of the Gospel with *parrhesia*, and describes himself as an 'ambassador' for the Gospel 'in chains'. The 'Paul' of the Pastoral Epistles conveys the same picture of the inspired confessor in rather different terms: 'At my first defence no one took my part...But the Lord stood by me and gave me strength to proclaim the word fully, that all the Gentiles might hear it. So I was rescued from the lion's mouth.'[66] So, too, Christians facing persecution are told in 1 Peter 4: 14 that if they are reproached for the name of

---

[64] Acts 6: 8–10, 15; 7: 55. [65] Philippians 1: 12–14, 19–20, 27–9.
[66] 2 Timothy 4: 16–17.

Christ they are blessed, because 'the Spirit of glory and of God' rests upon them; and the Fourth Gospel repeats the promise given in the Synoptic tradition: the warning that disciples will be persecuted is followed by the assurance that the Paraclete, the Spirit of truth, will bear witness to Jesus, and they also are witnesses (see Prof. Lindars, pp. 62–4 above). It is in their mission that the Paraclete will 'convince the world of sin and of righteousness and of judgment'.[67]

The negative side of the assurance of inspiration, the extreme seriousness of the sin of apostasy, can also be traced through the New Testament writings. Passages such as Revelation 2: 13 and 3: 8, which praise those who have stood firm and not 'denied', reveal, as does Hermas, *Sim.* IX.28.4, the anxiety of Church leaders lest their people should apostatise, and the warnings in the Gospels are echoed in the hymnal fragment quoted in 2 Timothy 2: 12: 'if we endure we shall also reign with him; if we deny him, he also will deny us'. Such denial is a repudiation of a Christian's baptismal allegiance,[68] and it involves participation in the corporate denial of Christ that Luke pictures Israel making in Pilate's court.[69] As the unforgivable blasphemy it evokes the rigorism of the Epistle to the Hebrews and of the attitude of 1 John towards the 'sin unto death'.[70]

Two passages relevant to this theme of witness and inspiration deserve special notice. The first is 1 Timothy 6: 12–13:

'Fight the good fight of the faith ($\dot{\alpha}\gamma\hat{\omega}\nu\alpha$ $\tau\hat{\eta}s$ $\pi\acute{\iota}\sigma\tau\epsilon\omega s$); take hold of the eternal life to which you were called when you made the good confession ($\dot{\omega}\mu o\lambda\acute{o}\gamma\eta\sigma\alpha s$ $\tau\grave{\eta}\nu$ $\kappa\alpha\lambda\grave{\eta}\nu$ $\dot{o}\mu o\lambda o\gamma\acute{\iota}\alpha\nu$) in the presence of many witnesses. In the presence...of Christ Jesus who in his testimony $\langle\mu\alpha\rho\tau\upsilon\rho\acute{\eta}\sigma\alpha\nu\tau os\rangle$ before Pontius Pilate made the good confession, I charge you to keep the commandment unstained and free from reproach.'

The view that Timothy is here represented as a confessor in a time of persecution goes back to Theodore of Mopsuestia who interprets 'you made the good confession' as meaning 'you suffered',[71] and it has more to be said for it than most commentators allow. It is usually understood to refer to Timothy's baptismal confession of faith, and $\dot{o}\mu o\lambda o\gamma\epsilon\hat{\iota}\nu$ could admittedly be used to denote this, as it is at Romans 10: 9–10. It is, however, most frequently employed in the New Testament to refer to confession, as opposed to denial, under persecution,[72] and to the

---

[67] John 15: 20–6; 16: 8.   [68] Romans 10: 9–10.   [69] Acts 3:13–14.
[70] Hebrews 6: 4–6; 10: 26–31; 12: 17; 1 John 5: 16.
[71] Theodore of Mopsuestia, *ad loc.*
[72] Matthew 10: 32; Luke 12: 8; John 9: 22; 12: 42; Revelation 3: 5.

corresponding 'confession' of his faithful disciples by Christ. Further, the parallel between Timothy's confession in the presence of many witnesses, which recalls the Synoptic allusions to testimony borne before 'governors and kings' and 'to the Gentiles', and the good confession made by Christ himself before Pilate, strongly suggests that Timothy's confession, too, was made in a trial in court. Possibly the reference may be to an actual historical event; possibly a picture of Timothy as an ideal Church leader is being presented to second-century readers, and is so designed as to include the element of faithful witness in time of persecution. In either case the imprisonment of Timothy implied by Hebrews 13: 23 may well be in the writer's mind.

The statement that Jesus witnessed or testified to the good confession raises other problems. According to the Synoptic traditions, the answer of Jesus to Pilate was no more than: 'You say [that I am king of the Jews]'.[73] It is Jesus' silence, rather than any utterance, before Pilate that the Synoptic Gospels emphasise. Behind 1 Timothy 6: 13 there may lie a different tradition, possibly also underlying the Fourth Gospel, of a more extended dialogue than the Synoptists record between Jesus and Pilate; or it is just conceivable that the author of the Pastorals actually knew the Fourth Gospel and its story of Jesus' witness to the truth in Pilate's court. The absence of information in the Gospels about any verbal ὁμολογία made by Jesus before Pilate has prompted a number of exegetes to interpret the 'good confession' as a synonym for Jesus' actual death.[74] This is, however, highly unlikely. Although the verb μαρτυρεῖν passes over from the sense of 'to witness' to that of 'to be a martyr' in such second-century writings as the *Martyrdom of Polycarp*[75] and Irenaeus, *Adversus Haereses*,[76] and may be approaching that meaning in 1 Clement 5.3–7, there seems to be no parallel to the combination of the verb in this sense with the noun ὁμολογία. The latter never means 'martyrdom' in the sense of a martyr's death as such; it is virtually a technical term for a martyr's verbal confession of his faith. If in this case, nevertheless, the phrase did refer to the death of Jesus, ἐπὶ Ποντίου Πιλάτου would have to mean, as in the Creeds, 'in the time of Pontius Pilate'. This, too, is unlikely. In the credal formulae that phrase is intended to locate the Gospel event in history;

[73] Mark 15: 2; Matthew 27: 11; Luke 23: 3.
[74] E.g. C. H. Turner, *JTS* 28 (1926/7), 270–3; J. Jeremias *Die Briefe an Timotheus und Titus* (Göttingen, 1937); J. N. D. Kelly *A Commentary on the Pastoral Epistles* (London, 1963); H. von Campenhausen, *Die Idee des Martyriums in der alten Kirche* (Göttingen, 1964); M. Dibelius, *Die Pastoralbriefe* (Tübingen, 1966).
[75] 1.1; 19.1; 21.1.   [76] III.3.4.

here the intention clearly is to state where Jesus made his confession, namely, in Pilate's court. The probability, then, seems to be that Timothy is being represented as a faithful confessor who testified in court, following the example of the Lord.

The remaining passage is the apparently somewhat similar allusion to the μαρτυρία Ἰησοῦ that is the Spirit of prophecy (Revelation 19: 10). This cannot be discussed here, partly for the reason that it forms the subject of the preceding study in this book (above, pp. 101–17), partly because I have treated it at some length in a contribution to another volume.[77] Suffice it now to say that I am unpersuaded by the large number of commentators who urge us to understand the phrase 'the testimony of Jesus' subjectively, as 'the witness borne by Jesus', and that I consider the correct interpretation to be that which takes the genitive objectively, so that the allusion is to 'witness borne to Jesus'. The expression is then parallel to the μαρτύριον τοῦ Κυρίου of 2 Timothy 1: 8, which means 'testimony borne to our Lord' (RSV, 'testifying to our Lord') and closely resembles both the Pauline use of μαρτύριον when it is practically synonymous with εὐαγγέλιον,[78] and also its use by Polycarp when speaking of the 'testimony of [i.e. 'to'] the Cross'.[79] The objective sense is supported by Revelation 1: 2, 9; 12: 17, and 20: 4. On the other hand, the many attempts to explain 'the testimony of Jesus' on the basis of taking the genitive subjectively seem unsuccessful. It is very hard to give a convincing account of what this testimony of Jesus actually was. To suppose that it was not any particular utterance, nor even his teaching as a whole or his general attitude, but rather his death, might be plausible if it could be explained how the death of Jesus, while it might indeed inspire martyrs to die, could be the spirit of *prophecy*, or be somehow identified with the Holy Spirit. On the other hand, the situation of crisis depicted in the Apocalypse, where the enemies of the faithful are trying to force them to apostatise, is a most appropriate setting for the angel's assurance that it is the Holy Spirit of prophecy that inspires every loyal witness to, or confession of, Jesus. That witness to Jesus is, as it were, the very essence of prophetic inspiration might be taken as a text to sum up the whole theme of the 'pneumatology of martyrdom'.

[77] The forthcoming Festschrift for Bo Reicke (Leiden, 1980).
[78] 2 Thessalonians 1: 10; 1 Corinthians 1: 6; 2: 1 (if μυστήριον is not read here).
[79] *Ep.* 7.1.

Suffering and martyrdom in the Odes of Solomon

BRIAN MCNEIL

It has been my privilege and my pleasure to know Geoffrey Styler for the past ten years, as a priest, a teacher and a scholar, and above all, as a friend of unfailing sensitiveness and delicacy of character. It is my aim in this short study to help round off the historical part of this tribute to him by pointing to something of the earliest developments of Christian reflection on martyrdom and suffering in the period after the writing (but before the canonisation) of the New Testament documents studied by other contributors. The most important texts of the second century for this question are well known: the letters of Ignatius of Antioch, the *Martyrdom* of Polycarp of Smyrna, the *Acts* of Justin and his companions, the accounts by Hegesippus of the persecution of the early leaders of the Church in Jerusalem, the *Letter* of the Churches in Gaul about the persecution there, the *Acts of the Scillitan Martyrs*, and the recently-discovered Second Apocalypse of James.[1] Light has been thrown on some of these texts in the previous contribution, and instead I shall discuss a body of literature that has not been much considered in this context, the Odes of Solomon.[2]

The Odes contain, on first inspection, little that has to do with Christian suffering. The references to the 'war' for which the believers must be prepared (Odes 8.7; 9.6ff) undoubtedly speak of a real conflict with human adversaries, but this is a 'war' fought against heretics (as in Odes 18 and 38), and the odist expects that he will conquer (cf. Ode

---

[1] On this last-named text, see Alexander Böhlig, 'Zum Martyrium des Jakobus', *NovT* 5 (1962), 207–13; S. Kent Brown, 'Jewish and Gnostic Elements in the Second Apocalypse of James (CG v, 4)', *NovT* 17 (1975), 225–37, with literature cited there; W.-P. Funk, *Die zweite Apokalypse des Jakobus aus Nag-Hammadi-Codex V: Neu herausgegeben, übersetzt und erklärt*, TU 119 (Berlin, 1976).

[2] I cite the Odes in the enumeration of James Hamilton Charlesworth, *The Odes of Solomon*, Texts and Translations 13, Pseudepigrapha Series 7 (Missoula, 1977), corrected reprint of 1st ed. (Oxford 1973). All translations are my own.

29.8–10). It is in this sense that the phrase ᵓ*ylyn dzkw* (8.11*b*) should be understood: it is 'those who have conquered' in the war concerning *truth* who are urged to 'put on the garland' (8.11*a*). There is little indication that such a conflict will entail physical suffering; we may compare the language used by Paul at 2 Corinthians 10: 3–5.

The Odes of Solomon do, however, have a great deal to say, usually *ex ore Christi*, about the sufferings of Jesus,[3] and it is here that we find something that has to do with the sufferings of his followers. If in Ode 42 the language is basically serene as he speaks of his sufferings and the redemption they brought –

'All those who persecuted me have died:
and those who trusted in me have sought me, because I am living.
And I arose and am with them,
and I shall speak by their mouths.
For they have rejected those who persecuted them,
and I have cast over them the yoke of my love.
As is the arm of the bridegroom on the bride,
so is my yoke on those who know me:
and as the bridal-chamber is spread forth in the house of the bridal pair,
so is my love on those who believe in me' (42.5–9)[4]

– the language used in Ode 39 is much more turbulent: after a description of the raging rivers that menace those who reject the Lord (39.1–4), the odist writes,

'And those who cross them in faith
shall not be shaken:
and those who walk on them without blemish
shall not be greatly moved.
Because the sign on them is the Lord,
and the sign is the way of those who cross in the name of the Lord.
Put on, therefore, the name of the Most High, and know him,
and you will cross without danger:
for the rivers will obey you.' (39.5–8)

---

[3] In a few cases, such as Odes 25 and 35, it is not wholly clear whether the poem is written *ex ore odistae* or *ex ore Christi*, nor on what grounds one could reach a decision. In the case of the Odes quoted in this study, it is sufficiently clear who the speaker is (see also the next footnote).

[4] I agree with August Vogl, 'Oden Salomos 17, 22, 24, 42: Übersetzung und Kommentar', *Oriens Christianus* 62 (1978), 60–76, that the whole of Ode 42 is to be read as *ex ore Christi*.

The meaning of these verses, which are not yet explicitly christological, is made clear in the remainder of the Ode (verses 9–13):

> 'The Lord has bridged them by his word (*bmlth*):
> and he walked and crossed them on foot.
> And his footsteps stood firm on the water and were not destroyed,
> but are like a beam that is fashioned in truth.
> On either side the waves were lifted up,
> but the footsteps of our Lord Messiah stood firm:
> and they are not blotted out,
> nor destroyed.
> And the way has been set for those who cross after him,
> and for those who complete the path of faith in him
>   [literally, 'of his faith']
> and adore his name.
> Hallelujah!'

Like his contemporary Hermas, the author of the Odes of Solomon steadfastly resists the temptation to call a spade a spade; unlike Hermas, however, he provides no authorised interpretation of what his imagery signifies.[5] The interpreter must therefore pick his way with care when he seeks to render the meaning of the Odes in more systematically theological language, for the danger of over-interpretation is always present. Bearing this in mind, we may go on to consider my statement that the meaning of Ode 39.5–8 is made clear in the verses that follow.

First, it is reasonably clear that the poet is drawing on the tradition of the walking of Jesus upon the waters (cf. Mark 6: 45–52; Matthew 14: 22–33; John 6: 15–21), however this story was transmitted to him,[6] and using this image not primarily to say something about the historical ministry of the Saviour, but to say something about his conquering of death. For the 'waters' that 'our Lord Messiah' crosses are the waters of death, the waters in which all the adversaries of God will perish; and in his crossing he has opened a path for those who believe in him, so that they may follow him and so escape drowning.

Secondly, we may say also that the notion of the death of Jesus is

---

[5] In the one case where there is a psychopomp, Ode 38, the interpretation given to the poet by the personified Truth is itself clothed in obscure imagery.

[6] With Ode 39.13c, *wsgdyn lšmh*, cf. Matthew 14: 33, προσεκύνησαν αὐτῷ – a further parallel, but, like all the other parallels, insufficiently close to permit us to conclude that the odist knew this story in the form in which the canonical Gospels transmit it to us. On the soteriological significance of the image of walking on the waters, see my 'Coptic Evidence of Jewish Messianic Beliefs (Apocalypse of Elijah 2: 5–6)', *Rivista degli Studi Orientali* 51 (1977), 39–45.

involved. The imagery of the waters of death in itself suggests this, as does the mention of 'waves' (verse 11*a*) when this is compared with the use of this imagery in the speech of the Saviour in Ode 31.6ff.[7] But more than this: the phrase *qysʾ dmtqn bšrrʾ* (39.10*b*), 'the beam [or, 'wood'] that is fashioned [or, 'framed'] in truth', is no arbitrary flowering of poetic fancy, but alludes directly to the Cross of Jesus.[8] His footsteps were not destroyed (verse 10*a*, 12*b*: in each case the verb *ḥbl* is employed): in other words, he himself was not destroyed (cf. the consistent use of *ḥbl* and its derivatives in the Odes to speak of physical or spiritual death),[9] and the path that his footprints left on the waters when he 'bridged' them has not been erased, but remains so that those who cross afterwards may walk in safety.

Thirdly, this path is 'the path of faith in him' (verse 13*b*), of those who have put on his name, of those who know him (verse 8),[10] and we are pointed here to the ecclesial dimension, and perhaps to the rite of

---

[7] Cf. Ode 31. 11:

> 'But I stood unmoved like a solid rock
> which is pounded by waves and endures.'

In verse 11*b* I follow the reading of MS H, *mn gllʾ*. MS N has undoubtedly the harder reading, *mn kʾpʾ gllʾ*, but since this requires emendation to make sense, it seems to me better to follow H. The plural *kʾpʾ* in verse 11*b* may have been produced by a scribe whose eye strayed to the singular *kʾpʾ* in verse 11*a*. For a different judgement, and proposed emendations, see Charlesworth, *Odes of Solomon*, pp. 117–18 (repeating the argument of his first edition), and G. R. Driver, 'Notes on Two Passages in the Odes of Solomon', *JTS* n.s. 25 (1974), 434–7. (After this study was concluded, Dr Michael Lattke kindly sent me a copy of his *Die Oden Salomos in ihrer Bedeutung für Neues Testament und Gnosis*, Orbis Biblicus et Orientalis 25/1 and 2 (Göttingen, 1979): I am happy to see that his judgement, vol. I, p. 49, n. 1, agrees with mine.)

[8] Cf. the use of the word *qysʾ* in Odes 27.3*b* and 42.2*a*, and my analysis in 'A Liturgical Source in Acts of Peter 38', *Vigiliae Christianae* 33 (1979), 342–6. There has been general agreement among commentators since the publication of the *editio princeps*, J. Rendel Harris, *The Odes and Psalms of Solomon* (Cambridge University Press, 1909), that in these two verses the odist has Christ's Cross in mind.

[9] Cf., for example, the use of *ḥbl* earlier in this Ode, verse 2*b*, where it is part of the extended metaphor of the death that the rivers bring; and 38.9, where the poet employs this verb or its derivatives five times in three lines to speak of the heretics who corrupt those who follow them.

[10] For the odist, to 'know' is the characteristic activity of the Christian (cf., for example, 6.6ff, which speak of missionary activity as spreading the knowledge of the Lord), and in this sense the Odes may certainly be called 'gnostic'. But I agree with J. H. Charlesworth, 'The Odes of Solomon – Not Gnostic', *CBQ* 31 (1969), 357–69, that one cannot call them 'gnostic' in the same sense as the writings of Valentinus or the Gospel of Mary are 'gnostic'. On this question, see the short but very illuminating study by Jonathan Z. Smith, 'Birth Upside Down or Right Side Up?', *History of Religions* 9 (1969–70), 281–303.

baptism in which the name of the Lord is put on. The pervasive use of the imagery of water in this hymn may be judged to increase the probability that an allusion to baptism is part of the poet's intention, and especially in view of the conceptual link between baptism and death that is made in the New Testament (cf. Luke 12: 50, and the Pauline (and ? deutero-Pauline) paraenesis of Romans 6 and Colossians 2) and in the *Peri Loutrou* of Melito of Sardis.[11]

Fourthly, in the choice of imagery there is at least a hint that the disciple's following is not envisaged in a general manner, but rather that he is called to suffer as Christ suffered. It is, indeed, true that Christ's act of crossing the waters has made it possible at all for the Christian to cross in safety: this is, so to speak, an affirmation that in the Saviour something objective has taken place with consequences for our understanding of man and his salvation (cf., in this connection, the soteriology expressed in the *homo renovatus* anthropology of Ode 15). Nevertheless, nothing is said to imply that the disciple's crossing will be upon waters of which the lethal character has been neutralised: the rivers will be obedient *only* to those who profess faith. Jesus declares in the Odes of Solomon that he did not perish (28.17), but not that he did not die;[12] the 'sign' (*'t'*) that is on the waters (39.7) is surely the sign of the Cross.[13]

We may now reconsider the apparent serenity of the language of the Saviour in the passage from Ode 42, the last in the collection, which I quoted earlier. There is a genuine serenity here, a serenity that shines through many of the Odes (cf., for example, the particularly beautiful Odes 3, 26, and 40): but it is a serenity that was paid for. The 'spreading-forth' of Christ on the Cross (42.1–2) made possible his spreading-forth of the bridal-chamber of his love for those who believe in him (verse 9): in verse 1*b* we have the noun *mth'*, a derivative of the verb *mth*, which we have in verse 9*a*. And these disciples, who love the Saviour (verse 4*a*), must reject those who persecute them *before* he will throw over them the yoke of his love (verse 7): yet, once again, this act of rejection is possible only because the Saviour has first risen (*wqmt ly*) and has spoken through their mouths (verse 6).[14] Comparison with

---

[11] I do not imply that the odist *need* have known any of these New Testament texts. He is undoubtedly still early enough for us to speak of oral transmission of traditions about Jesus and patterns of catechesis.

[12] On the proper framework for interpreting the christological language of the Odes, see my 'Le Christ en vérité est Un', *Irénikon* 51 (1978), 198–202.

[13] Cf. the use of *'t'* in Odes 27.2 and 42.1, and p. 139, n. 8 above.

[14] The referent of the imagery (if we may so speak) in verses 11ff, drawn from the tradition of the harrowing of hell, adds a further dimension to this picture. The Saviour 'formed a synagogue of the living among the dead' when he 'spoke with living lips' (verse 14). This language moves on several

other Odes might suggest that verse 6*b* has to do with the act of the composition of hymns of praise (cf., for example, 6.1f; 14.7f), but the whole context of Ode 42 surely requires us to see it as more tightly bound to verse 7*a*, which immediately follows it, and to understand it on the lines of the promise of Jesus in the Gospels that those on trial will be given words to speak (cf. Mark 13: 11 and parallels). Here, as in Ode 39, the *imitatio Christi*, made possible only by the prior fact of his victory, involves persecution.

But, in the persecution, the presence and support of the Lord are promised. And so, in Ode 5, the poet can express confidence that his persecutors (*rdwpy*, verse 4) will not have the final word. The reality of the suffering is not denied, but its ultimacy is so decisively rejected that here, as in Ode 18, the poet can use the past tense (5.8–9) to speak of the defeat of his foes for which he prays fervently in 5.2–7. He trusts in the Saviour:

> 'And though all that is visible should perish,
> I shall not die:
> because the Lord is with me
> and I am with him.
> Hallelujah!' (verses 14–15)

Here there may be a faint echo of Song of Songs 2: 16: 'My beloved is mine and I am his' (cf. also Song of Songs 6: 3), just as there may be in Ode 42.8, 'As is the arm of the bridegroom over the bride...', an echo of Song of Songs 2: 6 and 8: 3: 'O that his left hand were under my head, and that his right hand embraced me!' If so, it is no lightly-obtained union with Christ that is spoken of in such intimate imagery, but one forged in fire:

> 'The dagger shall not divide me from him,
> nor the sword'. (28.5)[15]

planes: we need not exclude a possible reference to the harrowing of hell, to the salvific work of the Saviour in his earthly ministry in gathering a community, and to his act in bringing those who have died at the hands of their persecutors to life with him. A similar sort of oscillation may be seen in Ode 24, where the thought of the poet embraces the baptism of Jesus, his descensus into Sheol, judgement, and the forming of the community of believers.

[15] W. Baumgartner, 'Das trennende Schwert. Oden Salomos 28: 4', in W. Baumgartner, O. Eißfeldt, K. Elliger and L. Rost (eds.), *Festschrift Alfred Bertholet zum 80. Geburtstag* (Tübingen, 1950) (reprinted in his *Zum Alten Testament und seiner Umwelt* (Leiden, 1959), pp. 274–81), argues that the image in this passage is a sexual one. Without wishing to exclude this interpretation altogether, I should prefer to interpret the image on the lines of Romans 8: 35ff.

In the self-understanding of the Christian Church, it has consistently been sensed that martyrdom and suffering have an ecclesial significance that transcends the appreciation of the heroism of individuals: for to speak of martyrdom is to say something that is, in a profound sense, christological – 'tu vincis in martyribus'.[16] Here, the Judaeo-Christian poet of the Odes of Solomon is wholly at one with the tradition of the *Großkirche*.

[16] From the Office hymn *Rex gloriose martyrum*, quoted from the *editio typica* of the Roman Breviary, *Liturgia Horarum iuxta Ritum Romanum*, 10th ed., vol. I (Vatican City, 1977), p. 1058.

Suffering and messianism in Yose ben Yose

WILLIAM HORBURY

'If the Sage ranked higher than a Prophet, the Precentor [*Vorbeter*] was at the least a Psalmist', wrote Zunz of the post-biblical development in Judaism;[1] but the Sage has had the lion's share of attention from students of rabbinic religion. This is partly, of course, a consequence of Zunz's own conclusion that the surviving relics of early synagogal poetry are post-Talmudic. Since he wrote, however, the Cairo Geniza has multiplied these relics,[2] and it has come to be generally recognised that the early *piyyuṭim* considerably antedate the Arab conquest.[3] Of the earliest poets known by name, Yose ben Yose, Yannai and Kalir, the first two are set at various times in the Amoraic period, up to and including the sixth century.[4] Talmud and liturgy are held to disclose still earlier poems, reciprocally related to midrashic literature in the process of formation.[5] Johann Maier nevertheless still constitutes an admirable exception when he gives space to the early *piyyuṭim* in an account of religion in the Talmudic period.[6]

A story current from the fifth century onwards relates it as remarkable that Eleazar, son of R. Simeon b. Yohai, should have been both a

---

[1] L. Zunz, *Die Ritus des synagogalen Gottesdienstes geschichtlich entwickelt* (Berlin, 1859), p. 6.

[2] P. E. Kahle, *The Cairo Geniza*, 2nd ed. (Oxford, 1959), pp. 34–48.

[3] On the *piyyuṭ* and its origins I. Elbogen, *Der jüdische Gottesdienst in seiner geschichtlichen Entwicklung*, 3rd ed. (Frankfurt a. M., 1931, repr. Hildesheim, 1962), pp. 280–305 is supplemented in the Hebrew translation, ed. J. Heinemann (Tel-Aviv, 1972), pp. 210–28 (cited below as Elbogen–Heinemann); cf. S. W. Baron, *A Social and Religious History of the Jews*, 2nd ed., vol. VII (New York, 1958), pp. 89–105; Petuchowski in J. Heinemann and J. J. Petuchowski, *Literature of the Synagogue* (New York, 1975), pp. 205–13; and G. Stemberger, *Geschichte der jüdischen Literatur* (Munich, 1977), pp. 96–100.

[4] Heinemann–Petuchowski, *Literature of the Synagogue*, p. 208.

[5] Elbogen–Heinemann, p. 211; Heinemann–Petuchowski, *Literature of the Synagogue*, p. 209.

[6] J. Maier, *Geschichte der jüdischen Religion* (Berlin, 1972), pp. 153–8.

William Horbury

teacher of Scripture and Mishnah and a precentor.[7] The discontinuity as well as the link between house of study and Synagogue is here underlined. *Piyyuṭim*, belonging to worship rather than to debate or homily, may therefore complement more strictly rabbinic sources.

There follows accordingly a modest venture in adding to the passages commonly discussed with reference to views of suffering and messianism in the rabbinic period. Valuable recent surveys of both subjects restrict themselves to rabbinic texts in the narrower sense, although the relevance of the *piyyuṭim* is noted.[8] Here attention is confined to Yose ben Yose, the earliest of the named poets.[9]

Yose's significance for our purpose derives especially from the *Sitz im Leben* of his poems, but is enhanced by their likely date. A. Mirsky, whose work in producing the first critical edition of Yose with commentary makes this attempt possible, dates him about the fifth century.[10] This means that he is an independent source from the period of the early haggadic midrashim. Genesis Rabbah and Lamentations Rabbah are ascribed to the beginning of the fifth century, and the earliest homiletic midrashim, Leviticus Rabbah and Pesikta de-Rav Kahana, are held to have been compiled during it. A number of parallels between Yose and the midrashim are consistent with such datings, but noteworthy differences in emphasis also emerge.

For Mirsky's dating, not the earliest that has been proposed, stylistic considerations are important. Whereas Yannai and Kalir are rich in characteristically rabbinic material, Yose uses it only occasionally, while hymn-like compositions that are probably earlier than Yose (such

---

[7] Pesikta de-Rav Kahana (PRK) 27.1 (ed. B. Mandelbaum (2 vols., New York, 1962), II, 403f); Lev. R. 30.1 (ed. M. Margulies (5 vols., Jerusalem, 1953–60), IV, 790, with citation of parallels including Cant. R. on 3:6). The texts of Mandelbaum and Margulies, each continuously paginated throughout, are cited below by editor's name.

[8] Rachel Rosenzweig, *Solidarität mit den Leidenden im Judentum*, Studia Judaica 10 (Berlin, 1978); P. Schäfer, 'Die messianischen Hoffnungen des rabbinischen Judentums zwischen Naherwartung und religiösem Pragmatismus', in C. Thoma (ed.), *Zukunft in der Gegenwart* (Bern, 1976), pp. 96–125 (on the *piyyuṭim*, p. 96) (not available to me as reprinted in Schäfer, *Studien zur Geschichte und Theologie des rabbinischen Judentums*, AGJU 15 (Leiden, 1978)); on a single important saying and its parallels, E. Bammel, 'Israels Dienstbarkeit', in E. Bammel, C. K. Barrett and W. D. Davies (eds.), *Donum Gentilicium* (for D. Daube; Oxford, 1978), pp. 295–305.

[9] Besides Mirsky, cited in the following footnote, see on Yose J. H. Schirmann in *Encyclopedia Judaica* XVI (1971), cols. 856f (literature); Baron, *History*, VII, 90–3, and nn. 38–41; Elbogen, *Der jüdische Gottesdienst*, pp. 306–8, with additional note in Elbogen–Heinemann, p. 231; Maier, *Gesch. der jüdischen Religion*, pp. 155–7.

[10] A. Mirsky, *Yosse ben Yosse: Poems* (Hebrew: Jerusalem, 1977), p. 13.

as the *Alenu* prayer[11]) have no trace of it at all.[12] In respect of rabbinic matter Yose's contacts appear to be with Palestinian rather than Babylonian tradition.[13] His name forms an independent ground for the view that he is of Palestinian origin.[14]

His surviving poems are mostly handed down in connection with the liturgy of the 'Days of Awe', New Year and Atonement. Saadia in his early tenth-century Order of Prayer gives a Tekiata for New Year and an Avodah for the Day of Atonement, both by Yose.[15] The Tekiata, thought to have been written originally as a version of this part of the New Year liturgy itself,[16] is used by Saadia rather as his choice among many current hymns. Its three poems *I will praise my God, I fear amid my doings* and *I will flee for help* (ʾahallelah ʾelohay, ʾefḥad be-maʿasay, ʾanusah le-ʿezrah) incorporate respectively the *catenae* of texts inserted in the Tefillah at New Year, known as *Kingdoms, Remembrances* and *Trumpets* (Mishnah, Rosh ha-Shanah 4.6). The Avodah of Yose chosen by Saadia is *I will recount the mighty works*, ʾazkhir gevuroth, Yose's longest composition in this genre, in which (below, p. 166) it was customary to recite the works of God from Creation to the institution of the Aaronic ministry of the Tabernacle, thereafter describing, with Mishnaic quotations, the Temple-service (ʿavodah) of the Day of Atonement; a debt to Ecclesiasticus, especially chapter 50, is apparent.[17] Shorter examples of the Avodah by Yose are *I will tell the great works*, ʾasapper gedoloth, recovered from Geniza fragments, and *Thou hast established the world in the multitude of mercy*, ʾattah konanta ʿolam be-rov ḥesed, preserved in the French rite and its North Italian offshoot of Asti–Fossano–Moncalvi (*Apam*).[18] 'Still to-day the visitor who...hears... the Avodah of Kippur in isolated communities like that of Asti is struck

---

[11] Elbogen, *Der jüdische Gottesdienst*, pp. 8of.

[12] Mirsky, *Yosse ben Yosse*, pp. 12f.

[13] *Ibid.* pp. 29–31, acknowledging and enlarging upon an observation of S. D. Luzzatto. At pp. 32–6 Mirsky lists parallels with *Pirqe Rabbi Eliezer*, the date of which, he suggests, should be reconsidered in their light.

[14] Mirsky, *Yosse ben Yosse*, p. 13.

[15] I. Davidson, S. Assaf and B. I. Joel, *Siddur R. Saadja Gaon* (Jerusalem, 1941), pp. 225–33, 264–75.

[16] [E.] D. Goldschmidt (ed.), *Maḥzor la-yamin ha-norʾaim* (2 vols., Jerusalem, 1970), I, p. 45 of the Introduction. He prints and annotates the Tekiata in the text, pp. 238–42, 251–6, 265–70. The ancient *Tekiata de-vey Rav*, used in present-day New Year rites, is translated and discussed in Heinemann–Petuchowski, *Literature of the Synagogue*, pp. 57–69.

[17] C. Roth, 'Ecclesiasticus in the Synagogue Service', *JBL* 71 (1952), 171–8.

[18] Goldschmidt, *Maḥzor la-yamim ha-norʾaim*, II, p. 23 of the Introduction. He prints and annotates Yose's ʾomnam ʾashamenu and ʾattah konanta ʿolam be-rov ḥesed in the text, pp. 20–4, 465–79.

by certain resemblances to the modes and phrasing of the Gregorian chant.'[19] Also for the Day of Atonement are *Truly our sins,* ʾ*omnam* ʾ*ashamenu*, a Selihah of the type known as Hataʾnu from its refrain 'we have sinned'; another lament, *We have no High Priest,* ʾ*eyn lanu kohen gadol*; and possibly *Once thou didst make us the head,* ʾ*az le-roʾsh tattanu*, a second Hataʾnu.

The simple style of these generally acknowledged poems, on which the remarks below are based, depends for effect on devices such as paronomasia, alphabetic arrangement, or the repetition of a final word or refrain. Rhyme is not used – a writer of the Geonic period indeed classed Yose as a poet without rhyme[20] – although it occurs in one of the four poems of less sure attribution printed by Mirsky in an appendix. Yose's characteristic beauty was singled out by Graetz as the terse phrase whereby, for example, the Hasmonaeans, in words recalling Romans 15: 16, are 'offering kingship as priestly service', *mekhahane melukhah*.[21]

So biblical a poet as Yose would perhaps have viewed the concerns designated in the title of this study by 'suffering' and 'messianism' under such headings as 'tribulation' and 'consolation'. However that may be, transposition into scriptural words underlines that biblical interconnection of the two topics which was memorably traced by E. C. Hoskyns.[22] Such an interconnection emerges also from the principal occasions for which Yose writes. The messianic hopes of New Year spring from present tribulation, and on the Day of Atonement that tribulation, token though it be of Israel's sin, is also the deep whence arises the cry for pardon and redemption.

The context of this volume, concerned with the christological interpretation of suffering in the New Testament, encourages attention to this constant association of suffering with messianic hope. The link appears with special clarity in Gershom Scholem's understanding of messianism as 'not so cheerful' as belief in progress, indeed as 'a theory of catastrophe'.[23] To unite the expressions of suffering and messianism

[19] Leo Levi, 'Sul rapporto tra il canto sinagogale in Italia e le origini del canto liturgico cristiano', in *Scritti in Memoria di Sally Mayer* (Jerusalem, 1956), p. 141.
[20] W. Bacher, 'Aus einer alten Poetik (Schule Saadja's)', *JQR* 14 (1902), 742–4 (742).
[21] H. Graetz, 'Die Anfänge der neuhebräischen Poesie', *MGWJ* 9 (1860), 20. The phrase is from ʾ*ahallelah* ʾ*elohay*, line 28.
[22] 'Tribulation – Comfort', in E. C. Hoskyns, *Cambridge Sermons* (London, 1938), pp. 121–9.
[23] G. Scholem, *The Messianic Idea in Judaism* (London, 1971), pp. 37f, 7f, and index s.v. 'Catastrophe'.

is a characteristic of the *piyyuṭ* throughout its history.[24] Yose's material on the two topics will be treated separately, but his words are often relevant to both at once.

SUFFERING

(a) The interpretation of suffering

Yose's poems bear out Rachel Rosenzweig's observation that the ancient Jewish sensitivity to communal suffering overshadows awareness of universal and individual pain.[25] The present sufferings most prominent in Yose are the twin corporate afflictions of servitude and the loss of the Temple-service. It is often hard to judge how far the descriptions of calamity are symbolic; but the bitterness of outward, historical experience certainly informs Yose's poems.

'The Service has failed from the House of Service;
  and how shall we serve the Pure One (*zakh*) when a stranger (*zar*)
  makes us serve?...
The joy (*gil*) of the Lots [Leviticus 16: 8] has ceased from us;
  and how shall we go up with joy (*gilah*) when we are in exile (*golah*)?'
  (*ᵓeyn lanu kohen gadol*, lines 3 and 5)

For this predominantly corporate outlook suffering is naturally comforted by messianic hope. Yose's regular consolations are derived especially from the Danielic scheme of the four kingdoms, foreshadowing the end of servitude, and the bridal imagery of the Song of Songs, to assure the return of the Beloved to his desolate dwelling. His biblical interpretations involve the biblical understandings of suffering as punitive, probative and meritorious. As in rabbinic texts, these views appear together without entire consistency.[26]

The punitive view of suffering makes intense awareness of corporate affliction the counterpart of an equally intense consciousness of sin. So, in a lament the closeness of which to historical experience is emphasised by Mirsky, *Yosse ben Yosse*, p. 56, 'we have eaten up the righteousness of our Fathers', the merits of the patriarchs are exhausted (*ᵓomnam ᵓashamenu*, 13, cf. *ᵓefhad be-maᶜasay*, 4; the question how long the merits

---

[24] L. Zunz, *Die synagogale Poesie des Mittelalters* (Berlin, 1855), esp. pp. 5f, 129; similarly Elbogen, *Der jüdische Gottesdienst*, p. 289.

[25] Rosenzweig, *Solidarität*, pp. xiv, 56, 83f.

[26] Rabbinic views of suffering are discussed by Rosenzweig, *ibid.* esp. pp. 56–8, 83f, 188, 224; S. Schechter, *Studies in Judaism*, first series (London, 1896), pp. 259–82; and J. W. Bowker, *Problems of Suffering in Religions of the World* (Cambridge University Press, 1970), pp. 32–7.

of the patriarchs endured is discussed in Lev. R. 36.6[27]). The congregation are thrown back on sheer grace, and still have not kept the commandments.

'Thou didst strengthen us when our hand failed [Leviticus 25: 35];
thou didst make known to us "This do, and live" –
yet hands were not stayed upon us, as her that was overthrown in a
    moment [Lamentations 4: 6].'

(ʾomnam ʾashamenu, 42–4)

Zunz paraphrases this last line: 'Yet we stretched out no helping hand,
behaving like Sodom that was overthrown in a moment',[28] refusal to
'strengthen the hand of the poor' being 'the iniquity of thy sister
Sodom' (Ezekiel 16: 49); and the reference is accordingly to failure in
the very commandment, the pattern of which is the divine grace mentioned two lines earlier. It is not surprising to find strong emphasis
(below, p. 174) on the effect of the Day of Atonement as making Israel
'perfect and upright' (ʾazkhir gevuroth, 275; ʾasapper gedoloth, 60).
The messianic significance of this consciousness of sin lies in the view
that sin delays the kingdom, an assumption manifest in prayers that
Israel may be purified and glorified for the return of the divine presence
(below, p. 161). Repentance, the precondition of redemption according
to one prominent but debated rabbinic view (below, p. 157), may be
implied but is left unmentioned.

The view that suffering may be a test is particularly clear in the lines
on Abraham (below, p. 152). It verges on the further view, vital to the
link between suffering and hope, that suffering will be compensated or
rewarded by God. Once again assumed rather than enunciated, it can,
for example, be combined with the punitive view in an explanation of
Roman dominion.

'The *hairy man* flattered his father with his venison,
    and inherited with the voice of weeping the sword and the KINGDOM.'

(ʾahallelah ʾelohay, 29)

Here Yose follows the midrash that Esau (Edom–Rome), because he
wept (Genesis 27: 38), was granted the *sword* and the *dominion* (Genesis
27: 40) (Mid. Teh. 80.4).[29] This is at once the reward of his suffering,

---

[27] Margulies, pp. 851–3.

[28] Zunz, *Die synagogale Poesie*, p. 163.

[29] References to this and other midrashim in Goldschmidt, *Maḥzor la-yamim
ha-norʾaim*, vol. I, text p. 241, and Mirsky, *Yosse ben Yosse, ad loc.* On Esau
see G. D. Cohen, 'Esau as Symbol in Early Medieval Thought', in A. Altmann
(ed.), *Jewish Medieval and Renaissance Studies* (Cambridge, Mass., 1967),
pp. 19–48.

the punishment of Jacob–Israel, and an implied promise that Israel's present tears will likewise be rewarded with the kingdom.

(b) The figure of the Synagogue

Yose's images for *kenesseth yisra°el*, the Synagogue of Israel, are at the heart of his poetry. The passages cited already exemplify a concentration on the fate of his people, which, natural though it be in liturgical settings, contrasts with the universalist language found together with the nationalist in the hymn-like prayers of the *Tekiata de-vey Rav*.[30] The Synagogue in Yose is a figure of past and future glory but present suffering. Central among his images is that of the bride, for which he combines the Song of Songs with Jeremiah 2 and Ezekiel 16 in a manner perhaps already apparent in 2 Esdras 5: 23–7, and familiar in rabbinic sources from tannaitic passages attributed to R. Akiba onwards.[31]

The three poems of Yose's Tekiata are especially rich in this imagery. The first, *I will praise my God*, °*ahallelah* °*elohay*, is mainly triumphant in tone. It begins confidently with the conquest of Canaan. Israel (lines 13–15) is the master, king Arad the Canaanite his slave; Israel are the seed of the blessed, Canaan the accursed; Israel 'the hosts of the KINGDOM' (*melukhah*, repeated at the end of each line from the *malkhuyyoth*-text Obadiah 21), whereas Canaan are (lines 17f)

'strangers
in the land of the children of Shem, the seed of the KINGDOM'

and victory is harshly evoked with 'the son of Nun slaughtered them'. Then, however, with an abrupt change of tone like that of Psalm 44: 10, Israel themselves are sheep for the slaughter (line 25, of Haman's plot) and doves (*yonim*) sold to Greeks (*yewanim*) (line 28, of Antiochus IV; cf. Joel 3: 6), until finally Esau, last of the 'four kingdoms' rules them. Yet his younger brother will surely inherit (line 30); and in a concluding passage of triumph incorporating the *malkhuyyoth* the Synagogue is the bride 'clear as the sun' of Song of Songs 6: 10, awaiting the divine glory in Zion (line 36, introducing Isaiah 24: 23), and, once again – now with a definitely present reference – God's hosts (line 52, introducing Numbers 23: 21). This messianic conclusion is discussed below (pp. 159–63); here it is only necessary to note the successive images for

[30] Mirsky, *Yosse ben Yosse*, pp. 15f; I. Elbogen, 'Die messianische Idee in den altjüdischen Gebeten', in *Judaica: Festschrift zu Hermann Cohens siebzigstem Geburtstage* (Berlin, 1912), pp. 669–79 (672f).

[31] R. Loewe, 'Apologetic Motifs in the Targum to the Song of Songs', in A. Altmann (ed.), *Biblical Motifs* (Cambridge, Mass., 1966), pp. 159–96 (161); Bammel, *Israels Dienstbarkeit*, p. 302; Rosenzweig, *Solidarität*, pp. 53–6.

Israel: master, seed of the blessed ones, army, seed royal, sheep, doves, bride, and again army. Those of triumph precede and follow those of suffering.

A forcible expression of suffering is the simple negation of the imagery of triumph. So, outside the Tekiata, the language of filiation and the metaphor of the bride recur in lamentation.

'We were reckoned *the holy seed, sons of the living God*:
  we are polluted, and called a people who bring defilement on the
  Name.'

(*'omnam 'ashamenu*, 35f; cf. Isaiah 6: 13; Hosea 2: 1 (1: 10); Ezekiel
22: 5)

'We have offered no frankincense (*levonah*) on the mount of *Lebanon*
  [the Temple, 1 Kings 7: 2]

  and how shall the sin be whitened (*yelubban*) of her that is *fair as the moon* (*levanah* [Song of Songs 6: 10])?'

'The pure myrrh has ceased from her that is *perfumed with myrrh* [Song of Songs 3: 6]

  and how, on the mount of myrrh [Moriah, the Temple-mount, 2 Chronicles 3: 1] shall there rest the *bundle of myrrh* [Song of Songs 1: 13]?'

(*'eyn lanu kohen gadol*, 23, 25)

These negations of course serve to intensify the hope that Synagogue may again be affirmatively described as a holy people, the children of God, a fair bride awaiting the divine bridegroom on his holy hill.[32]

Bridal imagery could be linked triumphantly in midrash with the four-kingdom scheme. Israel 'looked forth as the morning' under Babylon with Daniel, was 'fair as the moon' under Media with Esther, 'clear as the sun' against the Greeks with Mattathias and his sons, and will be 'terrible as an army with banners' to Edom (Song of Songs 6: 10 interpreted in Exod. R. 15.6).[33] Yose uses the same link more subtly in a sustained evocation of alternating fear and hope as Israel moves from tribulation to comfort. In *I will flee for help* (Isaiah 10: 3), the third poem of the Tekiata, he frames the bridal imagery with the symbolism

---

[32] For Song of Songs 1: 13 applied to the resting of the Shekhinah in the rebuilt Temple see Pesikta Rabbati 20.8, edited, with commentary discussing parallels, by K.-E. Grözinger, *Ich bin der Herr, dein Gott!: Eine rabbinische Homilie zum Ersten Gebot* (*PesR 20*), Frankfurter Judaistische Studien 2 (Bern and Frankfurt a. M., 1976), pp. 36, 124–6, 6*.

[33] Text with translation and notes in S. Krauss, *Griechen und Römer*, Monumenta Talmudica 5.1 (repr. Darmstadt, 1972), p. 34.

of timorous creatures such as sheep and dove, met already in the mournful central section of the first poem of the Tekiata (p. 149 above). Synagogue, convinced of the divine presence in her worship, takes heart (lines 2–3) to 'chirp' (Isaiah 10: 14) for help for the 'scattered sheep' (Jeremiah 50: 17), dumb before the (Gentile) 'shearers' who oppress her (Isaiah 53: 7). Yet though the bridegroom said 'Let me hear thy VOICE' (Song of Songs 2: 14; each line of the poem ends with *qol*), he fled when he found no Law in her (line 6). Encouraged by recollection of patriarchs and prophets (lines 7–12), Synagogue goes in search of him like the bride of the Song of Songs (lines 13f). The bridegroom is no longer to be found, as of old, at the Sea or in the Wilderness; he once spoke from the Temple, but 'I have defiled his beloved dwelling' (lines 15–18). This 'I', where 'they' might have been expected, strikingly marks the acute consciousness of sin already noted, especially apparent at this stage in the poem. The first person singular, for which no scriptural source is suggested by Mirsky and Goldschmidt *ad loc.*, may perhaps arise from Ezekiel 8, interpreted as 'the lodger turning out the master of the house' in Lev. R. 17:7 (Margulies, p. 387).

Synagogue remembers, however, that she was precious in the bridegroom's sight (Isaiah 43: 4); for her he cast down the kingdoms in their order until this present (Roman) dominion of the 'Beast of the reeds' (Psalm 68: 31), and, although the time of deliverance is hidden from her in her misery, she knows (here Yose prepares for the *Shofaroth*-texts) that she will rejoice to hear (Song of Songs 5: 2) the Beloved knocking at the doors (lines 19–29). 'For ever will he make me the seal upon his heart, as once under the apple tree he raised me up with a VOICE.' This line 30, with its allusions to Song of Songs 8: 6 and 5, is at once given its (standard)[34] interpretation by 'the voice of the trumpet exceeding loud' in Exodus 19: 16, now cited as the first of the *Shofaroth*. Emboldened as she recalls the giving of the Law, Synagogue prays earnestly for the gathering of the dispersion, reverting to the imagery of desolate biblical birds (Hosea 11: 11; Psalms 84: 4; 56: 1 (title); Isaiah 27: 13; Zechariah 10: 8).

'The sparrow from Egypt has cried from the wilderness,
  and the dove from Assyria has sent forth her VOICE.
Visit the house-sparrow, seek out the silent dove:
  blow for them on the trumpet and hiss for them with a VOICE.'

(lines 36f)

---

[34] For the Song of Songs interpreted of divine love in the giving of the Law, see Loewe, 'Apologetic Motifs', p. 161 and (on 8: 6) p. 172.

There follows immediately the third of the *Shofaroth* (Isaiah 27: 13), and the poem ends with twenty further lines of messianic hope, considered below (pp. 163–5). Its treatment of the Song of Songs is comparable with that of PRK 5.6–9, but the midrash is more consolatory in tone. Thus, whereas PRK 5.8 (Mandelbaum, p. 90) notes positively from Song of Songs 2: 8 that Israel saw the 'leaping' Holy One in Egypt, at the Sea and at Sinai, Yose's lines 15–18, alluding to the same verse, depend on the thought that this was once the case, but is so no longer.

(c) The fathers, the slain, and the disciples of the Wise

The suffering of Israel is also expressed in the sufferings of representative figures. Patriarchs and martyrs (the 'fathers' and the 'slain', *ʾefḥad be-maʿasay*, 4, 47) are prominent here, and it is probable that the rabbis and their pupils also have a place.

The patriarchs are frequently described in terms of glory. They are the 'ancient mountains' of Deuteronomy 33: 15, through whose worth Israel was redeemed from bondage (*ʾefḥad be-maʿasay*, 41, with Targum Ps.-Jon. *ad loc.*; Lev. R. 36.6 (above, n. 27)). In the *sidre ʿavodah*, as in contemporary midrash, Adam has the *wisdom* and *beauty* of Ezekiel 28: 12–15, and God spreads his jewelled couch within the wedding-canopy of Eden (*ʾazkhir gevuroth*, 39f; *ʾattah konanta ʿolam be-rov ḥesed*, 27f; cf. PRK 4.4; Lev. R. 20.2).[35] Jacob's wrestling is viewed not as affliction but as victory; 'blazing fire flees when it wrestles with him', (*ʾazkhir gevuroth*, 102; cf. *ʾattah konanta ʿolam be-rov ḥesed*, 64). Like the division of the sea by Moses, the halting of the sun by Joshua, and the raising of the dead by Elijah and Elisha, it can be cited to demonstrate man's God-given lordship over creation (*ʾattah konanta ʿolam be-rov ḥesed*, 24; cf. PRK 1.3).[36]

Equally strong, however, is the emphasis on patriarchal suffering. Adam received divine comfort after Abel's murder.

'This One bound up the wound of the primaeval creature
when he began to drink the cup mixed for the generations.'
(*ʾazkhir gevuroth*, 65)

The consolation, as in Genesis 4: 25, was Seth; and with an allusion to Psalm 147: 3 the verse expresses the straightforward view stated in messianic form in 2 Corinthians 1: 3–5. Tribulation is interpreted as testing especially in the case of Abraham. God 'tested him ten times' (*ʾasapper gedoloth*, 16), as in Mishnah, Aboth 5.3. The most important

[35] Mandelbaum, pp. 66f; Margulies, p. 446.
[36] Mandelbaum, p. 5.

of these tests in Yose is the sacrifice of Mount Moriah, to which *ʾasapper gedoloth* immediately proceeds. The Akedah is considered separately below at pp. 169–71; here we need only note the benefits of this testing for Israel. Abraham can be appealed to as advocate: 'Perhaps he will accept of you, because you obeyed the VOICE'; and Isaac's silent self-oblation gives a ground for petition: 'Look upon the lamb of Moriah; may the dumbness of his mouth be righteousness for her that did not obey the VOICE' (*ʾanusah le-ʿezrah*, 8f; for the patriarchs as advocates cf. PRK 23.7 (Mandelbaum, pp. 339f)). Readiness to die is also seen in Moses and Aaron. Moses prayed: 'Blot me out, I pray thee', for the sake of the people; and Aaron braved the plague: 'he bounded with the censer until the plague was stayed' (*ʾefḥad be-maʿasay*, 5, 8; Exodus 32: 32; Numbers 17: 11–13 (16: 46–8)).

The 'martyrological' character of the Akedah has often been noted, and the epithet is applied specifically to Yose's version in *ʾazkhir gevuroth*, 91–4 (below, p. 170) by Maier, *Gesch. der jüdischen Religion*, p. 119. It is worth gathering a few other passages in Yose that for convenience may be called martyrological, even though they speak neither of witness, with the New Testament, nor of sanctification of the Name, with the rabbis (but note the phrase 'defilement of the Name', above, p. 150). In all of these passages the sufferers are once again closely linked, or even identified, with the people as a whole. Earlier quotations have described Israel as 'sheep for the slaughter' and 'doves' (above, p. 149), or as a 'scattered' and 'dumb' sheep 'driven away' in exile (above, p. 151; cf. Jeremiah 50: 17, immediately followed by a promise of punishment on the Gentile nations). A line on the Synagogue as bride, however, departs from an otherwise closely followed scriptural model, the *zikhronoth*-text Jeremiah 2: 2, in order to mention the slain as especially remembered by God:

'The High One has greatly longed for the bride of youth:
her slain and her afflicted have come to REMEMBRANCE.'
(*ʾefḥad be-maʿasay*, 47)

'Her slain', *harugeyha*, recalls the rabbinic phrase *haruge malekhuth*, 'those slain by the Empire', applied especially to the so-called 'Ten Martyrs' under Hadrian. The 'fourth kingdom' was regarded in rabbinic thought as worse than its predecessors precisely in this respect, that it made many martyrs.[37] Suffering under the empire is also probably described in *ʾomnam ʾashamenu*, 40: 'we have been slaughtered, great

[37] Krauss, *Griechen und Römer*, p. 20n., p. 24.

and small, as fish swallowed up in the net'; and it is clearly lamented in
ᵓeyn lanu kohen gadol:

'How can we toss the blood [Mishnah, Yoma 1.2] when our blood is
    shed?
...How can we be purified by wood [Ezekiel 41: 22] when we have
    stumbled under the wood [Lamentations 5: 13]?'

(lines 8 and 32, second halves)

Mirsky notes that Targ. Lam. 5.13 interprets 'have been crucified'. It is
possible that the last line also constitutes a bitter hint at the Christian
Empire in particular; 'wood' comes to be used in anti-Christian
polemic.[38] In any case, in accord with the constant use of the first
person throughout the poem, the slain are again identified with the
whole people. The refrain 'we have sinned', after every second line,
immediately follows both references. Martyrdom is thus contextually
interpreted as punishment for the nation's sin; the positive values
attached to suffering elsewhere in Yose may be in the mind of poet and
congregation, but remain unexpressed.

Lastly, the Wise and their disciples are by no means so prominent in
Yose as in contemporary rabbinic homily, but the poet is aware of them
and appears to think of them in connection with representative suffering.
His awareness emerges in a significant adaptation of Psalm 123: 2;
Isaiah 30: 20, where he says of the High Priest in divination that 'his
eyes are to his teacher [the Shekhinah] as those of disciple to master',
ke-thalmid ·la-rav (ᵓazkhir gevuroth, 154). The disciples of the Wise
seem to be regarded as suffering figures in the concluding prayer of
ᵓefḥad be-maᶜasay, which incorporates the *zikhronoth*. The poet has just
mentioned the good works of the generation redeemed from Egypt
(lines 33f, introducing Psalm 111: 4), and is about to speak of the merits
of the patriarchs (line 41, introducing Exodus 2: 24). At this point he
prays (lines 36f):

'Look, O God, upon the dwellers in the gardens [Song of Songs 8: 13]
    hearkening to those who converse on the law for REMEMBRANGE;
Their work is before thee, and their reward is with thee –
    theirs who *eat the bread of carefulness* [Psalm 127: 2] – in the *book of*
    REMEMBRANCE,

    as it is written by the hand of thy prophet, Then they that feared the
    LORD spake one with another; and the LORD hearkened, and heard, and

---

[38] Thus Deuteronomy 21: 23 is applied polemically to the Cross, as noted by
    Jerome, *In Ep. ad Gal.* 2.3, on 3: 13 (14) (*PL* XXVI, 387); cf. B. Lindars,
    New Testament Apologetic (London, 1961), pp. 232–7.

a book of remembrance was written before him, for them that feared the LORD, and that thought upon his name [Malachi 3: 16].'

Israel as a whole is the garden-dweller, according to Canticle Rabbah *ad loc.*; but here the feminine singular participle of Massoretic Text becomes masculine plural, and the verses closely follow Malachi 3: 16, which is applied to converse on Torah in Aboth 3.3. It is likely, therefore, as Mirsky shows, that the 'gardens' (*gannim*) here are houses of study (compare the metaphorical use of *tarbiṣ* for 'academy'), and their 'dwellers' the disciples of the Wise who 'eat the bread of carefulness'. The context in Yose means that the rabbinic students' costly devotion must be regarded as meritorious and representative. His thought will then be close to that vividly expressed in the homily of PRK 11.24, where Simeon b. Yohai's son Eleazar says, when he has laboured in Torah as much as he can, 'Let all the sufferings of Israel come upon me.'[39]

Yose's allusions to patriarchs and martyrs have a hagiographical ring. Abraham is an intercessor, Isaac's death is atoning, and the martyrs are especially remembered by God. Miracles, as is natural in writing of this tendency (cf. Hebrew 11: 33f), are regarded for the moment as man's work rather than God's (compare Professor Lampe on the 'anthropology' of martyrdom; above, pp. 121f). Jewish veneration of the tombs of the patriarchs and the Maccabaean martyrs is attested well before Yose's time, and it is in the century after him that a pilgrim describes Jews as well as Christians offering incense at the patriarchal shrine in Hebron.[40] Yose's relatively slight reference to the disciples of the Wise is in so similiar a vein as to recall that the tombs of rabbis, too, had begun to be venerated. The *pièce justificative* of the Meronites, who in response to dream-apparitions of R. Simeon b. Yohai stole his son Eleazar's body and translated it to the father's tomb in Meron, is found among other places in a composition of Yose's time, PRK 11.23. In such contexts suffering is seen as meritorious and beneficial; 'the sufferer . . . becomes an object of veneration';[41] Israel benefits, and the sufferings of the Synagogue as a whole tend to be seen as a precious sign of favour rather than, or at least as well as, retribution.

'What then is there left to you to say, since the prophets speak of fixed periods concerning the other [three] captivities, whereas for

---

[39] Mandelbaum, p. 200; the parallel Ecc. R. 11.2 edited with notes by G. Dalman, *Aramäische Dialektproben*, 2nd ed. (repr. Darmstadt, 1960), p. 35 and discussed in connection with Matthew 26: 28 by Dalman, *Jesus – Jeschua* (Leipzig, 1922), pp. 158f; these traditions and related account of Rabbi discussed by Rosenzweig, *Solidarität*, pp. 176–88.

[40] E. Bammel, 'Zum jüdischen Märtyrerkult', *TLZ* 78 (1953), cols. 119–26.

[41] Schechter, *Studies in Judaism*, p. 275.

this [present] one they fix no period, but on the contrary add that the desolation will last to the end?'

'Your affairs have gone beyond all tragedy... Where now are the things that you hold sacred? Where is the high priest? Where are the garments, the breastplate and the Urim?'

(Chrysostom, *C. Iud.* 5.10 (resumed in 6.2) and 6.5)[42]

So Chrysostom rhetorically addresses the Jews in 387, when Church members were inclined to frequent the Synagogue for festivals including those 'Days of Awe' for which Yose wrote. There is a striking identity between the twin afflictions – servitude and loss of the Temple-service – singled out in the patristic commonplaces vigorously echoed by Chrysostom, and those that have figured most prominently in Jewish communal expression as represented by Yose. Chrysostom goes on to treat Leviticus 8, which is remembered at the heart of the Day of Atonement Avodah. In both the external and the inner-Jewish source, moreover, the connection is made between these sufferings and the sin that they imply. To note the extent of these shared presuppositions is also, however, to be made more keenly aware of the wholly different general tendency of Yose's poems. Deeply though they lament present suffering, they offer assurance even in the negations of former glory of *We have no high priest* (above, p. 150).

Here the link between Yose and contemporary midrash emerges clearly. Instances in which both draw on a common stock of ideas have already been noted. Rachel Rosenzweig is able to present the midrash as a mode of overcoming suffering,[43] and the compilations ascribed to the fifth century are indeed rich in words of comfort. Joseph Heinemann finds a leading theme of Leviticus Rabbah to be that the sufferings of Israel are in reality 'nothing but loving-kindness and atonement'.[44] He refers especially to chapters 16, 17 and 20, the last-named (on the Day of Atonement) belonging in his view originally to Pesikta de-Rav Kahana (where chapter 26 is parallel). Similarly, quite apart from this chapter, a large section of Pesikta de-Rav Kahana (chapters 16–22) is devoted to consolation.[45] These and other works likely to stand near in time to Yose's poems contain sayings that give the corporate afflictions themselves a strong positive interpretation. So a homily in the name of the

---

[42] *PG* XLVIII, 899, 905, 911.

[43] Rosenzweig, *Solidarität*, pp. 7, 52.

[44] J. Heinemann, 'The Art of Composition in *Leviticus Rabba*' (Hebrew), *Hasifrut*, 2 (1971), 808–34 (822*a*); cf. Heinemann, 'Profile of a Midrash', *JAAR* 39 (1971), 141–50 (148).

[45] W. G. Braude and I. J. Kapstein, *Pesikta de-Rab Kahana* (London, 1975), p. xxi.

third-century Palestinian Samuel bar Nahmani, current in several versions, says that the destruction of Jerusalem (Jeremiah 38: 28) is in fact a cause of rejoicing, since it brought Israel the ἀποχή, quittance (Gen. R. 41(42).3)[46] or ἀπόφασις, annulment (Lev. R. 11.7)[47] of her iniquities. According to Lam. R. 1.51,[48] on that day Menahem ('Comforter', the Messiah) was born, giving hope for the Temple's rebuilding.[49] Again, the saying ascribed to Akiba; 'Poverty is as becoming to the daughter of Jacob as a red band on the neck of a white horse', occurs at Pesikta de-Rav Kahana 14.3 and Lev. R. 13.4; 35.6.[50] E. Bammel shows that it is implicitly messianic: servitude is a part of redemption itself.[51]

Contrasts, however, also appear between Yose and such otherwise comparable midrashic material. They arise in part at least from the fact that Yose speaks in the name of the congregation, while the midrash is closer to words spoken in homily *to* the congregation. Yose expresses, in the manner appropriate to the day of the Jewish year, the sufferings that the preacher addresses as consoler and apologist. Hence Yose allows himself, as with the figure of the Synagogue in *I will flee for help* or in the lines on patriarchal suffering and martyrdom (above, pp. 152–4), to enter with less explicit allusion to comfort than is typical of these midrashic passages into the corporate affliction and longing for redemption. Hence also, perhaps, the strong midrashic tie between suffering and repentance[52] is absent from Yose. He takes no side on the question whether redemption depends on Israel's prior repentance.[53] His concern is not (unless implicitly) to urge repentance, but to express the communal confession of sin and prayer that *God* will purify and redeem his people. His poems thus recall the significant closing words of Mishnah, Yoma: 'The Holy One, blessed be he, cleanses Israel'; and, though they are hardly intended as argument, suggest something of the weight behind the view that redemption is in God's hand alone. Inevitably thereby they lack something of that strongly ethical emphasis on man's

[46] J. Theodor and Ch. Albeck (eds.), *Bereschit Rabba* (repr. Jerusalem, 1965), I, 407.
[47] Margulies, p. 337, apparatus to line 5.
[48] Dalman, *Dialektproben*, pp. 14f.
[49] The traditions cited here are discussed by Rosenzweig, *Solidarität*, pp. 32f.
[50] Mandelbaum, pp. 241f; Margulies, pp. 281, 824.
[51] Bammel in Bammel–Barrett–Davies, *Donum Gentilicium*, p. 303.
[52] Rosenzweig, *Solidarität*, pp. 153f, 223f, brings out the strength of the belief that suffering implies sin.
[53] The rabbinic material is surveyed by A. Marmorstein, 'The Doctrine of Redemption in Saadya's Theological System', in E. I. J. Rosenthal (ed.), *Saadya Studies* (Manchester, 1943), pp. 103–18 (106–12); cf. Schäfer, 'Hoffnungen', esp. pp. 98–100, 110–12, 118 and Bammel in Bammel–Barrett–Davies, *Donum Gentilicium*, pp. 302–4.

co-operation with divine redemption that Schäfer identifies as an important rabbinic contribution to messianic hope.[54]

Despite these points of contrast in treatment, Yose's interpretations of suffering are close to those of the rabbinic midrash. Just as, in Solomon Schechter's exposition of rabbinic thought, 'by a series of conscious and unconscious modifications' the sufferer 'passed from the state of a sinner into the zenith of the saint',[55] so the suffering Synagogue in Yose receives at one and the same time chastenings for sin and the tokens of divine favour. Here Yose may be comparable with the New Testament as well as the rabbis. As Professor Hooker shows above, the Apostle appears to include all his sufferings, without discrimination of cause, in the fellowship of Christ's sufferings.[56] For Yose, however, the present sufferings of the community are messianic in a sense less bound up with the messianic figure. Servitude and the loss of the Temple-service contain within themselves the hope of their reversal in redemption.

MESSIANISM

'King Messiah will arise and restore the kingdom of David to its former dominion. He will *build up* the sanctuary *and gather together the outcasts of Israel* [Psalm 147: 2]. All the laws will be restored in his days as they were of old, and sacrifices will be offered' (Maimonides, *Mishneh Torah* XIV.11.1).[57]

The twin afflictions lamented by Yose become in reverse the twin hopes of messianism. The summary of Maimonides shows these hopes for the kingdom and the Temple-service to be at the heart of messianic tradition, even though he goes on to restrict them by his own this-worldly interpretation. A miraculous redemption, in keeping with earlier tradition, is however expected by his predecessor Saadia, in whose *Beliefs and Opinions* (A.D. 933) the same hopes inform a synthesis of rabbinic messianism in which thirteen stages have been discerned.[58] They include the death of Messiah son of Joseph at the advent of the antichrist Armilus, the battle of Gog and Magog, and the advent of Messiah son of David, before the three fundamental events of the gathering of the exiles, the resurrection of the dead, and the rebuilding

[54] Schäfer, 'Hoffnungen', p. 118.
[55] Schechter, *Studies in Judaism*, p. 281.
[56] M. D. Hooker above, at p. 80.
[57] (Amsterdam, Joseph and Emmanuel Athias, 1702), IV, f. 306*b*; translation and discussion of this passage in Scholem, *Messianic Idea*, pp. 28–32.
[58] Marmorstein in Rosenthal, *Saadya Studies*, p. 113.

of the Temple. Saadia admitted Yose's poems into his Order of Prayer no doubt largely because they were widely current; but his deliberate choice of them from among a great many others also suggests that their messianism, less elaborate than his own though it may well be, did not strike him as inconsistent with the views that he was to synthesise.[59] His scheme of redemption is in fact close to apocalyptic works such as the early seventh-century *Zerubbabel*.

The works mentioned so far present messianism in a unified manner. In rabbinic writings, not least the midrashim likely to be near Yose's time, it is of course reflected fragmentarily. Yose's poems have the interest of appearing to presuppose a connected scheme of redemptive events. One cannot, however, expect such a scheme to be precisely described in poetry. Kalir's poem *In those days and at that time* is very close to *Zerubbabel*, but fails to mention Armilus by name; and a messianic *piyyuṭ* in Saadia's name is far from giving the detail of his prose account.[60] With this caution in view Yose's messianic passages are now considered. The headings of the kingdom and the Temple-service roughly correspond, with certain overlaps, to the principal themes of the Tekiata and the Avodah poems respectively.

(a) The Kingdom

Kingdom is the explicit and traditional theme of the first poem of the Tekiata (Mishnah, Rosh ha-Shanah 4.6). Yose's *kingdom* at the end of each line takes up the last word of Obadiah 21 (above, p. 149), the much-quoted *malkhuyyoth*-text, which unites the national and theocentric elements of messianism.[61] The opening description of the conquest has

---

[59] Saadia is likely to have compiled the *Siddur* after his travels ending in 921, and probably, though not certainly, before he received the title of Gaon in 928; so Assaf in Davidson–Assaf–Joel, *Siddur R. Saadja Gaon*, pp. 22f. Saadia's principles in choosing *piyyuṭim* are summarised by Assaf at p. 21; for his testimony to the great number from which he selected Yose's Tekiata, see p. 225.

[60] Kalir's poem is printed with comments by J. Kaufmann (Even-Shemuel), *Midrashe Geʾullah*, 2nd ed. (Hebrew: Jerusalem–Tel Aviv, 1954), pp. 109–16; for that in Saadia's name see S. Stein, 'Saadya's Piyyut on the Alphabet', in Rosenthal, *Saadya Studies*, pp. 206–26.

[61] Thus it forms the last words of Lev. R. 13, in which the four unclean beasts of Leviticus 11: 4–7 are the four kingdoms, Rome the swine (*ḥazir*) 'returning (*maḥzereth*) the crown to its owners' (text and notes in Krauss, *Griechen und Römer*, p. 20, no. 35); and it is the climax of *Zerubbabel* (A. Jellinek, *Bet ha-Midrasch* (6 parts, repr. Jerusalem, 1967), II, 57, line 4 from bottom). Cohen, 'Esau as Symbol', pp. 19f, gives a general discussion; for the question how far the theocentric climax of I Corinthians 15: 28 is comparable, see, e.g., W. D. Davies, *Paul and Rabbinic Judaism*, 2nd ed. (London, 1962), pp. 292–8.

prepared for the allusion to the downfall of Edom, which, after the mournful central section (above, p. 149), opens the concluding passage. The *hairy man* inherited for a while (above, p. 149), but (lines 30ff):

'the *smooth man* was exalted to be *lord over the brethren* [Genesis 27: 29], and to Jeshurun again shall there turn back the KINGDOM
[cf. Lev. R. 13, n. 60 above];

> as it is written in the law, And he was [or, 'And there was a'] king in Jeshurun, when the heads of the people and the tribes of Israel were gathered together [Deuteronomy 33: 5].'

This text is the first of the *malkhuyyoth*, which are now interwoven with couplets from the poet into a series of prayers and predictions concerning redemption. These appear to form two successive sequences dealing largely but not entirely with the same events. First, the lines on the downfall of Edom, just quoted, are followed by prayer for the establishment of the messianic kingdom in Jerusalem (in words close, as Mirsky notes, to the fourteenth Benediction of the Tefillah[62]):

'Stir and awake the *joy of the whole earth*, and establish thy throne in the city of the KINGDOM.'

(line 33, introducing Psalm 48: 3)

Before Israel, the bride in the 'fair city', the divine glory is to be revealed (lines 35f, introducing Isaiah 24: 23). The link between bride and city is now grounded by lines 39f, recalling that 'the redeemed from Zoan' in the Exodus foresaw in the Spirit their plantation in the holy place (Exodus 15: 17, about to be quoted). One of the scarce Pentateuchal kingdom-texts is thereby incorporated,[63] and a confident recollection of past redemption is introduced. The line on the divine glory is then elucidated, in the same tone of confidence, by a prediction that the Shekhinah will indeed come back to the Temple.

'The gates of the Dwelling were cut down, of the everlasting House [1 Kings 8: 13]
for from between them there ceased the KINGDOM.

---

[62] Translated and discussed in E. Schürer, G. Vermes, F. Millar and M. Black, *The History of the Jewish People in the Age of Jesus Christ*, rev. ed., vol. II (Edinburgh, 1979), pp. 458, 461.

[63] L. J. Liebreich, 'Aspects of the New Year Liturgy', *HUCA* 34 (1963), 125–76 (140) notes the great shortage of kingdom-texts in the Pentateuch.

The Holy One shall come within them for ever,
  and then shall they *lift up their head*, when thou renewest the
  KINGDOM.'

(lines 43f, introducing Psalm 24: 7f, 9f)

Now Yose reverts to the sombre present, hopefully interpreted as a
permitted lengthening of the days (in implied answer to arguments like
that of Chrysostom) before Edom's appointed end (line 48). Here there
accordingly seems to begin a second sequence of references to what is
fundamentally the same series of redemptive events. Obadiah 21 is
introduced (line 49) by a prayer for victory:

'Contend, O *saviours*, take the glory from Edom:
  and set upon the Lord the majesty of the KINGDOM.'

It is followed by an equally earnest prayer for the national purity
appropriate to redemption, quoting and introducing Numbers 23:21.

'Vanity God hates, and he upon our tongue
  sought truth, and there was none; and far away went the KINGDOM.
Shaddai, turn aside iniquity from thy hosts:
  and let them shout unto thee the *shout* of the KINGDOM.'

(lines 51f)

This sharply messianic exegesis, interpreting captivity as punishment
and praying for divine cleansing that the kingdom may be hastened, is
partly paralleled in Targum Pseudo-Jonathan, where 'the shout of a
king' is indeed 'the call to arms of king Messiah'. There is no comparable urgency in the Targum, however, where Israel is seen as already
free from iniquity, interpreted as idolatry – that *he hath not beheld
iniquity in Jacob* being similarly emphasised in the midrash.[64] There is
an even more marked contrast between Yose and the non-messianic
Onkelos on this verse (seeing Israel are not idolators, the Memra and
Shekhinah abide with them), followed later by Rashi (God abides with
Israel despite her sins).[65] Here Yose's messianism clearly diverges from
what was to become the royal road of interpretation.

---

[64] The Targums are surveyed by S. H. Levey, *The Messiah: an Aramaic
  Interpretation* (Cincinnati, 1974), p. 19. Neofiti's version of 'the shout of a
  king' is close to Ps.-Jon. (A. Diez Macho, *Neophyti I*, vol. IV (Madrid, 1974),
  p. 227). The first words of the verse are cited in Lev. R. 1.12 (Margulies,
  p. 27) and PRK S. 1.4 (Mandelbaum, p. 44).
[65] A. Berliner, *Der Kommentar des Salomo b. Isak über den Pentateuch*, 2nd ed.
  (1905, repr. Jerusalem, 1962), p. 329.

The next couplet, introducing Psalm 93: 1, takes up its words beforehand and gives them two messianic interpretations; these are analogous with its application especially to the Exodus and Sinai in contemporary homily.[66]

'Thou shalt *bind on majesty*, and *gird thyself with strength* –
   that no more may there be rule by a stranger in the KINGDOM;
Thou shalt *establish the world* – for the wicked one shall be *shaken out*
   [Job 38: 13]
   but one has set righteousness for his feet [Isaiah 41: 2], and he shall
   be crowned with KINGDOM.'

(lines 54f)

The verbs in the allusions to the Psalm-verse can be construed as either prayers or predictions; the latter sense seems more probable in view of the causal clause in the second line of the Hebrew. The 'stranger', then, will rule no longer, the 'wicked one' will be 'shaken out', and a righteous figure will be crowned (*yuṣnaf*; the royal association of *ṣanif* (Isaiah 62: 3) is taken up by Yose in respect of the sacerdotal mitre, *miṣnefeth*, at *ʾazkhir gevuroth*, 161). It is probably the Messiah who is crowned (Mirsky). The 'wicked one' may therefore be the current ruler of the 'kingdom of wickedness', the downfall of which is closely linked in contemporary midrash with Messiah's advent (e.g. PRK 5.9, Mandelbaum, p. 97).[67] The existing plural 'wicked' of Job 38: 13, to which allusion is made, would, however, have suited a reference to the 'wicked kingdom' equally well. Thus 'the time has come for the wicked men to be broken', PRK, *loc. cit.* (Mandelbaum, p. 97). It is striking, therefore, that Yose, without obvious metrical reason, has changed the word into the singular. He very possibly means, although the passage is not clear enough for certainty, to indicate the Gentile ruler conceived as antichrist, who in *Zerubbabel* is termed 'that wicked one' and is indeed, as in Targ. Isa. 11: 4, 'the wicked' slain by the Messiah 'with the breath of his lips' (Isaiah 11: 4).[68]

---

[66] PRK 22.5 (Mandelbaum, p. 330) (the sending of the Flood and the giving of the Law); PRK S. 6.5 (Mandelbaum, p. 469) (the division of the Sea); Midrash Tehillim *ad loc.*, quoted in *Yalkut Shimeoni* on the Writings (Wilna, 1909), no. 847, p. 946 (both the Sea and Sinai).

[67] The passage is quoted as typical of many others by S. Schechter, *Some Aspects of Rabbinic Theology* (repr. New York, 1961), p. 101.

[68] Jellinek, *Bet ha-Midrasch*, II, 56, lines 11f, 14 (*ʾotho rashaᶜ*); 'Armilus the wicked' (*rashaᶜ*) in the commentary on the Song of Songs under the name of Saadia reprinted by Even-Shemuel, *Midrashe Geʾullah*, p. 131, line 7. Job 38: 13 is comparably interpreted of the days of antichrist by Gregory the Great, *Moralia* 29.6 (10–11) (*PL* LXXVI, 482).

The last couplet, introducing Deuteronomy 6: 4, predicts that God shall 'break the staff of wickedness that rules in the KINGDOM' ('the staff of the wicked' (Isaiah 14: 5), is mentioned at PRK, *loc. cit.*), shall abolish idols, and for ever shall be called 'the only One to reign in KINGDOM'. If the previous couplet does indeed refer to antichrist, the train of thought will be comparable with that of *Zerubbabel*: 'and at once after him [Armilus] *the kingdom shall be the LORD's*' (Obadiah 21).[69]

The events of the first sequence are: downfall of Edom, Messiah's throne set up in Jerusalem, return of Shekhinah to Temple. Those of the second sequence are: downfall of Edom, destruction of 'the wicked one' (probably antichrist), God rules alone. The first sequence significantly fails to end with this reference to the final sole rule of God. The omission enhances the likelihood that the second reference to the downfall of Edom (line 48) leads back into the same series of events at a slightly later stage. The servitude envisaged is clearly continuous with that of the present. Line 48 cannot then itself refer to resurgence of 'the wicked kingdom' during the messianic age. Such resurgence would, however, be presupposed by the line on the 'wicked one', if it is rightly taken of antichrist. The midrashim likely to be near Yose's time envisage a threat to the messianic kingdom well after its beginning. Thus Messiah will come and then disappear for a time, during which his faithful followers will have tribulation; or at his advent Gog and Magog will plan their war 'against the LORD and against his anointed' (Psalm 2: 2); or 'the days of the Messiah' can be distinguished from, and placed before, 'the days of Gog and Magog'.[70] Yose appears to expect the attack at the end of the messianic age, or of a distinct stage in it. Herein he would be close to the third midrashic passage and to Revelation 20: 7f as well as to *Zerubbabel*.[71] The events envisaged in the poem as a whole would accordingly be: downfall of Edom, messianic reign in Jerusalem, Shekhinah returns to temple, antichrist rises and is destroyed, God rules alone.

The third poem of the Tekiata, *I will flee for help*, has comparable but not identical messianic references. Synagogue, recalling how the three kingdoms have been cast down for her (above, p. 151), prays 'from the teeth of iron' of the fourth beast (Daniel 7: 7):

[69] Jellinek, *Bet ha-Midrasch*, II, 57, line 4 from the bottom.
[70] PRK 5.8 (Mandelbaum, p. 92) (on Song of Songs 2: 9); PRK 9.11 (Mandelbaum, p. 159) = Lev. R. 27.11 (Margulies, p. 646); Lev. R. 30.5 (Margulies, p. 701).
[71] Gog and Magog come before the days of the Messiah, by contrast, in the tradition of Hanan bar Tahlifa in Sanh. 97*b* (discussed, without reference to this point, by Schäfer, 'Hoffnungen', pp. 15f).

'The measure of my end he has not made known to me:
when in my land shall *the turtle-dove* give VOICE?'

(line 25)

'The voice of the turtle' (Song of Songs 2: 12) is 'the voice of king Messiah' in an exegesis ascribed to the third-century R. Johanan and found among other places at PRK 5.9 (Mandelbaum, p. 97). This interpretation fits well here, and is followed by Mirsky, who cites the parallel from Pesikta Rabbati 75.1. God himself, however, is certainly the subject of the further allusion to the Song of Songs: 'when I hear my Beloved knocking at my doors' (5: 2), which shortly afterwards introduces the first of the *shofaroth*, Exodus 19: 16 (lines 29f; above, p. 151).

Further *shofaroth* are now introduced by couplets describing the giving of the Law (before Psalm 47: 6), praying for the gathering of the exiles (Zechariah 10: 8; version at p. 151 above), praying that the commandments may be treasured (Exodus 19: 19), and noting that the end symbolised by New Year is accompanied by judgement (Psalm 81: 4f). Isaiah 18: 3 is introduced by lines on the resurrection:

'A sound from the grave, a cry from *the rock* [Isaiah 42: 11]
   as the *dry-boned* from *the dust* give VOICE.
See, *an ensign on the mountains*, and the voice of *a trumpet* in the land,
   to cause a cry of joy to be heard from the silent with no VOICE.'

(lines 47f)

The circumstances are unclear. The resurrection is not expressly separated from the events of the messianic age, such as the ingathering. The 'end' looked for in line 25 is the beginning of the messianic age, and the same word *qeṣ* is taken up in the couplet on New Year and judgement immediately preceding that on the resurrection. Further, Isaiah 18: 3, 'earth', is so re-used in line 48 as to make the rendering 'land' adopted above possible. These indications are not conclusive, but they are consistent with the view that Yose is presupposing the widespread rabbinic association of the resurrection with Palestine in the messianic age (Ezekiel 37: 11–14). Saadia says that most in his time expected the resurrection at the messianic redemption; *Zerubbabel* expresses this expectation, and it is the principal theme of Kalir's messianic poem already mentioned.[72] Yose is perhaps more likely to

---

[72] Saadia, *ᵓEmunoth we-Deᶜoth*, 7.1, E T by S. Rosenblatt (New Haven, 1948), pp. 264f; *Zerubbabel* in Jellinek, *Bet ha-Midrasch*, II, 56; Kalir in Even-Shemuel, *Midrashe Ge'ullah*, pp. 113–16. The dead in Palestine rise first, according (for example) to PRK 22.5*a* (Mandelbaum, p. 330 (apparatus to

have envisaged it before the defeat of antichrist, with the two last-named sources, than afterwards, as in the specially-constructed scheme of Saadia.

The next couplet, introducing Exodus 20:18, predicts that the 'deceived heart' (Isaiah 44:20) shall no more be led astray (cf. *ʾahallelah ʾelohay*, 51; above, p. 161), and prays: 'Bring back to me as of old the law, the inheritance,' doubtless reckoning with the complete observance possible in the messianic age (Maimonides (above, p. 158) sums up this well-marked topic).[73] A couplet introducing Psalm 150 tells of the 'understanding' poured forth in David's psalms, which teach praise to the ruler of all. The reference to David in prophetic terms as 'the man understanding in speech' (line 54) may perhaps have messianic overtones; compare 'all the words of the songs and praises of David, son of Jesse, thy servant and anointed' at the end of the Sabbath morning *Nishmath*.[74] The next and last couplet, introducing the final text, Zechariah 9:14, recalls first the victory of the sons of Zion over the sons of Greece (Zechariah 9:13), and then predicts battle against Teman (Edom) in the words of the text.

In the whole passage three sequences can be discerned, each beginning from present corporate recollection of the past. In the first, the congregation, longing with Synagogue to know 'the measure of my end', look forward to the coming of the messianic age and the ingathering; in the second, they recall the giving of the Law (Exodus 19:19), looking to the 'end' (of the year and the present captivity), with its accompanying heavenly judgement, and to the resurrection; in the third, again recalling Sinai (Exodus 20:18), they look once more to the overthrow of Edom and the beginning of the messianic age. The newly-mentioned events are the ingathering and the resurrection.

The messianic events encountered in the two poems accordingly are: downfall of Edom, messianic reign in Jerusalem, Shekhinah returns to Temple, ingathering of exiles, resurrection of the dead, antichrist rises and is destroyed, God rules alone. The events have been linked with texts from the *malkhuyyoth* and *shofaroth*, but there is likely to have been a degree of free choice among these texts in Yose's

line 12)). On the continuity between rabbinic texts and apocalyptic like *Zerubbabel* on this topic, see A. Marmorstein, *Studies in Jewish Theology* (London, 1950), p. 160.

[73] So Synagogue says (Song of Songs 5:2): '*I sleep* – in lack of God's commandments; *nevertheless my heart wakeneth* – ready to obey them', PRK 5.6 (Mandelbaum, p. 87).

[74] T. Kronholm, *Seder R. Amram Gaon*, Part II (Lund, 1974), p. 71, and p. 14 of the Hebrew text.

time.[75] Yose nevertheless draws on a fund of messianic ideas according to need rather than versifying them systematically.

His strong messianism has so far evinced two characteristics generally seen as typically rabbinic. It is theocentric, clear allusion to the messiah being rare; and it is concerned with Law, as emerged especially in the prayer 'Bring back the law.' A fuller characterisation must, however, also take into account the messianism of the Avodah poems, with their special concentration on sanctuary and sacrifice.

(b) The Temple-service

A description of the Day of Atonement service, quoting and paraphrasing Mishnah, Yoma, is the kernel of the Avodah poems. It begins from a citation of Leviticus 8: 34, well compared and contrasted by L. Ligier with the Gospel-citation opening the narrative of institution in the eucharistic anaphora.[76] Elbogen argued, on the basis of Geniza texts, that this description originally constituted the Avodah in its entirety.[77] Since before Yose,[78] however, it had been prefaced with a recital of God's works from Creation to the institution of the Tabernacle-service: in Elbogen's view, a poetic device of one early writer, who was then imitated by most others.[79] In view of the many parallels with Ecclesiasticus, Roth suggested that the form grew from an original that combined the relevant parts of the Praise of the Fathers with Mishnah, Yoma.[80] Mirsky reinforces this view by pointing to the Creation-poem, Ecclesiasticus 42: 15 – 43: 33, which precedes the Praise of the Fathers; and he compares the belief, evinced for example at Gen. R. 1.4, that both the Temple and repentance (the business of the Day of Atonement) existed before Creation. The recital in the Avodah shows that the Temple-service completes the tale of the works of Creation, and that the world is founded upon it.[81]

---

[75] Heinemann in Heinemann-Petuchowski, *Literature of the Synagogue*, p. 60; Liebreich, 'New Year Liturgy', pp. 139–41, argues that the prophetic verses had to be eschatological passages from the Latter Prophets.

[76] L. Ligier, SJ, 'Autour du sacrifice eucharistique: anaphores orientales et anamnèse juive de Kippur', *Nouvelle revue théologique*, 82 (1960), 40–55 (52, 54).

[77] I. Elbogen, *Studien zur Geschichte des jüdischen Gottesdienstes* (Berlin, 1907), pp. 56f; Mirsky, *Yosse ben Yosse*, p. 25, also refers to J. M. Grintz's identification of a Qumran 'Prayer for the Day of Atonement' as an Avodah.

[78] The Avodah ʾattah baraʾtha ʾeth ha-ʿolam kullo (discussed below at p. 172) published by Elbogen, *Studien*, pp. 116f, is set earlier than Yose by Mirsky, *Yosse ben Yosse*, p. 26.

[79] Elbogen, *Studien*, pp. 58f.

[80] Roth, 'Ecclesiasticus', p. 177.

[81] Mirsky, *Yosse ben Yosse*, pp. 26–9.

The literary form of the Avodah thus reflects the conviction that the Temple-service is bound up with the work of Creation. The deep roots of this conviction, in such biblical passages as Psalm 78:69, are also probably to be traced beneath other liturgical institutions of Yose's time. Mishnah, Taanith 4.2–3 obliges the lay members of a *maamad* to read the story of Creation while the priests of the course concerned are ministering in the Temple. The Babylonian Gemara, 27*b*, gives the reason as 'were it not for the *maamadoth*, heaven and earth could not stand'. The priestly courses appear to have continued after 70 to fast and to read daily the relevant portion of Genesis 1 as 'part of the trend commemorating the ancient Temple ritual'.[82] Among midrashic echoes of the same conviction a special kinship with the Avodah form appears in the interpretation of Numbers 7:1 at PRK 1.4 and 5 (Mandelbaum, pp. 9 and 11): 'After the Tabernacle was set up, the earth became stable.'

The *anamnesis* of the Temple-service in these poems is, despite the bitter sense of loss already noted, in some degree an actualisation. 'Whenever they read the order of sacrifices I will deem it as if they had offered them before me, and I will grant them pardon' (Taanith 27*b*). Hence the recital, made in lively awareness of the service as the crown of Creation, in a measure anticipates the restoration expected in redemption.

S. Stein has observed that that the Gemara of Taanith in the Babylonian Talmud, which in a section already quoted (27*a*–28*a*) deals with the duties of the priestly courses, significantly ends by describing a dance of the redeemed (31*a*).[83] His observation is confirmed by the arrangement of Lev. R. 11, in which the first ministrations of Aaron and his sons (Leviticus 9:1) are interpreted by Proverbs 9:1–4 (Wisdom's 'house' being expounded successively of the world, the Temple and the days of Gog and Magog, the Torah, and the Tabernacle), and the chapter is ended (11.9) by the same tradition, with different attestation and proof-texts, on the dance of the righteous round the Holy One in the Time to Come. Discoveries of poems and synagogal inscriptions concerning the priestly courses have confirmed that throughout the Talmudic period Palestinian priests were ready, in

---

[82] E. E. Urbach, '*Mishmarot* and *Maᶜamadot*', *Tarbiz* 42 (1973), 304–27; the quotation is from the English summary, p. v. Cf. Urbach, 'Additional Note', *Tarbiz* 43 (1974), 224; Z. Ilan, 'A Broken Slab Containing the Names of the Twenty-Four Priestly Courses Discovered in the Vicinity of Kissufim', *ibid.* 225f; Stein in Rosenthal, *Saadya Studies*, p. 221; Baron, *History*, VII, 90; Schürer–Vermes–Millar, *History of the Jewish People*, II, 245–50.

[83] Stein in Rosenthal, *Saadya Studies*, p. 221.

S. W. Baron's words, 'to spring into immediate action upon the advent of Messiah, and without delay to restore the ancient ritual to full operation'.[84]

The whole Avodah-form accordingly possesses messianic overtones. The restoration of the Service, which it looks to and in some degree realises, will be the fulfilment of God's purpose from before the world and the sure token of his redemption. Some more specific allusions to redemption in Yose's interpretation can now be noted.

(i) *The rebuilding of the Temple.* The throne of glory, to which the Temple corresponds, is mentioned, as Mirsky notes, immediately after the Law as created before the world.[85]

'Then before a thousand generations it [the Law] came into mind,
    and from it is the preparation of all the works of the pattern [1 Chron-
      icles 28: 19].
In the height he set the throne of his majesty,
    spread his cloud and stretched it out as a curtain for a tent.
It shall not be taken down, and none of its stakes shall be removed,
    until its end come and it is renewed with a word.'

(*azkhir gevuroth*, 10–12)[86]

Here the Law, as in Gen. R. 1.1, is the plan of Creation, but line 10*b* uses the words of 1 Chronicles 28: 19, which refer to the building of the *Temple* after the heavenly pattern. Murtonen brings this out by rendering *mal**akhoth*, 'works', as 'services', and noting *tavnith*, 'pattern', as an allusive name for 'sanctuary'. In the next line 'height' is linked by Mirsky with Jeremiah 17: 12: 'a glorious high throne from the beginning is the place of our sanctuary'; and *ohel*, tent or tabernacle, taken here from the description of the heavens in Isaiah 40: 22, has an obvious sacred application, to occur shortly in line 26 where Joshua is *meshareth* *ohel*, the minister of the tabernacle. The double meaning is sustained in line 12, which alludes to Isaiah 33: 20, where the 'taber-nacle that shall not be taken down' is Jerusalem. Thus line 12*b*, on the appointed end and renewal of the heavens, speaks also of the end and renewal of the earthly Temple.

(ii) *The Messianic Banquet.* Genesis 1: 21, on the creation of sea-monsters, fish and fowl, is linked with the Banquet, as in Targum and

---

[84] Baron, *History*, VII, 90.
[85] Mirsky, *Yosse ben Yosse*, p. 27, also quoting *attah konanta* *olam be-rov ḥesed*, 3 and 5, and *asapper gedoloth*, 2.
[86] This poem is translated (apart from a passage at the end) with comments by A. Murtonen, *Materials for a Non-Masoretic Hebrew Grammar*, vol. 1 (Helsinki, 1958), pp. 107–13.

midrash, in both the longer Avodah-poems. In *Thou hast established the world in the multitude of mercy*, lines 18–22, the Banquet is connected with the dietary laws, as in Targ. Ps.-Jon. *ad loc.*; Leviticus Rabbah at 13.3; 22.10 (Margulies, pp. 278f, 522f) indeed presents it as the future compensation for eating *kosher*. In *I will recount the mighty works*, however, the Banquet receives a sacrificial interpretation also. From 'the fleeing ones of the deeps' (Isaiah 27: 1; Psalm 148: 7) created on the Fifth Day

'He stored up some for the everlasting banquet...
Tall fowl sprouted from the pool of waters
    for them that *eat at the king's table*, and the army of his hosts...
There multiplied from the earth horned beasts for sacrifice,
    creatures to eat, cattle and creeping things.
He fattened Behemoth with the produce of *a thousand hills* [Psalm 50: 10],
    for on the day of his sacrifice *he will bring near his sword* [Job 40: 19].'
                                        (ʾazkhir gevuroth, 28a, 29, 31f)

Although the question of uncleanness is expressly mentioned in the omitted line 30, the emphasis here falls, by contrast with the sources already noted, less on diet than on sacrifice. Creation provides both for the priests who 'eat at the king's table' (Ezekiel 41: 22) and for the lay Israelite. The messianic banquet will be just such a sacrificial meal. With the due slaughter implied in line 32 we may contrast Lev. R. 13.3, where the monsters kill one another, although this too is interpreted as ritual slaughter. A similarly 'sacrificial' view of the Banquet may also be found at 1QSa 2.11–22, where however the model appears to be not the whole-offerings but the priestly participation in the Shew-bread from the altar-table of Ezekiel 41:22, associated with the meal of the messianic Prince in the Temple described at Ezekiel 44:3ff.[87] Likewise, in Targ. Cant. 8.2, Israel conducts Messiah into the Temple for 'the feast of Leviathan'.[88]

(iii) *The Akedah*. The binding of Isaac (already discussed by Dr O'Neill, above, pp. 13–15) is interpreted as the equivalent of 'a lamb for a burnt

[87] M. Black, *The Scrolls and Christian Origins* (London, 1961), pp. 108–11, 146f.
[88] Levey, *The Messiah*, pp. 130–2; on the monsters' deaths in Kalir, other poets including Yose, and the midrash, see J. Schirmann, 'The Battle between Behemoth and Leviathan According to an Ancient Hebrew *Piyyut*', *Proceedings of the Israel Academy of Sciences and Humanities*, 4 (1969–70), 327–69 (338–40, 362).

offering' (Genesis 22: 8) and the pledge of future redemption. Isaac is
'the basket of first-fruits' (Deuteronomy 26: 2) and 'the lamb' (ʾ*azkhir*
gevuroth, 92f; cf. ʾ*anusah le-ezrah*, 8; above, p. 153). Zunz drew attention
to the emphasis in the Avodah poems on readiness for sacrifice.[89] This
emphasis may well come to Yose by inheritance. In an Aramaic poem
dated earlier than Yose by J. Heinemann 'the father did not spare his
son, and the son did not delay' (language almost identical with that of
ʾ*azkhir gevuroth*, 92*b*, quoted below); and Isaac declares, in heavily
Graecised diction: 'Happy am I that *Kyrios* has chosen me from the
whole *kosmos*.'[90] The link between freely-accepted trials, sacrifice and
atonement is very close (above, p. 153).

'He bore like a giant the weight of temptations,
> and by command to slaughter his only son thou didst try him, and he
> stood.
The father rejoiced to bind, and the son to be bound;
> for by this will be justified [God's] carried ones in the chastisement.
Thou didst appoint his atonement (*kofer*) a ram, and it was reckoned to
> him righteousness;
> on this day will *we* hear: I have found atonement.'

(ʾattah konanta ᶜolam be-rov ḥesed, 58–60)

Zunz brings out the emphasis of the last line by rendering 'we also', and
for *kofer* has *Lösung*, 'setting free' or 'absolution'.[91] ᶜ*aqad*, 'bind', is the
term for tying the lamb of the *Tamid* before slaughter.[92]

Similarly in ʾ*azkhir gevuroth*, 92–4, 'the father did not spare, the son
did not delay' and 'the Good and Merciful One' said 'We will accept
your [plural] deed as that of priest and victim' (*zoveaḥ we-nizbaḥ*,
'sacrificer and sacrificed'). Again, in ʾ*asapper gedoloth* Abraham's ten
trials (above, p. 152) culminated in the command

'to make his son an offering,[93] and he did not hesitate.
The lamb was delivered to the sword, and the burning of fire:
JAH will look upon him as ashes when we are in distress.'

(ʾasapper gedoloth, 16f)

Throughout, the efficacy of the Akedah is expressed as that of a
burnt offering. The terms are mainly those known from Amoraic

---

[89] Zunz, *Die synagogale Poesie*, pp. 136f.

[90] J. Heinemann, 'Remnants of Ancient *Piyyutim* in the Palestinian *Targum*
Tradition', *Hasifrut* 4 (1973), 362–75 (366f).

[91] Zunz, *Die synagogale Poesie*, p. 137.

[92] Mishnah, *Tamid* 4.1; the point is emphasised by P. R. Davies and B. D.
Chilton, 'The Aqedah: A Revised Tradition-History', *CBQ* 40 (1978), 535.

[93] *shay*, often used for *qorban* in Yose; see Mirsky, *Yosse ben Yosse*, p. 69.

texts, the last quotation being close to those, like Ber. 62*b*, which speak as if Isaac had in truth been offered.[94] In the context of the Avodah, however, emphasis falls rather on the importance of the sacrificial rites prefigured on Mount Moriah (the Temple-mount, *ʾeyn lanu kohen gadol*, 25; above, p. 150) than on the value of the binding of Isaac as their substitute. The recital of the Day of Atonement offerings will soon follow. Ligier has noted the striking resemblance between Yose and contemporary eastern and western Church teaching on Christ as both priest and victim.[95] There is probably an element of conscious or unconscious reaction to such teaching in Yose's presentation of the binding of Isaac; but in the setting of the Avodah his interpretation remains true to the early understanding of the passage as a prefiguration of the Temple-service, and of the atonement and future redemption that the service betokens.[96]

(iv) *The redemption from Egypt*. The Exodus, foreshadowing redemption to come, is described with markedly sacerdotal emphasis. The similarly coloured Ecclesiasticus 45 only hints at the story, but Yose tells it to the glory of the house of Levi. Jacob became father of the twelve tribes, and

> 'The third was set aside to behold the King's face,
> to sing and to minister, to enter his chambers.'
>
> (*ʾazkhir gevuroth*, 105)

This line on Levi is echoed in the account of the service at line 186 of the same poem; the high priest, seeming like an angel in his vesture (line 157), will be 'seeing the King's face and entering his holy chamber'. This stress on the angelic privilege shared by the priesthood recalls the view expressed in contemporary Day-of-Atonement homily that Nadab and Abihu abused it by 'eating and drinking' the vision of God (Exodus 24: 11 in PRK 26.9 (Mandelbaum, p. 396) and Lev. R. 20.10 (Margulies, pp. 466f)); the High Priest could indeed be described as an angel, Lev.R. 21.12 (Margulies, p. 493). These passages, like Yose here, continue the tendency to compare priests with angels seen at Jub. 31.14; 1QSb 4.24–6 (from 'Recueil des Bénédictions').

[94] S. Spiegel, *The Last Trial* (New York, 1967), pp. 41–4; cf. pp. 102f (willingness of father and son), pp. 114f (atonement, Cant. R. on 1: 14).

[95] Ligier, 'Autour du sacrifice eucharistique', p. 55, citing among other texts the Liturgies of S. Basil and S. Chrysostom in F. E. Brightman, *Liturgies Eastern and Western*, vol. 1 (Oxford, 1896), p. 318, lines 34–5, and p. 378, lines 5–6 (σὺ γὰρ εἶ ὁ προσφέρων καὶ προσφερόμενος).

[96] See P. R. Davies, 'Passover and the Dating of the Aqedah', *JJS* 30 (1979), 59–67, on the early interpretation of the passage, and apologetic elements in its development; cf. Dr O'Neill's comments, above, pp. 13–15.

Meanwhile, however, the poem describes the blossoming of Levi's rod or tribe in his three sons (Exodus 6: 16) until like 'a goodly vine' (Ezekiel 17: 8) Amram his grandson sprouts into 'a priest, a shepherd, and a woman that is a prophetess' – Aaron, Moses and Miriam (line 110). The order of reference, following Exodus 6: 20 (Aaron and Moses, only) rather than Micah 6: 4 (the three, with Moses first), is significant of what follows (line 111):

'When the *time of love* drew near [Ezekiel 16: 8] his blossom was established
  to break the bonds of Zoan, and to breach the hedge of the handful [the sea, Isaiah 40: 12].'

It is, then, through the blossoming of the levitical vine that redemption was accomplished, when Israel was brought near to the Bridegroom. After three lines on Moses' sanctification in the cloud, and his miracles, and a line on Miriam and her merits, Yose ascribes the pillar of cloud and fire to Aaron's merit (lines 116f, each beginning with Levi's *lamed*):

'The escort of clouds of majesty was granted to the beloved ones
  at the hands of a priest ministering *in peace and equity* [Malachi 2: 6];
With him and with his seed a covenant of salt was made
  that there might never fail the covenant of the salt of offerings of sweet savour' [Numbers 18: 19; Leviticus 2: 12f].

An entirely priestly passage on the company of Korah (in the spirit of Ecclesiasticus 45: 18–20) and the duties of the priests as laid down by Moses in Leviticus 8 now leads to the quotation of Leviticus 8: 34: 'As he hath done this day, so the LORD hath commanded to do, to make an atonement for you.' This text, as noted above, opens the narrative of the rites and ceremonies of the Day of Atonement.

The redemption from Egypt has been presented as part of the annals of Levi. The same pattern is followed more briefly in *ʾattah konanta ʿolam be-rov ḥesed*, 66–72, on the blossoming of the 'stem of Levi' (line 67, cf. Isaiah 11: 1). The much briefer *ʾasapper gedoloth* encompasses the matter in lines 20–3, without mentioning the Exodus. The three offspring of Amram were 'for a king, and for a seeress, and to minister and do priestly service' (line 20), Aaron receiving the last but the fullest and most honorific reference. Lines 21f immediately begin the description of priestly duties, Leviticus 8: 34 being quoted after line 22.

That this presentation was traditional in Yose's time is suggested by the bare bones of it visible in what is considered an earlier Avodah, *ʾattah baraʾtha ʾeth ha-ʿolam kullo*, lines 12–16.[97] Here Levi 'the third' (cf. *ʾazkhir gevuroth*, 105, above, p. 171) is separated; God's eyes are set on one of his descendants, 'Aaron the chief of thy saints' (Psalm 106: 16); to him it has been explained how he shall enter the holy place. Yose has adorned this structure with the momentous narrative of redemption, which now appears as wrought through the fruitful vine of the Levitical priesthood; the effect is to underline the redemptive significance of the recital of the order of priestly service that follows.

(v) *The Day of Atonement.* The high priest's glory is described first when he vests himself and secondly when he comes forth from the holy of holies. The atoning value of each garment that he puts on is described (*ʾazkhir gevuroth*, 152–86; *ʾattah konanta ʿolam be-rov ḥesed*, 93–119; no treatment in *ʾasapper gedoloth*). Among the collective sins of Israel thus absolved are the selling of the 'righteous one', Joseph (the vestment, *ʾazkhir gevuroth*, 160; *ʾattah konanta ʿolam be-rov ḥesed*, 98) and the making of the golden calf (the jewel of the breastplate, *ʾazkhir gevuroth*, 174; *ʾattah konanta ʿolam be-rov ḥesed*, 110). Strong consciousness of the first of these sins emerges also in the midrash *ʾElleh ʾezkerah*, where the Hadrianic martyrs suffer for this fault of their forefathers; for the second, compare *I fear amid my doings*, line 51. The messianic significance of this acute awareness of corporate sin has been noted above at p. 148. Atonement for these sins may be presumed to hasten the messianic age.

Two items in the vesture in fact recall kingdom rather than atonement. It is at once noted that the 'anointed for war' divines by these garments, and that the Urim forecast defeat or victory (Numbers 27: 21). Hence 'Praise God, sons of a *great nation* (Deuteronomy 4: 7); the herald of salvation is near at all times' (*ʾazkhir gevuroth*, 156). The phrase is taken up at the end of the poem, where the high priest is the herald of salvation .(line 269, quoted below). The priest 'anointed for war' (Deuteronomy 20: 2–9, Mishnah, Sotah 8) is a messianic figure at PRK 5.9 (Mandelbaum, p. 97) where together with Elijah, king Messiah and Melchizedek he is one of the 'four carpenters' of Zechariah 2: 3 (1: 20) who are 'the flowers' to 'appear on the earth' at the messianic age (Song of Songs 2: 12). A similarly messianic note is struck in the description of the mitre (above, p. 162).

'The crown of his head was in royal majesty (*be-hod ha-melukhah*), mitred in fair linen *for glory and for beauty*.'

(*ʾazkhir gevuroth*, 161)

[97] Text in Elbogen, *Studien*, p. 117.

In the parallel, *ʾattah konanta ʿolam be-rov ḥesed*, 161, it is 'a royal diadem', *nezer ha-melukhah*. The description recalls the Hasmonaean priest–kings, *mekhahane melukhah* (*ʾahallelah ʾelohay*, 28; above, p. 146), whose victory over the third kingdom Yose can mention in a messianic context, as at the end of *ʾanusah le-ʿezrah* (above, p. 165).

At the end of the Avodah the High Priest emerges from the holy of holies.

> 'His appearance shines out as when the sun comes forth *in his might* [Judges 5:31, Revelation 1:16];
>> he is sending to those that sent him *righteousness* and *healing* [Malachi 3:20].
>
> The hope of the congregation is for the coming forth of a skilled man, a herald of salvation and proclaimer of forgiveness.'
>
> (*ʾazkhir gevuroth*, 268f)

The high priest speaks of God's forgiveness, and the attendant of the scapegoat 'gives good tidings of forgiveness' (*ibid.* 273) by attesting that the scarlet thread is whitened (Yoma 6.8); then

> '*Perfect and upright* they lead him to his dwelling,
>> and they make rejoicing as he comes forth without harm.
>
> *Happy are the people that are in such a case...*' [Psalm 144:15]
>
> (*ibid.* lines 275f)

The high priest coming forth as the sun represents all Israel as 'the messenger of the congregation' (line 268); cf. 'faithful messenger' (*ʾasapper gedoloth*, line 59). The righteousness and healing that he brings make them perfect and upright.

The sacerdotal vesture in Yose is both priestly and kingly, the token at once of divine forgiveness and reunion with Israel, and of royalty to be restored. The emphasis laid on the proclamation of forgiveness by 'the herald of salvation' so vested corresponds not only to acute consciousness of sin, but also to a longing for the kingdom that sin delays.

The messianic events expected by Yose can now be listed as: downfall of Edom, messianic reign in Jerusalem, Shekhinah returns to Temple, ingathering of exiles, messianic banquet, resurrection of dead, antichrist rises and is destroyed, God rules alone. As has been noted, they are not described by the poet in this sequence, and the place given here to so important an event as the resurrection can be no more than probable (above, pp. 164f). It is nevertheless significant that a relatively compact body of liturgical poetry for the 'Days of Awe' can yield so full a picture of messianic expectation. To note the importance of the subject in Yose is the first step towards the fuller characterisation of his messianism that can now be attempted.

Its thematic importance corresponds, first of all, to Yose's striking *urgency* of tone. This is especially audible in the Tekiata, where each poem builds up to a final section on redemption. The *malkhuyyoth* pray (above, pp. 160f):

> 'Stir and awake the *joy of the whole earth*...
> Contend, O *saviours*, take the glory from Edom...
> let them shout unto thee the *shout* of the KINGDOM.'

(where Yose's messianism diverges from the line to be taken by classical exegesis of Numbers 23: 21). The *zikhronoth* move from the petition: 'Look, O God, upon the dwellers in the gardens' (above, p. 154) to: '*Purchase* us *the second time* [Isaiah 11: 11], for we are forgotten out of REMEMBRANCE' (line 57, introducing Psalm 74: 2: 'Remember thy congregation whom thou didst purchase of old'). In the third poem, 'When in my land shall *the turtle-dove* give VOICE?' (p. 164), is soon followed by the petitions of the *shofaroth* (pp. 151, 165): 'Visit the house-sparrow...bring back to me as of old the law, the inheritance', and the final militant prediction (Zechariah 9: 14; p. 165): 'Thou shalt blow *the trumpet; with the whirlwinds to Teman* then *shall go forth* the VOICE.' In the Avodah-poems 'the hope of the congregation' (*'azkhir gevuroth*, 269; above, p. 174) is directed primarily towards the Day-of-Atonement declaration of divine pardon. 'The end of days' (Daniel 12: 13; *'attah konanta 'olam be-rov ḥesed*, line 1) is also in mind, however; the Temple will be renewed, and the day of sacrifice for the everlasting banquet will come (above, p. 169); the remembrance of the work of creation culminating in the servicè of the Tabernacle, and the recital of the order of sacrifice for atonement, are themselves implicitly messianic (p. 168). Similarly, the systematic account of Temple rites and ceremonies that can no longer be performed, in *We have no high priest*, intensifies hope for the restoration of God's presence (p. 150). The specially clear note of urgency in the Tekiata recalls that it was intended not as hymnody simply, but as liturgy (above, p. 145); it is formally comparable with the messianic prayers of the *Tekiata de-vey Rav* (p. 145, n. 16). Earnest petition is therefore appropriate to its purpose. An estimate of Yose's messianism must still reckon with the fact that its expression has the 'fervent piety' (S. W. Baron[98]) suited to this traditional form, and that it won for itself a place in the mainstream of Jewish liturgy.

A second obvious characteristic is Yose's *nationalism*. The synagogue

---

[98] Baron, *History*, VII, 93.

of Israel, rather than mankind or the individual, is at the heart of his thought (p. 147). This might seem too commonplace for comment, did it not contrast, as seen already (above, p. 149), with the messianism of the hymn-like prayers – among the most important antecedents of Yose's poetry – that introduce *malkhuyyoth*, *zikhronoth* and *shofaroth* in the *Tekiata de-vey Rav*. These exhibit, not entirely without particularist passages, a universalism marked by such expressions as 'all sons of flesh shall call upon thee'.[99] From the same *malkhuyyoth* (including Obadiah 21) quoted after this passage Yose, so bitterly lamenting the oppression of the fourth kingdom, characteristically emphasises not only the kingdom of the LORD, but his vengeance on the heathen (above, p. 161).

Obadiah 21, promising that when the saviours judge the mount of Esau the kingdom shall be the LORD's, links nationalism with a characteristic picked out above as typically rabbinic, Yose's *theocentricity*. This was especially noticeable in the third poem of the Tekiata, where an allusion to the messiah in the language of the Song of Songs (above, p. 164) occurs in the midst of a sustained application of the imagery of bridegroom and bride not to the Messiah, but to God himself and his people. Similarly, suffering, closely bound up with messianism as we have seen it to be, marks the Synagogue and her representative patriarchs, martyrs and wise men, but not the Messiah himself. There is little trace of that meditation on the messianic figure, in which he can appear as a sufferer, that is evident in rabbinic tradition before Yose's time. The theme of the Deity himself as Israel's bridegroom and earth's sovereign by far preponderates over that of the Messiah, to whom only two reasonably clear allusions have been noticed. As quotation has made plain, this theocentricity combines intense reverence with extreme boldness, in the manner of the haggadah. Hence the bridegroom-imagery that in Church tradition, from 2 Corinthians 11: 2 onwards, is characteristically christological (although the christology is itself theocentric; 1 Corinthians 3: 23), in Yose is directly theological.

Concern with Torah, the other characteristic already noted as rabbinic, is present but not pre-eminent. Torah is the pattern of the universe, and the dietary laws are envisaged in Creation (above, p. 169); the Wise and their converse are dear to God (pp. 154f), and Israel longs to keep the Law, given at 'the time of love' in the first redemption, wholly and wholeheartedly in the messianic age (p. 165). Yet Yose does not strongly emphasise the place in the divine economy of the Oral Law and its rabbinic elucidation. Herein he differs from such a rabbinic presenta-

---

[99] Translation from text in Goldschmidt, *Maḥzor la-yamim ha-norʾaim*, I, 243; cf. p. 145, n. 16 above.

tion of Israel's relation with God as the Targum to the Song of Songs
(below, p. 178); and his position seems to correspond to the fact that
linguistically he is only moderately influenced by rabbinic terminology
(above, p. 144).

More obvious, especially in the Avodah poems, is the *levitical
flavour* of Yose's messianism. The rebuilding of the Temple is central to
his hopes; the messianic banquet is sacrificial, and the Akedah pre-
figures the sacrifices to be restored, the promise of pardon going with
them; the first redemption was wrought through the levitical priesthood,
whose ministry is the appointed means of reconciliation between Israel
and her Beloved (above, pp. 168–74). Outside the Day-of-Atonement
compositions, the return of the Shekhinah to the Temple is a prominent
theme of the *malkhuyyoth* (p. 160). Like the midrashic passages compared
above, Yose's poems attest the lively continuance of the concern with
priesthood and sacrifice manifest in the Qumran writings (cited above
at pp. 169, 171) or the Epistle to the Hebrews.

With his concern for the Temple-service we may link a last important
note of his messianism, *consciousness of sin* and desire for reconciliation
with God. When Israel sinned, 'far away went the KINGDOM'; God is
asked to purify her for the messianic age (above, p. 161), when the heart
will no more be led astray (the evil *yeṣer*, in rabbinic terms that Yose
does not use, will lose its power) (p. 165); then, as the first redemption
promised, forever will she be the seal upon his heart (p. 151).

CONCLUSIONS

(a) The relations of suffering with messianism in Yose

The corporate sufferings underscored by Yose, servitude and the loss
of the Temple-service, answer (as we saw) to the twin hopes of his
messianism, with its series of redemptive events in realm and sanctuary
culminating in the sole rule of God. The foregoing summary has shown,
however, that suffering is not related to messianism simply as depriva-
tion to the hope of restoration, in precise correspondence. Such a
correspondence is indeed envisaged, as appears in the characteristics of
urgency, nationalism and levitical concern identified above. There is
also, however, a more integral relation between suffering and hope.
Yose indeed, as noted above, has no suffering Messiah among the
representatives of suffering Israel; Isaiah 53:7 is characteristically
applied to Synagogue herself (*ʾanusah le-ʿezrah*, line 3; above, p. 151).
Yet, as seen in the first part of this study, Yose gives the Synagogue's
present suffering a double interpretation as at once punitive and

meritorious; and this theological interpretation is related to the theo-centricity of his messianism, his levitical concern as concern with the means of atonement, his consciousness of sin and love of God's Law. An approach to his consolation from its biblical links with tribulation, the messianic significance of which Scholem has emphasised, thus leads to the miraculous as well as the this-worldly elements in his view of redemption. In present, historical suffering he hopes indeed for the overthrow of Edom and the restoration of Israel; but present suffering itself, viewed as punishment and merit, implies a larger hope of recon-ciliation and reward with God – who returns to the bride of youth in the beloved dwelling, who receives acceptable sacrifice and service, and who raises the dead.

(b) *Yose and rabbinic messianism*

Yose's messianism hopes above all for the establishment of God's kingdom and the return of the divine Bridegroom to his sanctuary and people. This hope embraces a series of expectations, from the downfall of Edom and the return of the Shekhinah to the resurrection of the dead, the defeat of antichrist and God's sole rule. His presentation of them is urgent, nationalist but theocentric; concerned with God's Law, and con-cerned still more obviously with sanctuary, sacrifice, sin and atonement.

These expectations are known from rabbinic sources, and their presentation has typically rabbinic features in its restrained treatment of the Messiah and its concern with Torah (although the latter is less strongly marked, as already noted, than we might expect). On the other hand, the reflection of so unified a series of expectations within a relatively confined space itself contrasts with the more fragmentary and unschematised presentations of messianic traditions in Talmud and midrash; and the unqualified urgency of Yose's petitions for the king-dom, like the fervency with which he affirms the value of sanctuary and sacrifice, is at variance with the more cautious tenor of the midrash. Thus Leviticus Rabbah, as Joseph Heinemann observes,[100] depicts messianic joys (e.g. 13.3; above, p. 169), but bridles expectation by reserve on the manner and time of their coming; and when it affirms sacrificial atonement (e.g. 11; above, p. 167), also inculcates the atoning value of good works.

A similar difference of emphasis emerges in comparison with the Targum of the Song of Songs, wherein, as in Yose, the Song is the story of Israel's relation with God. The redaction of the Targum is ascribed

---

[100] Heinemann, 'Art of Composition', pp. 821, 825f, and 'Profile of a Midrash', pp. 146–8.

to rabbinic circles in seventh-century Palestine by R. Loewe, who also draws attention to its contact with interpretations in the name of the third-century Palestinian R. Johanan (above, p. 164) and his contemporaries.[101] Four features of the Targum are specially noted by Loewe: the prominence that it accords to Oral Torah as the central theme in Israel's story of salvation; emphasis on Israel's sin (which can receive apparently gratuitous notice, as in Yose; above, p. 151); affirmation of atonement through Tabernacle, Temple and sacrifice; and restriction of Messiah's role in redemption, with concentration on that of the Deity himself. These points add up, Loewe suggests, to a mute repudiation of the Christian understanding of atonement. The striking fact that Yose shares the last three of the Targum's notable features may further suggest, in line with Loewe's indication of possible sources, that both draw on a common exegetical tradition, perhaps already marked by the apologetic concern that has also seemed possible in Yose (above, pp. 154, 171). However that may be, Yose, who has so much in common with the Targumist, fails to share (as noted above) his characteristically rabbinic emphasis on Oral Torah. Further, Yose's urgency is opposed to a lesser feature of the Targum, its dissuasion from premature messianism.

These contrasts may in part correspond, as in the case of the treatments of suffering discussed above, to the formal contrast between congregational self-expression in Yose and the address *to* the congregation that in different modes lies beneath the literary traditions of midrash and Targum. Yose's characteristic concerns are shared, however, by the other two sources, which simply balance them with other emphases. These answer not merely to the pastoral demands of homily and biblical paraphrase, but also to the conviction that Israel's present life according to *halakhah* is an acceptable offering. Had this fundamental rabbinic conviction been close to Yose's heart, he would probably have expressed it in connection with his unmistakable love of the commandments. Instead, more strongly conscious of the tendency to sin in suffering Israel's present life, he characteristically prays: 'Bind on the commandments, lest they fly from me as an eagle' (*ʾanusah le-ʿezrah*, 39, introducing Exodus 19: 19; above, p. 164).

Yose's failure to magnify the Oral Torah and to neutralise his messianic urgency thus corresponds to a lack of emphasis in these poems on the validity of Israel's present observance. Without this emphasis, but with a lively awareness of present suffering, concern for sin and the appointed means of atonement is thrown into bolder relief, and the hope for redemption is correspondingly intensified. This muting of a

[101] Loewe, 'Apologetic Motifs', pp. 161, 168.

characteristically rabbinic note in the sphere of thought recalls Yose's limited use of rabbinic terms in the sphere of language. Yose's messianism constantly draws, as we have seen, on the material of rabbinic midrash; but its distinctiveness over against the *ethos* of the midrash is epitomised in his introduction to Numbers 23: 21 (above, pp. 161, 177). Here he avoids expressing the midrashic confidence, echoed in Rashi's comment, that God 'hath not beheld iniquity in Jacob'; but prays instead for the removal of iniquity and the hastening of the kingdom.

(c) *Yose and the New Testament*

Yose's poems, largely scriptural in language, draw on biblical writings and interpretations known in New Testament times, together with exegesis of later date. This material subserves an integration of experienced suffering with messianic hope. The corporate afflictions of the Synagogue are interpreted not only as deserving compensation, but as constituting tokens of coming reconciliation and reward with God. The voice of the congregation cries directly to the divine Bridegroom.

Among the few New Testament passages formally comparable with Yose's poems are the hymns in Revelation to God – and the Lamb. Other literary forms attest this same new Church-consciousness of relation to God through Christ. The Bridegroom now is the crucified Messiah (above, p. 176). Yose's bold biblical images of the Almighty's longing for the bride of youth are not far from the spirit of contemporary midrash, wherein God's 'undefiled' in the Song of Songs is his 'twin' whose pain he shares.[102] Nevertheless these poems are, in Rachel Rosenzweig's phrase, projecting on to God himself Israel's own human solidarity in woe.[103] For the New Testament writers, by contrast, the historical Passion of Christ means that the Bridegroom's sufferings are primary and determinative in a way for which there is no parallel in Yose. The corporate sufferings of the New Testament Church are accordingly related, as earlier contributions show, to those of the Lord. The contrast is heightened by Yose's combination of theocentric fervour with reserve on the Messiah's role. A comparable difference is discerned by P. Prigent between the christocentric visions of Revelation and their Jewish apocalyptic counterparts, wherein specifically messianic concern is often subsumed in the longing for intervention by God

---

[102] PRK 5.6 (Mandelbaum, pp. 87f); the parallel Cant. R. on 5: 2 is discussed with other passages on God's identification with Israel's suffering in Rosenzweig, *Solidarität*, pp. 93–9.
[103] *Ibid.* p. 203.

himself.[104] Yet Yose's poems also highlight the debt that he shares with the New Testament writers to their common source, the application of bridal imagery to redemption in such passages of Hebrew scripture as Jeremiah 2.[105]

The importance of suffering and messianism in Yose's poems evinces their thematic closeness to the New Testament. The Mishnah and other rabbinic texts often appear far removed from the interests of the early Church. Thus Jacob Neusner's voluminous studies of Mishnah-Tosefta lead him to suggest that the *tannaim* and their successors are constituting a world of reality to replace that of the cult. Their system of regular observance in daily life corresponds to the perpetuity of the Temple-rites and of nature itself in an 'effort to replicate eternity and perpetual order'. Neusner explicitly contrasts this piety with that of the New Testament, rooted in the disruptive and historical Passion of Christ.[106]

The complexity of post-biblical Judaism, which Neusner also emphasises, is underlined by the fact that a not-dissimilar contrast could be drawn between rabbinic piety as Neusner depicts it and that of Yose's poems. The mass of Mishnah-Tosefta is incommensurable with the small body of poems from the Amoraic period studied here, but Yose speaks for the congregation and was subsequently felt to have done so worthily. Hence it is not insignificant that in Yose tranquil daily observance is galvanised, as we saw in comparison with rabbinic messianism, by consciousness of sin and urgent hope for redemption. Herein, as already noted from time to time, Yose takes up themes of other Jewish sources as well as the New Testament. Concern with sin and redemption is comparably prominent in the Qumran hymns and the Eighteen Benedictions. Atonement through the ministrations of the priesthood in sanctuary and sacrifice is important not only in Yose, but at Qumran, in the background of such New Testament books as

[104] P. Prigent, 'Apocalypse et apocalyptique', in J.-E. Ménard (ed.), *Exegèse biblique et judaïsme* (= *RSR* 47 (1973), 157–407) (Strasbourg, 1973), pp. 126–45 (133).

[105] The general New Testament debt to such passages is vividly expounded by J. P. M. Sweet, *Revelation* (London, 1979), pp. 279, 301f (on Revelation 19:7; 21:9); a post-biblical instance is Od. Sol. 42, discussed by Dr McNeil, above, pp. 137, 140f.

[106] J. Neusner, 'The Use of the Later Rabbinic Evidence for the Study of First-Century Pharisaism', in W. S. Green (ed.), *Approaches to Ancient Judaism: Theory and Practice*, Brown Judaic Studies I (Missoula, 1978), pp. 215–28 (225); cf. Neusner, *A History of the Mishnaic Law of Purities*, vol. XXI (Leiden, 1977), esp. pp. 322f, and 'Comparing Judaisms', *HR* 18 (1978), 177–91 (185f). I have made a brief attempt to take stock of Neusner's great contribution in *Exp T* 91 (1980), 233–40 (236–8).

Hebrews and Revelation, in midrashic and Targumic passages noted above, in patristic references to Judaism like that of Chrysostom,[107] and perhaps also in the explanation of archaeological evidence such as the course-inscriptions or the representation of a censer in the Beth Alpha synagogue.[108] For assessment of the development of Judaism in the New Testament period it is not irrelevant that Yose's poems attest the influence of concerns that, as Neusner's presentation of rabbinic piety shows, may emerge less vividly from the traditions of the sages than from the New Testament itself. However G.M.S. may view these remarks in his own capacity as sage, he may perhaps accept the interspersed renderings from Yose's liturgical poems as a thank-offering for many pleasant discussions of hymnody with the Precentor.

[107] With Chrysostom, *C. Iud.* 6.5 (above, p. 156) cf. Origen, *In Num. hom.* 10.2 (Jewish lament that without sacrifice sin remains unforgiven, *PG* XII, 638) and *Princ.* IV.1.3 (loss of priestly ministrations, *PG* XI, 347f; J. A. Robinson, *The Philocalia of Origen* (Cambridge University Press, 1893) p. 10, discussed by N. R. M. de Lange, *Origen and the Jews* (Cambridge University Press, 1976), pp. 45, 97; further comments in *JTS* n.s. 30 (1979), 326.

[108] The fire-pan, *maḥtah*, used by Aaron when staying the plague (Numbers 17: 11 (16: 46), *ʾefhad be-maʿasay*, 8; above, p. 153), was centrally important on the Day of Atonement (Leviticus 16: 2, 12f; Mishnah, Yoma 5.1f; and Yose, *ʾazkhir gevuroth*, 230f; *ʾattah konanta ʿolam be-rov ḥesed*, 158f; *ʾasapper gedoloth*, 43–5). Its representation at Beth Alpha and elsewhere is linked with suggested synagogal use of incense by E. R. Goodenough, *Jewish Symbols in the Greco-Roman Period*, vol. XII (New York, 1965), pp. 78, 91.

What might martyrdom mean?

NICHOLAS LASH

Most of the members of the New Testament seminar attend its meetings clad in the robes of professional exegesis. Wearing these same robes (or, perhaps, their 'festal' version) the other contributors to this volume have come suitably attired to the feast. I feel a little naked. I am not wearing, and cannot wear, a wedding garment. And yet, just as the seminar, and its secretary, have so often in the past made me welcome and encouraged me to feel at home, so the editors have been kind enough to invite me, ill-clad as I am, to share in this celebration.

Nevertheless, the question cannot be avoided: what am I doing here? As one whose work includes consideration of problems of theological method, and aspects of systematic theology and the philosophy of religion, what contribution can I make to a discussion of suffering and martyrdom in the New Testament? Perhaps the question already suggests one form of an answer. All Christians, and not only New Testament scholars, seek to understand the New Testament. But the standpoints from which understanding is sought are manifold. The individual Christian, meditating on the text, the preacher, the textual critic, the systematic theologian and the exegete, are all concerned with understanding the New Testament. And yet they are clearly not engaged in identical enterprises. How might these different enterprises be characterised, and what relationships obtain, or should obtain, between them?

There is a received account, in this country, both of the character of these enterprises, and of the relationship between them, which goes something like this. Christian hermeneutics is principally concerned with negotiating the 'gap' between what was once said and what might appropriately be said today. The biblical scholar, and the historian of doctrine, are expected to recover, today, what the text meant; the systematic theologian is supposed to transpose the recovered meanings into contemporary idiom; and Christian living is conceived as the practical application or implementation of meanings thus recovered and transposed.

In this paper I propose to indicate some of the reasons why I regard this hermeneutical model as profoundly unsatisfactory. The relationships between exegesis and preaching, on the one hand, and between exegesis and critical or systematic theology, on the other, that are inscribed in this model, are often expressed in terms of a distinction between what the text 'meant' and what it 'means', or might mean, today. I shall therefore discuss Professor Krister Stendahl's use of this distinction and Professor Dennis Nineham's variation on the theme. From this discussion it will, I hope, emerge that the model is defective both in its neglect of questions of interpretative truth and in its failure to locate problems concerning the relationship between theory and practice *within* the description of the interpretative process. The paper is thus an invitation to my New Testament colleagues to reconsider, on the one hand, their view of the relationships between their activity and other aspects of theological inquiry and, on the other hand, their view of the relationship between the 'obedience of faith' and critical, scholarly reflection. Whether or not it thereby also constitutes an invitation to them to reconsider some features of their own exegetical activity is for them rather than for me to say.

'MEANING', PAST AND PRESENT

According to the article on 'Exegesis' in the Supplementary Volume to the *Interpreter's Dictionary of the Bible*, 'the distinction between what the text meant and what it means is fundamental, even though it should not be pressed'.[1] The article also tells us that 'When exegesis is distinguished from exposition, the former refers to the process of ascertaining the original meaning, and the latter, the meaning for today.'[2] This formulation, so slipshod as not to merit detailed commentary, at least reminds us of the abiding influence of Krister Stendahl's article on 'Contemporary Biblical Theology' in the original edition of the dictionary.[3] In that article, Stendahl observed that 'the *religions-geschichtliche Schule* had drastically widened the hiatus between our time and that of the Bible... The question of meaning was split up in two tenses: "What *did* it mean?" and "What *does* it mean?"'[4]

---

[1] L. E. Keck and G. M. Tucker, 'Exegesis', *The Interpreter's Dictionary of the Bible. Supplementary Volume* (Nashville, 1976), p. 297.

[2] *Loc. cit.*

[3] Cf. K. Stendahl, 'Biblical Theology, Contemporary', *The Interpreter's Dictionary of the Bible I* (New York, 1962), pp. 418–32.

[4] Stendahl, *ibid.* p. 419.

According to Stendahl, attention to the first of these questions is the responsibility of 'the descriptive task', while the movement from the first to the second is a matter of 'hermeneutics'. In undertaking the 'descriptive' task, 'our only concern', he tells us, 'is to find out what these words meant when uttered or written by the prophet, the priest, the evangelist, or the apostle – and regardless of their meaning in later stages of religious history, our own included...The meaning for the present...is not involved.'[5] Later, commenting on the relationships between what the text originally meant, and what it subsequently came to mean or might mean today, he insists that this is 'a relation between two highly developed types of theology',[6] and he describes 'the task of systematic theology' as being 'by its very nature one of translation from one pattern of thought into another'.[7]

The importance of the point upon which the article was concerned centrally to insist is beyond question. The exegete is an historian, and any historian, whatever the motives that lead him to undertake his inquiry, seeks to understand and to exhibit some aspect of the past 'in its pastness'.[8] Christians are not alone in being tempted to 'read' the past anachronistically, to find in it what they expect or hope to find, but they are peculiarly exposed to this temptation because of their conviction that certain words spoken and deeds enacted in the past are of unique and enduring significance. Nevertheless, the framework within which Stendahl expresses this concern is, for a number of reasons, highly questionable.

In the first place, his characterisation of the respective tasks of the historian and the systematic theologian, in terms of a distinction between 'description' and 'hermeneutics' comes dangerously close to endorsing the positivist myth that exegesis is not yet interpretation. Let us suppose that the textual critic has done his work, and provided the exegete with the materials for his task.[9] What are these materials? They are 'just a series of signs'[10] or notations. And 'anything over and above a reissue of the same signs in the same order will be mediated by the experience, intelligence, and judgement of the interpreter'.[11] Moreover, the perspective within which the exegete works, and the language he employs, have been shaped by the history of the culture to

---

[5] *Ibid.* p. 422.   [6] *Ibid.* p. 425.   [7] *Ibid.* p. 427.

[8] Cf. D. E. Nineham, 'New Testament Interpretation in an Historical Age', *Explorations in Theology I* (London, 1977), p. 163.

[9] I should in fact wish to argue that even textual criticism is inevitably an interpretative activity.

[10] B. J. F. Lonergan, *Method in Theology* (London, 1971), p. 157.

[11] *Loc. cit.*

which he belongs. To insist on this self-evident truth is by no means necessarily to subscribe to some form of radical hermeneutical relativism, nor to espouse the strange view that different cultural contexts are always mutually 'impermeable', rendering good historical interpretation impossible. It is merely to issue a reminder that the notions of 'objectivity' and 'scientificity' presupposed by some New Testament scholars betray the influence of a discredited positivism all the more insidious for being unrecognised.

In the second place, the concept of 'meaning' with which Stendahl works is dangerously imprecise. If we say that the exegete, as historian, is concerned to understand and exhibit what the text 'originally meant', to what are we referring? Do we have in mind some notion of 'authorial intention', such that what we are after is what Luke, or Paul, was 'trying to get at'? Or, bearing in mind that what people intend to say, or suppose themselves to be saying, is often by no means identical with what they succeed in saying, do we read the text, as a cultural artefact, in the light of the cultural conditions in which it was produced? Or do we have in mind that which the text was 'heard' to say by its original audience – and, if so, is not the idea of some single, uniform, 'original audience' itself highly problematic? If these considerations seem unhelpfully abstract, consider the following question: what was the 'original meaning' of *King Lear*, or of Mr Whitelaw's speech, at the 1979 Conservative Party Conference, announcing the government's intention to set up detention centres to administer 'short, sharp shocks' to juvenile offenders?

In the third place, we have seen that Stendahl describes 'the task of systematic theology' as being 'by its very nature one of *translation* from one pattern of thought into another'.[12] That description distracts attention from the fact that, as I have already insisted, the exegete's task, the historian's task, is itself already an interpretative enterprise. This being so, if the metaphor of 'translation' is to be used, it should be used, not only of the task of systematics, but also, as Bultmann claimed, of 'the task of historical science'.[13] Stendahl admits that the model of 'original' and 'translation' is only an analogy,[14] but he seems to suppose that the analogy is appropriate. Whereas I should wish to argue, following Professor David Kelsey, that from many points of view the analogy is singularly *in*appropriate. 'The metaphorical use of "translation"', says Kelsey, 'stretches the concept into unintelligi-

---

[12] Stendahl, 'Biblical Theology', p. 427 (my italics).
[13] R. Bultmann, *Existence and Faith* (London, 1964), p. 346.
[14] Cf. Stendahl, 'Biblical Theology', pp. 427, 430.

bility';[15] it 'obscures the fact that there may be a *conceptual discontinuity* between what the biblical texts say and what the theological proposals say';[16] and, for all its apparent methodological neutrality, it is in fact parasitic upon certain *theological* decisions concerning the nature of revelation.[17]

In the fourth place, the metaphor of 'translation' and, more generally, the assumption that the task of the systematic theologian is that of transposing meanings recovered by the New Testament scholar into contemporary idiom presupposes what we might call the 'relay-race' model of the relationship between the two enterprises. When the New Testament scholar has done his job, produced his completed package of 'original meanings', he hands this over to the systematic theologian, whose responsibility it is to transpose the meanings received into forms intelligible within the conditions of our contemporary culture. Systematic theologians who subscribe to this model are sometimes irritated by the fact that, because the work of New Testament interpretation is never finished, the baton never reaches them. The New Testament scholar appears to be 'running on the spot'; he never arrives at the point at which the baton could be handed over. The New Testament scholar, for his part, either ignores what the systematic theologian is doing (it is not his business: he is only running the *first* leg of the race) or disapproves of the fact that the baton is continually being wrenched prematurely from his hands.

It is, however, the model that is defective and, especially, the assumption that there is a one-way dependence between New Testament scholarship and systematic theology. I should wish to argue that the relationship between the two enterprises is, or should be, dialectical: that it is, or should be, a relationship of mutual dependence.

As I have put it elsewhere:

'If it is true for us, as creatures of history, that some understanding of our past is a necessary condition of an accurate grasp of our present predicament and of our responsibilities for the future, it is also true that a measure of critical self-understanding of our present predicament is a necessary condition of an accurate "reading" of our past. We do not *first* understand the past and *then* proceed to understand the present. The relationship between these two dimensions of

---

[15] D. H. Kelsey, *The Uses of Scripture in Recent Theology* (London, 1975), p. 186.
[16] *Ibid.* pp. 189–90 (his italics).
[17] Cf. *ibid.* pp. 185–6.

our quest for meaning and truth is dialectical: they mutually inform, enable, correct and enlighten each other.'[18]

The more peripheral that aspect of the past with which the historian is concerned, the more fragile the validity of this claim. In order to decide whether it was a cloak or an overcoat that Paul left at Troas and, if a cloak, what kind of a cloak it was likely to have been, no very profound existential and cultural self-awareness is demanded of the historian. But most of the New Testament is concerned with weightier matters. Let us suppose that Professor Lindars is correct in saying that, according to the Fourth Gospel, 'The works of Jesus reveal not only his identity as the Father's agent, but also his unity with the Father.'[19] Or let us suppose that Mr Beck is justified in proposing 'a martyrological interpretation of Luke's Passion narrative'[20] as at least one strand in what that narrative 'originally meant'. In both these cases, is there not a sense in which it is a necessary condition for understanding, with any depth and sensitivity, what either of the texts in question 'originally meant', that we have some articulated grasp of those fundamental features of the human predicament to which those texts were constructed as elements of a response? (This would only not be the case on the supposition that the affirmation of Jesus' unity with the Father, or the construal of his Passion in martyrological terms, 'meant nothing' for the hope and self-understanding of those who thus interpreted his fact and significance.) I am not saying that this condition is always, or even frequently, capable of being fulfilled. It may be the case that the culture, the 'structure of feeling', that we inhabit is such as to render us incapable of seriously entertaining those questions to which the authors of the New Testament sought to respond. It may be the case that the world of the New Testament is, at least for the time being, so different from ours as to be quite opaque, illegible. I am only saying that, when we have to do with texts which treat of, and embody particular responses to, fundamental aspects of the human predicament: questions of life and death, innocence and freedom, hope and suffering, then, in order to 'understand' those texts, the technical skills of the historian, although indispensable, are inadequate for the task.

If the questions to which ancient authors sought to respond in terms available to them within their cultural horizons are to be 'heard' today with something like their original force and urgency, they have first

[18] N. L. A. Lash, 'Interpretation and Imagination', in *Incarnation and Myth: the Debate Continued*, ed. M. D. Goulder (London, 1979), pp. 24–5.
[19] Lindars, above, p. 61.
[20] Beck, above, p. 40.

to be 'heard' as questions that challenge us with comparable serious-ness. And if they are to be thus heard, they must first be articulated in terms available to us within *our* cultural horizons. There is thus a sense in which the articulation of what the text might 'mean', today, is a necessary condition of hearing what that text 'originally meant'. And, once again, there can be no *a priori* guarantees that this condition is or can be fulfilled. Just as certain features of the past may be rendered quite opaque or illegible by the differences between past and present contexts of meaning, so also certain features of the present may be rendered quite opaque or illegible by the circumstances of contemporary existence. It is no part of my argument that we should suppose it to be a straightforward matter to 'make sense' either of the past or of the pre-sent, let alone to make a sense that would be recognisably Christian. Moreover, it is no part of my argument to suggest that the distinction between our attempts, in the present, to understand the past on its own terms, and our attempts, in the present, to articulate self-understanding and hope, and thus to formulate coherent and responsible policies for future action and attitude, is not fundamental and irreducible. I am only concerned to insist, as a matter of general hermeneutical principle, that understanding what an ancient text 'originally meant', in the cir-cumstances in which it was originally produced, and understanding what that text might mean today, are mutually interdependent and not merely successive enterprises.

It is not, I think, irrelevant to point out that exegetical practice frequently neglects its own theoretical stipulation consistently to distinguish what the text 'meant' from what it might 'mean'. As a matter of fact, New Testament scholars frequently conduct their discussion in the present rather than the past tense. They insist that 'this is not what Paul is saying', or 'this is what the text means', and so on. It seems likely that certain awkward questions concerning the adequacy of the theory of meaning presupposed by the distinction are thereby obscured from view. It would be interesting to discover what modifications of exegetical practice resulted from a rigorous adherence to the 'past tense' rule.

CONSUMERS AND TOURISTS

So far, I have taken Professor Stendahl's influential and controversial article as the background to my remarks. A somewhat different approach to the distinction between past and present meaning is to be found in the work of Professor Dennis Nineham. 'What', asks Nineham, 'is an interpreter of the New Testament...seeking to do? So far as he aims to go beyond the satisfaction of simple antiquarian curiosity and bring his readers contemporary enlightenment of some sort, how should he conceive and set about his task?'[21] An historian would, I suspect, find Nineham's distinction doubly puzzling. It is puzzling, first, in its apparent depreciation of the historian's craft. 'Antiquarian' has overtones of cobwebbed eccentricity; the implication is that historical study is a harmless and slightly self-indulgent hobby: its goal is the 'satisfaction' of 'curiosity'. It is puzzling, secondly, because when an historian publishes a piece of work, he presumably does so in the expectation, or at least the hope, that his readers will find it 'enlightening'. And I fail to see how such 'enlightenment' as the reader receives could be other than 'contemporary': it is, after all, *today* that I am reading the historian's text, not yesterday or tomorrow.

It could be objected that I am obscuring the perfectly straightforward distinction that Nineham is drawing between information or 'enlightenment' concerning the past and the 'enlightenment' of present perplexity. The trouble is that I do not find that distinction, thus drawn, at all straightforward. Self-understanding, whether of an individual or of a group, is a matter of producing, or being able to produce, an autobiography. And in so far as historical research concerning some aspect of my past, or the past of some group to which I belong, or of some tradition within which I seek to stand, results in 'the discovery of new knowledge, the connection of previously unrelated facts, the development of new theory, or the revision of older views',[22] it constitutes a challenge to reassess some features of my autobiography and hence of my self-understanding.

In other words, someone who acknowledges the origins of Christianity to be an aspect of *his* past, and not merely of 'the past of mankind' in general, is thereby precluded, in logic, if not necessarily in psychological fact, from regarding the historical study of Christian origins as being 'simply' a matter of 'satisfying antiquarian curiosity'. The contrast drawn by Professor Nineham, and the manner in which he draws it, could be the expression of a particular *theological* judgement of a kind with which students of Bultmann are familiar. Not that Nineham, I think, regards himself as a Lutheran. And yet it seems to be being suggested that the human work of the antiquarian profiteth nothing unto salvation or, should we say, unto 'contemporary enlightenment'.

[21] Nineham, 'NT Interpretation', p. 145.
[22] From the Cambridge Board of Graduate Studies description of requirements for the Ph.D. Degree.

Nearer the surface of his text, Nineham's question concerning the interpreter's task reflects his dissatisfaction with certain ways of drawing distinctions between what the text 'meant' and what it 'means' or might mean today. And he answers his own question as follows:

'We ask the New Testament exegete to help us to pass over into the beliefs and relationships with God witnessed to in the New Testament, not in the belief that they were necessarily better than our own, but in the faith that they will prove complementary to our own, revealing to us new insights, new dimensions of relationship with God...which, once they are revealed, must, and can, be dealt with in our own terms.'[23]

What particularly interests me in that passage (aside from problems concerning the force of 'better', the grounds of that 'faith', the sense of 'complementary', and the legitimacy of the shift from 'must' to 'can') is the enthusiasm with which here, as in other places in his recent writing, he appropriates Professor John Dunne's metaphor of 'passing over'. Dunne himself defines 'passing over' as 'a shifting of standpoint, a going over to the standpoint of another culture, another way of life, another religion. It is followed by an equal and opposite process we might call "coming back".'[24]

Dunne's allusive and evocative study makes no pretence to be a work of disciplined theoretical rigour. Even so, I confess that I find his repeated use of this favoured metaphor underdeveloped, uninformative and not particularly illuminating (were I seeking for a sign, I would take comfort from the fact that the first reference to 'passing over', in the index to the edition of *The Way of All the Earth* that I consulted, is to a page that, on examination, turns out to be blank). And yet, passing over(!) decades of sustained and often rigorous debate on problems of interpretation-theory – in historiography, literary criticism and the philosophy of the social sciences – this metaphor is served up to us as a description of the interpreter's task.

Professor Raymond Williams has complained that

'nearly all forms of contemporary critical theory are theories of *consumption*. That is to say, they are concerned with understanding an object in such a way that it can profitably or correctly be consumed. The earliest stage of consumption theory was the theory of "taste",

---

[23] Nineham, 'The Genealogy in St Matthew's Gospel and its Significance for the Study of the Gospels', *Explorations*, p. 186.
[24] J. S. Dunne, *The Way of All the Earth* (London, 1972), p. vii.

where the link between the practice and the theory was direct in the metaphor.'[25]

Not the least serious deficiency of 'consumption theories' is their mistaken assumption that a literary text is, as an embodiment of meaning, a kind of 'material object'. If this were the case, then 'reading' a text would be a process similar to that whereby we seek to 'understand', say, a piece of rock or a plate of food, by isolating its constituent components. There is undoubtedly a sense in which some cultural artefacts – a building, for example, or a painting – do have 'specific material existence'. But the same is not true of literary, dramatic and musical works.

'There is no *Hamlet*, no *Brothers Karamazov*, no *Wuthering Heights*, in the sense that there is a particular great painting. There is no *Fifth Symphony*...which is an object in any way comparable to those works in the visual arts which have survived... In literature, especially in drama, in music and in a very wide area of the performing arts, what we have are not objects but *notations*. These notations have to be reinterpreted in an active way, according to particular conventions.'[26]

A performance of *Hamlet* is an interpretation of the text. The history of performances of *Hamlet* is the history of successive interpretations of the text. An historian of Tudor drama, exploring the circumstances of that text's 'original production', is engaged in the second-order activity of constructing an 'interpretation' of that original 'interpretation'. That way of putting the matter may seem cumbersome, but it serves to remind us not only that there are irreducibly distinct aspects of the hermeneutic process, but also that there is a sense in which a text, any text, becomes an expression of meaning only in so far as it becomes an element in the human activity that is its production, use or interpretation. Williams' criticism of 'consumption' theories of interpretation thus helps us to see what is wrong with a statement such as the following: 'Exegesis is a process by which one enables *the text's own meaning* to come forth in its own terms.'[27] Here we are clearly confronted with the mistaken belief that texts 'have meaning' in somewhat the same way that material objects 'have mass'. (It should perhaps be added that considerations of this generality concerning the relationship between sign and signified,

[25] R. Williams, 'Base and Superstructure in Marxist Cultural Theory', *New Left Review* 82 (1973), 14.
[26] *Ibid.* p. 15.
[27] Keck and Tucker, 'Exegesis', p. 297 (my italics).

text and meaning, are equally applicable to texts – such as many New Testament passages – interpretative of particular historical events and persons, and texts – such as those mentioned by Professor Williams – which lack such particularity of concrete reference.)

Taking our cue from Raymond Williams, we might describe that received account of the relationships between New Testament study, systematic theology and Christian living, which I sketched at the beginning of this paper, as the 'consumption' model of Christian hermeneutics. According to some versions of this model, the historian of Christian origins provides the 'raw materials', and the systematic theologian 'cooks' them, according to taste, for contemporary consumption. According to others, such as Professor Stendahl, with his insistence that the relation between past and present meanings is 'a relation between two highly developed types of theology',[28] the historian is an importer of foreign manufactured goods, while the systematic theologian's task is that of repackaging ('translating') them for local use.

If I understand Professor Nineham, he is unhappy with sharp distinctions between the provision of goods and their adaptation. His disapproval of 'antiquarianism' seems to spring from a suspicion that the importer may be insufficiently concerned about the usefulness of, or likely demand for, his goods on the home market. I confess that I do sometimes have the impression that some biblical scholars, in their apparent lack of interest in questions concerning the disproportion between energy expended and results achieved, and in questions concerning the wider implications and significance of their work, do exhibit a tendency towards the dilettantism against which Nineham is protesting. (It will, I hope, nevertheless be clear from remarks I made earlier that I believe Nineham's criticism, with its implied blanket disapproval of historical study 'for its own sake', to be far too indiscriminate.)

Be that as it may, we can perhaps suggest that, in recommending a unified account of the interpretative process, Nineham turns for his hermeneutical model to another aspect of modern life: tourism. There are, of course, some tourists who derive little benefit from the experience of foreign travel, because they insist on ascribing normative status to the customs, language and eating-habits of their domestic context. Foreign countries are experienced as defective forms of England. There is an analogy between such tourists and those whose 'reading' of ancient texts is vitiated by the 'eisegetical' tendencies that Nineham rightly deplores.

28 Stendahl, 'Biblical Theology', p. 425.

There are also more open-minded and less ethnocentric travellers who allow the experience of foreign travel to modify and enlarge their domestic horizons of experience. These are the tourists whom Nineham would propose to us as paradigms of Christian interpretation (even though it must be admitted that his insistence that ancient texts 'must, and can, be dealt with in our own terms',[29] is not lacking in traces of ethnocentricity: within what limits are 'our own terms' sacrosanct?).

There are, however, at least two reasons why the model of 'tourism' is hardly more satisfactory than that of 'consumption' as a characterisation of the process of the Christian interpretation of the New Testament. In the first place, both models focus on considerations of 'meaning' to the neglect of questions of truth. In the second place, both models assume that the poles of the interpretative enterprise are expressions of 'meaning' rather than patterns of human action. Let us briefly consider these two issues in turn.

MEANING AND TRUTH

Dr O'Neill's paper addresses itself to the question: 'Did Jesus think that his death would do for mankind what no one else could do?'[30] He answers this question in the affirmative. Other New Testament scholars may contest O'Neill's interpretation of 'the Cross sayings and the servant sayings'.[31] But let us suppose that his interpretation is broadly correct and can be shown to be correct. This still leaves untouched the far more interesting question: was Jesus right?

The essays in this collection exhibit something of the variety both of the responses offered to this question by the authors of the New Testament and of the interpretations of their response provided by contemporary exegetes. But, notwithstanding this twofold pluralism, it appears to be agreed that the authors of the New Testament shared a common conviction that, in the death and vindication of Jesus, that was done for mankind which was uniquely and unrepeatably done.

We now have two questions, rather than one: Was Jesus right? Were the authors of the New Testament right? If we addressed these questions to a representative group of contemporary New Testament scholars we would, I think, be told by most of them that it is beyond the competence of the exegete, as an historian, to answer either question and, especially, the former.

[29] Nineham, 'The Genealogy in St Matthew's Gospel', p. 186.
[30] O'Neill, above, p. 10.
[31] Cf. O'Neill, above, p. 27.

To what extent is this modesty becoming, and on what grounds does it rest? It sometimes seems to be grounded on the conviction that exegesis, as historical interpretation, is concerned not with questions of 'truth' but only with questions of 'meaning'. But this distinction, thus employed, is less than satisfactory. A history of the Peninsular War, or of the October Revolution, in which the author systematically refrained from all judgements of appropriateness, correctness or truth concerning Wellington's conduct of the campaign and his estimation of the chances of success, or concerning Lenin's analysis of a turning-point in Russian history, which restricted itself to exhibiting what Wellington's diaries or Lenin's letters 'originally meant', would be a very queer kind of history. Historicism, in the sense of a refusal to risk judgements of truth or appropriateness, has its limits.

The exegete, as an historian, cannot, it would seem, legitimately evade responsibility for assessing, however tentatively, the truth, correctness or appropriateness of those interpretative judgements concerning the fact and significance of Jesus that are expressed or implied in the writings of the New Testament. And yet there are considerations that may help to explain, and that in some measure justify, the exegete's hesitation. The most important of these considerations arise from the fact that the truth-conditions of the proposition, 'In Jesus' death that was done for mankind which was uniquely and unrepeatably done', are hidden in the mystery of divine action and do not lie open for historical scrutiny. To put it very simply, oversimply: the exegete is correct in supposing that the question 'Was Jesus right?' is not one that he is competent, as an historian, to answer.

And yet the question remains, shall we say, interesting. If the New Testament scholar cannot answer it, who can? Should we turn to some other field of expertise or professional competence: to philosophy, perhaps, or to systematic theology? No. It is not that kind of question. It is at once more general, more personal and more particular. To refrain from answering it, or to answer it in the negative, is to refrain from giving, or to refuse to give – not to a 'meaning', but to a man – the kind of trust that the authors of the New Testament gave and, in giving it, exhibited their intention to maintain 'the testimony of Jesus'.[32]

It appears to be the case, therefore, that recognition of the fact that the interpretative process is concerned not only with 'meaning' but also with 'truth' obliges us to consider questions concerning the relationship between the practice of faith and the goal and function of academic reflection and inquiry as constitutive features of the hermeneutical

[32] Cf. Sweet, above, pp. 101, 103f.

problem. I submit that any model of Christian hermeneutics that ignores such questions, or treats them as marginal or merely consequential, is *theoretically* deficient. And I suggest that the two models that I earlier considered – the 'consumption' and 'tourism' models – are deficient on precisely this score.

LOCATING THE 'GAP'

This conclusion can be reinforced by considering the second charge that I brought against the two models of interpretation previously considered: namely, that they both mistakenly assume the poles of the interpretative process to be expressions of 'meaning' rather than patterns of human action. (That formulation may be misleading. 'Action' and 'speech', 'deeds' and 'words', are not to be contrasted dualistically. All human actions 'speak', and all uses of language are aspects of human action and behaviour. The contrast that I wish to draw is between the abstract and the concrete: between expressions of meaning and judgements of truth considered, on the one hand, 'in themselves' and, on the other hand, as aspects of concrete, historical, human practice and behaviour.)

Mr Flemington's essay is instructive in this regard. He expresses the worry that 'Pauline theology may seem utterly remote and unreal'[33] to many people today. And he attempts to meet this difficulty, not by producing some fresh abstract description, in contemporary concepts and images, of what it was that he supposes Pauline theology to have 'originally meant', but by offering us the pattern of Maximilian Kolbe's action, the manner of his witness, as a correct or faithful *interpretation of Pauline theology.*

Following up a suggestion at which I hinted in my discussion of Raymond Williams, I would wish to argue that the fundamental form of the Christian interpretation of scripture is, in the concrete, the life, activity and organisation of the Christian community, and that Christian practice consists (by analogy with the practical interpretation of dramatic, legal and musical texts) in the performance or enactment of the biblical text: in its 'active reinterpretation'. The elucidation of this suggestion would demand another paper, but Mr Flemington's evocation of the example of Maximilian Kolbe may perhaps serve as a parable. Flemington does not suggest, nor am I suggesting, that the attribution of primacy to interpretative performance dispenses those

[33] Flemington, above, p. 90.

ancillary interpreters, the textual critics, exegetes and theologians, from the need to pursue their enterprises with relentless scholarly and intellectual rigour (any more than the attribution of primacy to dramatic, legal or musical interpretative performance dispenses with the need for submitting scripts, statutes and scores to continual historical and theoretical scrutiny and assessment). We are, however, reminded of the need to situate academic tasks appropriately in that broader context of interpretative practice of which they form an indispensable part.

Moreover, it is not only the contemporary pole of the interpretative process that demands description in concrete, rather than abstract, terms: the same is true of the *interpretandum*. The practice of Christian faith is not, in the last resort, a matter of interpreting, in our time and place, an ancient text. It is, or seeks to be, the faithful 'rendering' of those events, of those patterns of human action, decision and suffering, to which the texts bear original witness. To acknowledge that the criteria of fidelity are hard to establish and are frequently problematic is to admit that there is, indeed, a hermeneutical 'gap'. But this 'gap' does not lie, in the last resort, between what was once 'meant' and what might be 'meant' today. It lies, rather, between what was once achieved, intended, or 'shown', and what might be achieved, intended, or 'shown' today. The poles of Christian interpretation are, on the one hand, 'the testimony of Jesus' in his own time and in the time of those who first sought to share that testimony and, on the other hand, such continued sharing in that testimony as may be demanded of us today.

There are, as any reader of Gadamer's *Truth and Method* will appreciate, general considerations of hermeneutical theory that point in the direction that I am indicating. But, in addition to such methodological or philosophical considerations, there are also theological considerations that can be adduced. Only an incorrigible idealist (in Marx's sense) could suppose that Christianity's primary concern is to 'make sense' of suffering – whether the suffering of Jesus or of anybody else. That would be to 'leave everything as it is'. It was not thus that Jesus – by his words and deeds and death – bore witness to God, interpreted the divine in his historical particularity. Nor was it thus that those who first interpreted him as God's self-interpretation sought to share his testimony. Nor was it thus (to put it theologically) that God 'interpreted himself' in those historical persons and events.

God's self-witness, the 'martyrdom' of God, is not the provision of a more or less satisfactory account of the human condition, but is rather the transformation of that condition: divine utterance is 'performative'. Similarly, the transformative power of Christian 'martyrdom', of 'sharing the testimony of Jesus', is a condition of its truthfulness.

What might 'witness' or 'martyrdom' mean, today? The form of the question, derived from models of interpretation the inadequacy of which I have tried to indicate, is unsatisfactory. It should rather be: What form might contemporary fidelity to 'the testimony of Jesus' appropriately take? And this is a practical and not merely a theoretical question. It is a question that will continue, often in darkness, strenuously to engage all those resources of integrity and discernment without which patterns of human action are not responsibly undertaken or pursued. And it will also continue to engage all those resources of textual, historical and literary criticism without which the New Testament scholar cannot competently perform his indispensable function. That function, I have suggested, is an aspect, but only an aspect, of the broader task of Christian interpretative practice, of the attempt to bear witness faithfully and effectively to God's transformative purpose and meaning for mankind.

INDEX OF AUTHORS

A page number in brackets (e.g., Lindars (188)) indicates that a contributor to this book discusses another essay in it.

Arndt & Gingrich, 40
Assaf, 145, 159

Bacher, 146
Baker, 84f
Bammel, (2f), 96, 98, 100, 144, 149, 155, 157
Baron, 143f, 166, 168, 175
Barrett, 41, 49, 61, 66, 78
Baumgartner, 141
Beasley-Murray, 52, 53
Beck, (3), (188)
Becker, 55, 63
Berliner, 161
Bethune-Baker, xiiif
Betz, 75
Black, 169 (and s.v. Schürer)
Blank, 126
Böhlig, 136
Bonwetsch, 96
Borgen, 59
Bornkamm, 17
Bousset, 96
Bowker, 113, 116, 147
Braude and Kapstein, 156
Brightman, 171
Brown, R. E., 48, 51, 62, 63, 67, 69
Brown, S., 33, 34, 35, 38, 39
Brown, S. Kent, 136
Brox, 104
Bruce, 112
Bultmann, 13, 40, 54, 55, 56, 61, 63, 68, 186, 190
Butler, xx

Caird, 110, 113, 114
von Campenhausen, 104, 126, 134
Carmignac, 38
Chadwick, xviii, 93

Charlesworth, 136, 139
Chilton, 13f, 170
Cohen, 148, 159
Conzelmann, 28, 37, 39
Craig, 90
Cripps, xvi
Cullmann, 48, 107

Dalman, 155, 157
Daube, xviii
Davidson, Assaf and Joel, 145, 159
Davies, P. R., 13f, 170, 171
Davies, W. D., 49, 51, 65, 159
Dibelius, 28, 36, 37, 91, 93, 134
Dillistone, xviif
Diez Macho, 161
von Dobschütz, 91, 92, 93, 100
Dodd, 53, 113
Driver, 139
Dunne, 191

Elbogen, 143, 144, 145, 147, 149, 166, 173
Ernst, 34
Even-Shemuel, s.v. Kaufmann

Farrer, 103
Fiorenza, 115
Flemington, (2), (6), (82), (196)
Foakes Jackson, xiif, xiv
Freed, 62
Funk, 136

Gadamer, 197
George, 37, 43, 46
Goldschmidt, 145, 148, 151, 176
Goodenough, 182
Goodspeed, 41
Graetz, 146

Green, 51
Grintz, 166
Grözinger, 150
Grotius, 93
Grundmann, 28, 38

Haenchen, 43
Hanson, A. T., 114
Hanson, R. P. C., 42
Hare, 51, 67
von Harnack, 99
Harris, 139
Haussleiter, 76
Hebert, 75
Heinemann, 143, 144, 156, 166, 170, 178
Heinisch, 44
Hemer, 106
Hengel, 65
Hill, 51, 105
Hooker, (2), 70, 75, 81, (158)
Horbury, (4ff), 181, 182
Hoskyns, 146
Hoskyns and Davey, 88

van Iersel, 52
Ilan, 167

Jellinek, 159, 162, 163, 164
Jeremias, 58, 134
Johnston, 63

Kahle, 143
Kaufmann, 159, 162, 164
Kelly, 104, 134
Kelsey, 186, 187
Kilpatrick, 42
Knox, J., 101
Knox, W., xviii, 85, 86
Kraft, 105
Krauss, 150, 153
Kronholm, 165
Kysar, 48

Lagrange, 28
Lampe, (4), 43, (63), 67, (104), 131, 135, (155)
de Lange, 182
Larcher, 43
Lash, (6), (7), 187f
Lattke, 139
Lawrence, 113
Levey, 161, 169
Levi, 145f

Liebreich, 160, 166
Lietzmann, 88
Lightfoot, 81, 86
Ligier, 166, 171
Lindars, xxi, (3), 53, 62, 112, (133), 154, (188)
Loewe, H., xviii
Loewe, R., xviii, 149, 151, 178f
Lonergan, 185
Longenecker, 76
Luzzatto, 145

MacLachlan, 44
Maier, 143, 144, 153
Mandelbaum, 144, 152, 153, 155, 162, 163, 164, 165, 180
Manson, T. W., 85
Margulies, 144, 148, 152, 157, 161, 163
Marmorstein, 157, 158, 165
Marshall, 28, 36, 37, 38, 43, 51, 53, Martyn, 49
Marxsen, 52
Mattill, 29, 46
McNamara, 113
McNeil, (5), 138, 139, 140, (181)
Metzger, 25f, 37, 40
Meyer, 13
Michaels, 112
Minear, 106
Mirsky, 144, 145, 146, 147, 149, 151, 154, 166, 167, 168, 170
Morris, 79
Moule, 10, 57, 70, 75, 76, 84, 86, 87
Murtonen, 168

Neusner, 181
Nineham, 184, 185, 189, 190, 191, 193, 194

Odeberg, 94
Oepke, 97
Oman, xiif
O'Neill, (1f), (5), (7), 113, (169), (171), (194)

Pancaro, 49
Parkes, 67
Peake, 88
Pesch, 29
Petuchowski, 143
Pobee, 28, 35
Preisigke, 100
Prigent, 180

Index of Authors

Reese, 44
Rengstorf, 59
Robinson, J. A., 181f
Robinson, J. A. T., 49, 53, 102
Roloff, 24
Rosenblatt, 164
Rosenzweig, 144, 147, 149, 155, 156, 157, 180
Roth, 145, 166

Schäfer, 49, 144, 157, 158, 163
Schechter, 147, 155, 158, 162
Schirmann, 144, 169
Schlatter, 13
Schmithals, 78
Schnackenburg, 53, 59, 61, 62, 63, 67, 68
Scholem, 94, 146
Schürer, Vermes, Millar & Black, 49, 160, 166
Schürmann, 51, 58
Schweizer, 20
Scott, 88
Selwyn, 107
Smith, 139
Spiegel, 171
Stauffer, 30, 38, 97
Stein, 159, 166
Steindorff, 94
Stemberger, 143
Stendahl, 184, 185, 186, 189, 192, 193
Stöger, 28, 31, 38, 43, 46
Strachan, 78

Strack & Billerbeck, 13, 45
Strathmann, 29
Styler, G. M., xi, xii, xx, 72, 85, 104
Surkau, 28, 38
Sweet, 3, (3f), 102, 107, 111, 113, 181 (195)

Taylor, 52
Theodor and Albeck, 157
Thyen, 53
Tinsley, 28
Torrance, 75
Torrey, 127
Trites, 104, 105, 107
Turner, 134

Urbach, 167

Vallotton, 76
Vermes, 14 (and s.v. Schürer)
Violet, 94, 96
Vogl, 137

Walaskay, 41
Westcott and Hort, 25
Wellhausen, 24
Whiteley, 93
Wilcox, 68
Williams, R., 191f, 193, 196
Williams, S. K., 37

Zehnle, 37
Ziener, 43, 44
Zunz, 143, 147, 148, 170

INDEX OF REFERENCES

Old Testament

Genesis
1	167
1: 21	169
3	110
4: 8	68
4: 25	152
22: 6	13
22: 8	169f.
27: 29	160
27: 38	148
27: 40	148
32: 24–32	38
49	101
49: 8–12	113

Exodus
2: 24	154
6: 16	172
6: 20	172
15: 17	160
19: 16	151, 164
19: 19	164, 165, 179
20: 18	165
24: 11	171
31: 18	105
32: 15	107
32: 32	153

Leviticus
2: 12f	172
8	156, 172
8: 34	166, 172
9: 1	167
11: 4–7	159
16: 2	182
16: 8	147
16: 12f	182
25: 35	148

Numbers
7: 1	167

17: 11–13 (16: 46–8)	153
17: 11 (16: 46)	182
18: 19	172
23: 21	149, 161, 175, 180
27: 21	173

Deuteronomy
4: 7	173
6: 4	163
20: 2–9	173
21: 23	154
26: 2	169
32: 7	115
33: 5	160
33: 15	152

Judges
5: 31	174

1 Samuel
6:5–8	109

1 Kings
7: 2	150
8: 13	160

1 Chronicles
21: 1	36
28: 19	168

2 Chronicles
3: 1	150
24: 20–2	29, 126ff
24: 20–1	124
36: 15–16	123

Nehemiah
9: 26	29

Job
1: 6 – 2: 10	38
38: 13	162
40: 19	169

Psalms
2	111
2: 2	163
9	111

10	111
22	35
22:8	32
24:7f	161
24:9f	161
31:6	32, 45
35:19	62
40:3	26
42:6	40
42:12	40
44:10	149
44:22	16
47:6	164
48:3	160
50:10	169
56:1	151
68:31	151
69:5	62
74:2	175
78:69	167
81:4f	164
84:4	151
86:9	19, 110, 111
87	111
93:1	162
106:16	173
109:3	62
111:4	154
116:1–10	78
119:41–6	123
119:161	62
123:2	154
127:2	154
130:3	18
144:15	174
147:2	158
147:3	152
148:7	169
150	165

Proverbs
9:1–4	167

Song of Songs
1:13	150
2:6	141
2:8	152
2:9	163
2:12	164, 173
2:14	151
2:16	141
3:6	150
5:2	151, 164, 165, 180
6:3	141
6:10	149, 150
8:2	169
8:3	141
8:5	151
8:6	151
8:13	154

Isaiah
3:10	43
6:13	150
10:3	150
10:14	151
11:1	172
11:4	107, 162
11:11	175
14:5	163
18:3	164
24:23	149, 160
27:1	169
27:13	151, 152
30:20	154
33:20	168
40:12	172
40:22	168
41:2	162
42:1	43, 123
42:11	164
43:4	151
43:9–12	105
43:10	123
44:8	105
44:9	105
44:20	165
49:17f	103
49:23	111
53:7–9	103
53:7	113, 151, 177
53:8	43
53:11	43
53:12	43
54:11f	103
60:10–16	111
62:3	162
63:1–6	113

Jeremiah
2	149, 181
2:2	153
9:15	110
17:12	168
23:15	110
38:28	157
50:17	151, 153

Lamentations
4:6	148
5:13	154

Ezekiel
2:10	107

8	151	16: 15 (8: 12 p)	42
16	149	Wisdom	
16: 8	172	1–5	43
16: 49	148	1: 16 – 3: 9	44
17: 8	172	2	47
22: 5	150	2: 12ff	123
28: 12–15	152	2: 12–20	106
37: 11–14	164	2: 12	43
41: 22	154, 169	2: 13	45
44: 3ff	169	2: 15	45
48: 35	116	2: 16	45
Daniel	118	2: 18	45
3	30, 31	2: 19	44, 45
3: 25	31, 38	2: 24	44
4: 28ff	110	3: 1–8	123
6	30	3: 2f	45
6: 4f	31	3: 5f	44
7: 7	163	3: 5	15, 45
7: 13	112	3: 7ff	45
10: 18f	38	4: 16ff	45
10: 20 – 11: 1	38	8: 7	44
12: 1	38	13–14	107
12: 2–3	123	14: 12	107
12: 13	175	Ecclesiasticus	
Hosea		42: 15–43: 33	166
2: 1 (1: 10)	150	45	171
11: 11	151	45: 18–20	172
Joel		50	145
3: 6	149	2 Maccabees	118
Amos		6: 12 – 7: 42	30
5: 6f	110	6: 12ff	35
6: 12	110	6: 18–7: 41	32
Obadiah		6: 18–20	35
21	149, 159, 161, 163, 176	7	15
Micah		7: 9ff	31
6: 4	172	7: 9–13	109
Zechariah		7: 14	35
2: 3 (1: 20)	173	7: 17	35
3: 1–5	38	7: 18f	35
3: 1	36	7: 18	24
4: 1ff	106	7: 19	35
9: 13–14	165	7: 24f	32
9: 14	175	7: 29	15
10: 8	151, 164	7: 30	35
12–14	101, 111f	7: 31–8	109
12: 10	112	7: 31–5	34
13: 2	112	7: 37f	15f
Malachi		9: 5–9	29
2: 6	172	2 Esdras	
3: 16	154f	5: 1	96
3: 20	174	5: 23–7	149
Apocrypha		6: 13ff	96
Esther (LXX)		6: 29	94
16: 15f (8: 12 p–q)	45	9: 3	96

10: 26 — 94
10: 30 — 94
10: 34 — 94
12: 6 — 96
12: 47 — 96
13: 30 — 96
16: 76 — 97

Pseudepigrapha
Apocalypse of Abraham
10.2–4 — 94
Apocalypse of Baruch (Syr.)
25.3 — 96
54.1 — 94
70.2ff — 96
Apocalypse of Elijah
2.5f — 138
3.33 — 15
Apocalypse of Sophonias
1.2 — 95
1.3 — 95
5.2 — 95
5.6 — 95
8.3 — 94f
12.5 — 95
13.5 — 95
18.3ff — 96
Ascension of Isaiah
5.7 — 95
Enoch (Eth., 1 Enoch)
10.30, 37 — 95
12.7 — 95
12.8 — 95
14.13f — 94
14.24f — 94
62.5 — 109
62.10 — 109
63.11–12 — 109
89 — 113
Enoch (Slav., 2 Enoch)
20.1 — 94
21.2 — 94
21.3 — 97
22.1ff — 97
39.8 — 95
Enoch (Hebr., 3 Enoch)
1.7 — 94
1.9 — 95
1.10f — 95
14.1 — 95
16.2 — 95
30.1 — 95
35.6 — 95
48(B) — 95
Jubilees

1.12 — 123
31.14 — 171
3 Maccabees — 39
3.1–10 — 31
5.6ff — 31
5.24 — 31
5.25 — 31
5.50f — 31
6.1ff — 31
6.18 — 31
4 Maccabees 13, 30ff, 37, 118, 121
1.11 — 15, 30, 121
6.5–6 — 121
6.10f — 31
6.17 — 124
6.23 — 124
6.27–9 — 15, 109
6.28f — 34, 37, 121
6.29 — 24
7.10 — 121
7.14 — 13
8–18 — 13
13.9 — 124
13.12 — 13
14.20 — 124
15.28 — 13
16.3 — 124
16.19f — 13
16.20–1 — 124
17.6 — 13
17.11–16 — 30
17.20–2 — 109
17.21f — 15, 34, 37
17.21 — 24
17.22 — 14, 121
18.1 — 142
18.3–5 — 14
18.11f — 142
18.11 — 13
18.23 — 142
Martyrdom of Isaiah — 30
4.11f — 30
5.1ff — 32
5.6f — 31
5.7 — 124
5.13 — 32
5.14 — 124
Odes of Solomon 5, 136–42 *passim*
3 — 140
5.2–9 — 141
5.14–15 — 141
6.1f — 141
6.6ff — 139
8.7 — 136

8.11	137	10: 32	133
9.6ff	136	10: 38	11, 15
14.7f	141	10: 40	60
15	140	12: 32	52, 130
18	136, 141	14: 22–33	138
24	141	16: 24	11
25	137	16: 28	17
26	140	17: 27	25
27.2	140	19: 28	21
27.3	139	20: 20–3	21
28.4f	141	20: 24–7	21, 22f
28.17	140	20: 28	11, 24ff, 121
29.8–10	136f	21: 33–46	19
31.6ff	139	23: 11	21
31.11	139	23: 29–33	124
35	137	23: 34–5	125ff
38	136, 138	24: 4ff	103
38.9	139	24: 9ff	129
39.1–4	137	24: 9	51
39.5–8	137ff	24: 10	97
39.9–13	138ff	24: 25	65
40	140	24: 29–31	103
42	137, 141, 181	24: 30	112
42.1–2	140f	24: 43–51	52
42.2	139	25: 1–13	17
42.5–9	137, 140f	26: 28	155
42.11ff	140	26: 31	65
Psalms of Solomon		26: 37	40
7.1	62	26: 39	32
Priesthood of Methuselah	96	27: 11	134
Testament of Benjamin		27: 51–3	108
3.1	15	27: 52	50
3.6–8	15	27: 54	46, 108f
Testament of Joseph		28: 2	108
19.8	113	Mark	
19.11	15	3: 10	45
Vitae Prophetarum	127	3: 23	36
New Testament		3: 26	36
Matthew		3: 28f	52
5: 10–12	125	3: 29	130
5: 11	34, 58	4: 15	36
5: 44	58	6: 45–52	138
6: 10	38	8: 34	11, 16, 34, 85
6: 20f	52	8: 38	130
6: 25–33	52	9: 1	17, 18
10	59, 62, 64, 66, 106	9: 35	19, 21
10:17–25	51	10: 32–4	96
10: 17–20	130	10: 35–40	21
10: 19f	63	10: 41–4	21, 22f
10: 22	58, 59, 60	10: 43	20
10: 23	51	10: 45	11, 24ff, 34, 121
10: 24f	59	12: 1–12	19
10: 26–33	52	12: 1–5	124
10:32f	130	12: 8ff	130

12: 8	113	8: 13	35
13: 5–31	52	9: 23	11, 16, 33, 34
13: 9–23	103	9: 26	130
13: 9–13	51	9: 27	17, 18
13: 9–11	129	9: 45	39
13: 9f	52, 107	9: 48	21
13: 9	34	9: 54	40
13: 11	107, 141	10	106
13: 12	34	10: 18	36, 37
13: 13	58	10: 21f	45
13: 14–20	35	11: 4	38
13: 19	102	11: 18	37
13: 23	65	11: 47ff	29
13: 30	52	11: 47–8	124
13: 32	52	11: 49–50	125
14: 27	65	12: 2–9	52
14: 30	65	12: 4f	34
14: 32	39	12: 8–10	130
14: 33	40	12: 8	133
14: 34	39, 40	12: 10	52
14: 36	32	12: 11–12	51, 63, 130
14: 38	39	12: 22–31	52
15: 2	134	12: 33f	52
15: 21	33	12: 39–46	52
15: 27	42	12: 50	33, 140
15: 34	45	13: 16	36, 37
15: 37–9	108	13: 32	33, 46
15: 38f	46	13: 33–4	29, 125
15: 39	41, 112	13: 33	105
16: 8	xviii	14: 27	11, 33
Luke		15: 8ff	xv
1: 6	126	16: 15	46
1: 11	40	17: 21	20
1: 14	91	17: 29	40
1: 20	40	18: 9	46
1: 26	40	18: 23	40
1: 67	126, 129	18: 34	39
2: 9	40	19: 11	96
2: 13	40	20: 20	46
2: 20	42	21: 11	40
3: 22	40	21: 12–19	51
4: 1–13	30	21: 12–17	52
4: 13	33	21: 12–15	129
4: 24	29	21: 12	33, 34
4: 29	113	21: 15	107
6: 19	45	21: 16	34
6: 20–49	46	21: 20–4	34
6: 22	34, 58	21: 20	52
6: 23	29	22: 3	30, 36, 37, 122
6: 27	58	22: 14–38	33
6: 40	46	22: 19f	34, 35, 37
7: 16	29, 42	22: 24–7	21, 22f
7: 36ff	xviii	22: 27	24, 34
7: 39	29	22: 28	21, 33, 37

22: 29f	21	23: 49	39
22: 31f	38	23: 50	42
22: 31	30, 122	24: 5	109
22: 33f	33	24: 7	36
22: 35f	36, 37	24: 19	29
22: 36	30	24: 23	40
22: 37	37, 43	24: 25–7	36
22: 39–43	37f	24: 26	39
22: 40ff	46	24: 35	39
22: 40	30, 33, 39	24: 37	109
22: 41–4	30, 31, 32	24: 39–43	40
22: 43f	37ff, 46	24: 44–9	36
22: 44	3	John	
22: 45	39f	2: 6	65
22: 46	30, 33, 39	3: 1	50
22: 49ff	39	3: 11	58
22: 50f	46	3: 14f	15
22: 51	33, 45	3: 20	59
22: 53	30	4: 14	58
22: 54–65	33	4: 21	65
22: 61	33	4: 23	65
22: 63–5	32	5: 16	48
22: 64	29	5: 20	61
22: 66–71	33, 36	5: 25	65
22: 68f	35	5: 28	65
22: 70	45	5: 35	91
23	36	5: 36–47	61
23: 2ff	36	6: 15–21	138
23: 2	31	6: 36	61
23: 3	134	6: 70	59
23: 4	31, 41	7: 7	59
23: 11	32	7: 30	65
23: 14f	31, 41	7: 37f	58
23: 18	43	7: 50–2	50
23: 19	42	8: 20	65
23: 22	31, 35, 41	8: 31ff	115
23: 25	36, 42	8: 55	60
23: 26	33	8: 56	91
23: 27–31	33	9	54
23: 28–31	35	9: 22	49, 50, 133
23: 32f	42	9: 34	49
23: 34–6	35	10: 1–18	54
23: 34	33, 43, 45	10: 18	39
23: 35–9	32	10: 19–21	54
23:35	36, 43	10: 22–39	61
23: 37	36	10: 26–9	54
23: 39	36, 42	10: 30	61
23: 41	31, 41, 42	10: 34	61
23: 42f	33	11: 51	129
23: 43	31, 45	12: 23	65
23: 44f	30, 31	12: 27	65
23: 46	31, 32, 45, 46	12: 42	49, 50, 133
23: 47	31, 41ff	12: 43	50
23: 48	32	13–17	53

13: 1	65
13: 14	20
13: 16–20	57, 59, 60, 62
13: 27	122
13: 38	65
14–16	55
14: 12	61
14: 16f	63
14: 25	64
14: 26	63, 64
14: 30f	39
14: 31	53
15–17	53
15: 1–17	55
15: 11	64
15: 13	68
15: 16	57, 59
15: 17	68
15: 18 – 16: 15	55
15: 18 – 16: 4	4, 48–69 passim
15: 18–25	54, 55ff, 64
15: 18–20	66
15: 18	68
15: 19	68
15: 20–6	133
15: 20	48, 119
15: 21–4	65, 69
15: 21	67
15: 26 – 16: 11	55
15: 26f	54, 62f
16: 1–4a	54, 62, 64f
16: 2	49, 50, 54
16: 4b–7	54
16: 6	40
16: 7	63
16: 8ff	107
16: 8–16	54
16: 8	133
16: 13–15	63
16: 15	54
16: 16–22	54
16: 21	65
16: 25	64
16: 32	65
16: 33	64
17: 1	65
17: 12–19	53, 54
17: 19	66
17: 20–3	53, 69
18: 1	53
18: 37	59, 104, 116
19: 30	105
19: 34–7	112
19: 35	58
19: 38f	50
20: 20–7	114
21: 24	58
Acts	21
1: 8	131
2: 2	40
2: 23–8	39
2: 46	91
3: 13–14	133
3: 14	43
3: 22f	29
4: 5ff	131
4: 29–31	131, 132
5: 19	40
5: 32	131
6: 8–10	132
6: 15	132
7: 10f	34
7: 30	40
7: 37	29
7: 52–7	125
7: 52	29, 43, 124
7: 55–6	124
7: 55	132
7: 58	113
8: 26	40
8: 32f	34, 43
9: 5	119
9: 18	40
9: 19	40
10: 3	40
11: 18	42
11: 19	34
12: 2	29
12: 5	40
12: 7	40
12: 11	40
12: 23	29, 40
13: 48	42
14: 15–17	107
14: 22	34
16: 30f	41
17: 29–31	107
20: 23	34
20: 28	34, 37
20: 29	67
22: 14	43
22: 15	29
22: 20	29
24: 25	107, 109
25: 19	41
26: 7	40
27: 23	40

Romans

1: 18ff	107, 115
1: 21	109
3: 25	89
4: 20	109
5: 1–5	74
5: 9f	74
5: 12–19	71
6	140
6: 2–14	12
6: 3ff	71, 72, 73
6: 3	119
6: 4	88
6: 6	88
6: 8	88
6: 10	74
8: 1	73f
8: 3	70, 86, 89
8: 11	88
8: 14	70
8: 15	98
8: 17	73f, 79
8: 26	98
8: 35ff	141
9: 3	82
10: 9–10	133
12: 1	90
15: 16	146

1 Corinthians

1: 6	135
1: 13	84, 89
1: 23f	113
1: 23	83
2: 1	135
2: 2	12
3: 23	176
4: 8	82
5: 3	88
9: 24–7	77, 79
10: 20	115
15: 17	72
15: 22	72
15: 28	159
16: 13	99

2 Corinthians

1: 3–5	81
1: 5–7	152
1: 8–10	77
1: 9	78
3	79
3: 18	78
4	79
4: 10–11	78ff
5	88f
	79f

5: 4	71
5: 19	86
5: 21	70
6: 4–10	80
7: 10 ,	110
8: 9	70, 80
10: 3–5	137
11: 2	176
12: 7–10	80
12: 10	81

Galatians

2: 20f	80
2: 20	88
3: 13 (14)	154
3: 13	70
4: 4	70
6: 14	12

Ephesians

2: 6	88
6: 11	18
6: 13	18
6: 14	18
6: 19–20	132

Philippians

1: 12–14	132
1: 19–20	132
1: 27–9	132
1: 27f	100
1: 27	92
1: 29	81
2–3	74–7
2	82
2: 6–10	70
2: 6–8	83
2: 6	76
2: 9	76
2: 12	77
2: 17	121
3: 9	75, 79
3: 10f	76, 79
3: 10	12
3: 12–16	77, 79
3: 18	76
3: 20f	70
3: 21	75

Colossians

1: 24	2, 8, 81f, 84–90 *passim*, 92, 97
2	140
2: 5	88
2: 8f	87
2: 12–15	12
2: 12	88, 119
3: 1	88

3:3	12	13:23	134
1 Thessalonians	80, 91, 97, 99f	1 Peter	66, 107f, 120
1:5	91	1:6	40
1:6	99, 100	1:11	124
1:9f	107	1:19f	114
2:2	100	2:12	108
2:12	98	2:19f	31
2:13	91, 100	2:19	40
2:14f	80, 98, 100	3:1-4	108
2:15	50, 124, 125	4:4	106
2:18	92, 100	4:13	120
2:19	91	4:14	132
3	100	5:8	122
3:1ff	92f, 97f	1 John	3
3:2	98ff	1:1-3	58
3:3	2, 91-100 *passim*	2:2	115
3:4	100	2:18-22	68
3:5	100	2:22f	69
3:7	99	3:1	67
3:8	99	3:10	67
3:10	92	3:12f	68
3:13	98, 99	3:16f	68
4:3-8	107	4:1-3	68
4:10	98	4:2f	69
4:11	98	4:5f	68
4:14	100	4:15	69
5:6	98	4:20	69
5:8	99	5:10	69
5:10	71	5:16	133
5:14	99	2 John	
5:17	99	9	69
5:24	98	3 John	
2 Thessalonians		9f	68
1	110	12	58
1:10	135	Revelation	
2:2	99	1-3	106, 181f
1 Timothy		1:2	103, 135
2:6	24	1:5	25, 104, 112, 114, 115, 116
6:12ff	4	1:6	106
6:12-13	133	1:7	108, 109, 111, 112, 114
6:13	104, 134	1:9	103, 105, 135
2 Timothy		1:16	174
1:8	135	2	103
2:10	82	2:9	106
2:11	12, 120	2:13	102, 122, 133
2:12	133	2:14	105
4:6	121	2:20	105
4:16-17	132	3	103
Hebrews	177, 181	3:1	106
6:4-6	133	3:4	15
10:26-31	133	3:5	106, 133
11:32ff	124, 155	3:8	133
12:17	133	3:9	106
13:11-14	113	3:10	102, 104

4–7	103	14: 7	109
4–5	110	14: 8–11	107
5	107	14: 9–11	103, 109
5: 5f	113	14: 20	109, 113
5: 10	106	15: 1 – 22: 5	103
6–20	109f, 114	15: 4	109, 110, 111
6: 1–8	107	15: 5	105
6: 2	108	16	116
6: 9–11	117	16: 6	15
6: 17	18	16: 9	109
7	105, 111	16: 11	109
7: 2f	104	16: 15	102
7: 14	102, 114	17: 1	111
7: 17	114	17: 8	114
8–14	103	17: 10	102
8–9	110, 116	19: 7	181
8: 8	110	19: 8	108
8: 11	110	19: 10	4, 103, 104, 135
8: 13	110	19: 11ff	103
9: 12	110	19: 11–21	109f
9: 20f	107, 109 ,110	19: 11–16	107f
9: 20	115	19: 12–15	113
10: 1 – 11: 13	105, 110	20–2	112
10: 9–11	105	20: 2	122
10: 10–11	107	20: 4	103, 135
11: 1–13	106	20: 7f	163
11: 3ff	107f	20: 8–10	112
11: 4	106	21: 1 – 22: 5	110
11: 5ff	105	21: 3ff	116
11: 5f	110, 116	21: 6	58
11: 7–13	109	21: 7	102
11: 7–10	105	21: 8	111
11: 7	114f	21: 9	111, 181
11: 13	110, 114	21: 10	108
11: 14	103, 110	21: 24 – 22: 5	110ff
12: 7	135	21: 27	111
12: 7–9	114, 116	22: 1	112
12: 9–12	116	22: 15	111
12: 9	122	22: 17	58
12: 11	101, 103, 114, 117		
12: 12 – 13: 18	116		
12: 12f	103		
12: 17	103, 105, 106, 116, 135		
13	102, 103, 106		
13: 3	102, 116		
13: 7	114f		
13: 8	114, 115		
13: 9f	102		
13: 12	102		
13: 14	102		
14: 1–5	103		
14: 4f	114		
14: 4	115		
14: 6f	107		

New Testament Apocrypha

Acts of Peter 38	139
Second Apocalypse of James	136
Gospel of Mary	139
Protevangelium of James	
8.3	128
8.23–4	128

Diogenes Laertius VIII.41   93

Josephus

B.J. IV.5.4	128
v.9.4. (419)	15
A.J. XI.6.12 (279)	42
XVII.6.4 (167)	31
C. Apion. 2.7	128

Philo

De Ag. 97	15

Pliny

Epp. x.96.3f	119

Acta Martyrum

Epistle of Lyons and Vienne

	119f, 129, 136
ap. Eus. *H.E.* v.1.10	125f
v.1.16	122
v.1.23	120
v.1.25	122
v.1.27	122
v.1.35	122
v.1.41	120
v.1.42	120
v.3.3	129

Acts of Justin 136

Martyrdom of Perpetua	10	122
Martyrdom of Polycarp	119f,	136
1.1		134
1.2		120
2.2		120
2.3		122
6.2		120
7.1		124
8.2		119
9.2–3		119
14.1–2		121
17.3		120
19.1		134
21.1		134

Acts of the Scillitan Martyrs 136

Church Fathers

Augustine

Civ. Dei XVII.20.1	43
De Cons. Evang. III.20.57	41
Epistle of Barnabas 7.3	14
12.7	15
1 Clement 5.3–7	134

Clement of Alexandria

Strom. IV.13ff	122
IV.56.2	121f
V.14	43

Cyprian

Ep. 81	129
Test. 2.14	43

Ephraem

Antichr. II.223	96

Epiphanius

Haer. 26.12	128

Gregory the Great

Moralia 29.6 (10–11)	162

Gregory of Tours

De gloria martyrum 49	126

Hegesippus	136
Hermas	138
Sim. IX.28.4	133
Ignatius	136
Eph. 3.1	120
21.1	121
Magn. 8.2	124
Rom. 4.2–3	120
5.3	120
6.3	120
Irenaeus	70, 102
Adv. Haer. III.3.4	134
IV.5.4	14

Jerome

Comm. in Matt. 23: 35–6	127f
In Ep. ad Gal. 2.3, on 3: 13 (14)	154
John Chrysostom	161
Hom. 74.2 *in Matt.*	127
C. Iud. 5.10	156
6.2	156
6.5	156, 182

Justin Martyr

Dial. 16	49, 65
47	49
93	49
95	49, 65
96	49
108	49
110	65
117	49
122	65
133	49, 65
137	49
Liturgy of S. Basil	171
Liturgy of S. Chrysostom	171

Melito

Peri Pascha 59	14
69	14
frs. 9–12	14
fr. 15.21	14
Peri Loutrou	140

Origen

In Num. hom. 10.2	182
Comm. ser. in Matt. 25	128
Fr. 457 *in Matt.*	128
Princ. IV.1.3	182
Dialogue with Heraclides	93
In Joh. 1.35	93
II.13 (7)	93
VI.9 (6)	93

Peter of Alexandria

Can. 13	128

Index of References

Polycarp
Ep. 7.1   135
Sozomen
H.E. 9.17   126f
Tertullian   91, 120
Adv. Iud. 10.6   13f
Adv. Marc. III.18.2   13f
Ad Nat. 1.11   128
1.18   122
Apol. 50   122
Mart. 1   129
Theodore of Mopsuestia
on 1 Tim. 6: 12–13   133
Qumran Texts   177, 181
1QS 8.6   15
8.10   15
9.4   15
1QSa 2.11–22   169
1QSb 4.24–6   171
CD 14.19   15
Targum
Genesis 1: 21, Ps.-Jon.   169
3: 15, Ps.-Jon.   116
4: 8   68
22, Frag. Tg. and Neofiti   15
49: 11, Ps.-Jon.   113
Numbers 23: 21, Onkelos,
Ps.-Jon., Neofiti   161
Deuteronomy 33: 15, Ps.-Jon.   152
Song of Songs   178f
8: 2   169
Isaiah 11: 4   162
Lamentations 5: 13   154
Mishnah
Yoma   166
1.2   154
5.1f   182
6.8   174
8.9   157
Rosh ha-Shanah 4.6   145, 159
Taanith 4.2–3   167
Sotah 8   173
Aboth 3.3   155
5.3   152
Tamid 4.1   170
Babylonian Talmud
Berakhoth 62b   171
Yoma 53b   96
Taanith 27a   167
27b   167
28a   167
31a   167
Hagigah 15   95
Gittin 57b   15

Sanhedrin 96b   15
97b   163
Palestinian Talmud
Taanith 69a   15
Midrash
Gen R.   144
1.1   168
1.4   166
41(42).3   157
56.3(35c)   13
Exod. R. 15.6   150
Lev. R.   144, 156
1.12   161
11   167, 178
11.7   157
11.9   167
13   159f
13.3   169, 178
13.4   157
16   156
17   156
17.7   151
20   156
20.2   152
20.10   171
21.12   171
22.10   169
27.11   163
30.1   144
30.5   163
35.6   157
36.6   148, 152
Num. R. 21.4   66
Ecc. R. 11.2   155
Cant. R. 1.14   171
3.6   144
5.2   180
8.13   155
Lam. R.   144
1.51   157
ʾElleh ʾezkerah   173
Pesikta Rabbati 20.8   150
31.2(143b)   13
75.1   164
Pesikta de-Rav Kahana   144
1.3   152
1.4f   167
4.4   152
5.6–9   152
5.6   165, 180
5.8   163
5.9   162f, 164, 173
9.11   163
11.23   155

11.24	155	51	173
14.3	157	57	175
16–22	156	'anusah le-'ezrah	
22.5	162, 164		145, 150–2, 157, 163
23.7	153	2–3	151
26	156	3	177
26.9	171	6–18	151ff
27.1	144	8f	153
S.1.4	161	8	170
S.6.5	162	19–30	151f
Tanhuma Wa'era 46	13	24f	163f
Tehillim 80.4	148	25	164, 175
on Ps. 93: 1	162	29f	164
Zerubbabel	159, 164f	30	151, 177
ap. Jellinek,		34–48	164
Bet ha-Midrasch, II, 56	164	36f	151
56, lines 11f, 14	162	39	179
57, line 4 from bottom	159, 163	47f	164
Prayers		50–64	165
Eighteen Benedictions	181	50	165, 177
Twelfth Benediction	49–51, 65, 67	61	165, 174
Fourteenth Benediction	160	'azkhir gevuroth	145
Nishmath	165	10–12	168
Tekiata de-vey Rav	145, 149, 175f	26	168
Piyyut		28–32	169
Yose ben Yose	4–6, 8, 143–82 passim	39f	152
'ahallelah 'elohay	145, 149	59	174
13–15	149	65	152
17f	149	91–4	153, 170
25	149	102	152
28	146, 149, 174	105	171, 173
29	148	106–26	172
30ff	160	110f	172
30	149	116f	172
33	160, 175	152–86	173
35f	160	154	154
36	149	156	173
39f	160	157	171
43f	161	160	173
48f	161	161	162, 173
48	163	174	173
49	175	186	171
51f	161, 165, 177, 180	230f	182
52	149, 175	268	174
54f	162, 165	269	173–5
57–60	163, 176	273	174
'efhad be-ma'asay	145	275	148, 174
4	147, 152	276	174
5	153	'attah konanta 'olam be-rov hesed	
8	153, 182		145
33–41	154f	1	175
36	154, 175	3	168
41	152	5	168
47	152f	18–22	169

24	152	8	154
27f	152	23	150
58–60	170	25	150, 171
64	152	32	154
66–72	172	ʾaz le-roʾsh tattanu	146
93–119	173	Yannai	143f
98	173	Kalir	143f, 169
110	173	Ba-yamim ha-hem	159, 164
158f	182	Saadia (?)	159
161	174	Anonymous	
ʾasapper gedoloth	145, 153, 173	ʾamar Yiṣḥaq le-ʾAvraham ʾavohi	
2	168		170
16f	170	ʾattah baraʾtha ʾeth ha-ʿolam kullo	
16	152		166
20–3	172	12–16	173
43–5	182	**Saadia** (*see also under* **Piyyut**)	
60	148	ʾEmunoth we-Deʿoth	158
ʾomnam ʾashamenu	146	7.1	164f
13	147	Siddur	145, 159
35f	150	(?) On the Song of Songs	162
40	153f	**Solomon ben Isaac of Troyes (Rashi)**	
42–4	148		
ʾeyn lanu kohen gadol		on Numbers 23: 21	161, 180
	146f, 156, 175	**Maimonides**	
3	147	Mishneh Torah XIV.11.1	158, 165
5	147		

INDEX OF SUBJECTS

Antipas, 102

apocalyptic, 2f, 51ff, 58, 94ff, 102ff, 158ff, 180; *also* 173f

baptism, 5, 7, 71ff, 89, 104f, 119, 133, 139f

binding of Isaac, 5, 13ff, 153, 169ff, 177; *also* 155

discipleship and suffering, 33, 49, 50, 57ff, 69, 80, 129; *also* 106f

educative character of suffering, 35, 44; *also* 77

heroic virtue of martyrs, 4, 44, 121f, 155

Imitatio Christi, 1, 9ff, 26f, 33, 46f, 66, 75, 80, 82, 85, 119f, 140f; *also* 72

Israel's suffering, 16, 143–82 *passim*; *also* 84f

Kolbe, M., 6, 90, 196

martyrs: Christian, 9–27 *passim*, 34f, 65f, 100, 102, 117, 118–35 *passim*; *see also* persecution; Jewish, 4, 13ff, 29ff, 35, 37, 43ff, 109, 118ff, 153f, 173, 176; pagan, 7, 30, 118, 122

persecution, 34, 108, 141, 124f, 132f; Jewish, 49ff, 54f, 57, 58f, 65ff, 80, 97f, 100; Roman, 35, 52, 102, 118, 122, 154; *also* 12, 31, 41f

Pliny the Younger, 102, 119

prophets, 4, 16, 29, 80, 102, 104, 105ff, 122ff, 132, 135, 143

resurrection, 31, 34, 39, 44f, 70ff, 89, 158, 164f, 174

sacrifice of Jesus, 1f, 9–27 *passim*, 34ff, 43, 65f, 81, 89, 101f, 113f, 116f, 121

sacrifice of martyrs, 14ff, 19, 23f, 26f, 37, 44, 102ff, 117, 121

Stephen, 28f, 35, 45, 120, 124f, 131f

Suffering Servant, 43, 103, 113, 123; *also* 177

Valentinus, 139

DATE DUE

27 Jan 82			

GAYLORD PRINTED IN U.S.A.